S0-BSB-256

B+T-2-18-74   5.48

FOURTH EDITION

# Personal and Professional Typing

**S. J. WANOUS, Ph.D.**
Professor of Education
University of California, Los Angeles

**JAMES C. BENNETT, Ed. D.**
Chairman, Department of Office
Administration and Business Education
California State University, Northridge

Copyright © 1973
by South-Western Publishing Co.
Cincinnati, Ohio

**ALL RIGHTS RESERVED**

The text of this publication, or any part thereof, may not be reproduced or transmitted in any form or by any means, electronic
or mechanical, including photocopying, recording, storage in an information retrieval system, or otherwise, without the prior written
permission of the publisher.

Standard Book Number: 0-538-20660-8

Library of Congress Catalog Card Number: 72-97894

1 2 3 4 5 6 7 H 9 8 7 6 5 4 3

LIBRARY
WAYNE STATE COLLEGE
WAYNE, NEBRASKA

Published by

**T66**   **SOUTH-WESTERN PUBLISHING CO.**

CINCINNATI   WEST CHICAGO, ILL.   DALLAS   PELHAM MANOR, N.Y.   BURLINGAME, CALIF.   BRIGHTON, ENGLAND

# Preface

PERSONAL AND PROFESSIONAL TYPING, Fourth Edition, is a unique typewriting book. It is designed for people in all walks of life—students, writers, speakers—who wish to learn how to use the typewriter for their written communications. The person who wishes to use typewriting skill as a career objective will find this book an excellent introduction from which he may progress into an advanced course.

The book is also unique in that it attempts to help the student learn not only how to "typewrite," but how to "write" on the typewriter—the composition of personal as well as professional papers.

**Organization of the Book.** The Fourth Edition contains 80 carefully developed lessons which can be adapted to meet a variety of instructional programs. These lessons are organized into nine units; each unit expands the skills developed in the previous unit. The successful elements from previous editions have been retained, and many new features have been added.

The skill-building and problem activities progress from the basic to the advanced in a logical sequence as the student develops a mastery of typewriting skill. Equal attention is devoted to the preparation of personal, school, and professional papers. Extra-credit problems, which appear throughout the book, provide the student with additional experience in composing papers similar to problems he has already covered.

**Part 1—Typewriting Fundamentals.** This part contains four units which are concerned with learning the letter keys, building typing facility, learning the number and symbol keys, and building typing continuity. Careful attention is devoted to the development of basic techniques. The skill-building drills have been improved and expanded. There are more drill lines in the early lessons and drills for the electric typewriter are given along with manual typewriter drills. Each new lesson begins with an intensive review of the keys introduced in the preceding lesson; then the new keys are introduced. The drill lines on new keys stress only one new key at a time in order to focus the student's attention on that key and to assist the teacher in varying the amount of new material to be covered in a lesson.

**Part 2—Basic Personal Applications.** The two units in this part of the book cover the memorandum, the short report, the personal note, and the personal letter. An effective learning sequence is established for problem copy. The first time a student encounters a new problem, he types it from an authentic model. He then types a similar paper from semiarranged form. Finally, he types additional papers from problem copy.

**Part 3—Applying Typewriting Skills.** The final three units enable the student to apply his skill in typing manuscripts and reports, tables, and a variety of business papers. He is given experience in working with the most frequently used media for conveying written business information.

**Special Features.** There are a number of special features that are emphasized in this edition:

1. Timed writings—extensive one-, three-, and five-minute timed-writing copy is provided—thirteen three-minute writings and ten five-minute writings. Both speed and accuracy are emphasized in these writings throughout the book.

2. Composition at the typewriter—skill in composing at the typewriter is developed through a logical sequence beginning with simple questions to which the student types brief answers and ending with the composition of a variety of papers on the typewriter.

3. Effective illustrations—more effective illustrations are found in this edition. Larger key-location illustrations of finger and hand positions are used in the preliminary pages. Keyboard illustrations appear on the same page with drills covering the new keys to be learned. Many full-page illustrations are shown in order to give the student an accurate model which he can follow when typing problems.

4. Arrangement of copy—all copy is attractively arranged and spaced. Clear directions are given at the beginning of a lesson and are printed in distinct type so that the student can readily identify what he is to read and what he is to type.

5. Technique- and skill-building drills—a wide variety of technique and skill-building drills are found throughout the book. Many drills are designed to enable the teacher to provide for individual differences in student abilities. Realistic goals are set for each practice, giving meaning and direction to the work of the students. The various parts of each lesson are timed as an aid in lesson planning.

6. Proofreading drills—new drills and problems have been added on proofreading typewritten copy. These are designed to make students aware of the types of errors they must look for in typewritten material. The drills involve spelling errors, transposition errors, errors in meaning, and errors in numbers and names.

**Acknowledgments.** Many colleagues, teachers, and students have been helpful to us in the preparation of this book. To these people we express our sincere appreciation.

*S. J. Wanous – J. C. Bennett*

# Contents

## PART 1
### TYPEWRITING FUNDAMENTALS

## PART 2
### BASIC PERSONAL APPLICATIONS

## PART 3
### APPLYING TYPEWRITING SKILLS

200448

# Operating Parts of the Typewriter

All typewriters have similar parts. These parts are identified in the four segments of a typewriter given below and on page v. Each segment is a composite and not an exact drawing of any one typewriter. For this reason, the exact location of a part may be slightly different from that on your typewriter, but the differences are, for the most part, few and slight.

Extra parts peculiar to your typewriter can be identified by reference to the instructional booklet prepared especially for your typewriter.

In using the illustrations below, follow the line from the number to the part. The function of each part is explained in the textbook. Learn to operate each part correctly, as it is explained to you.

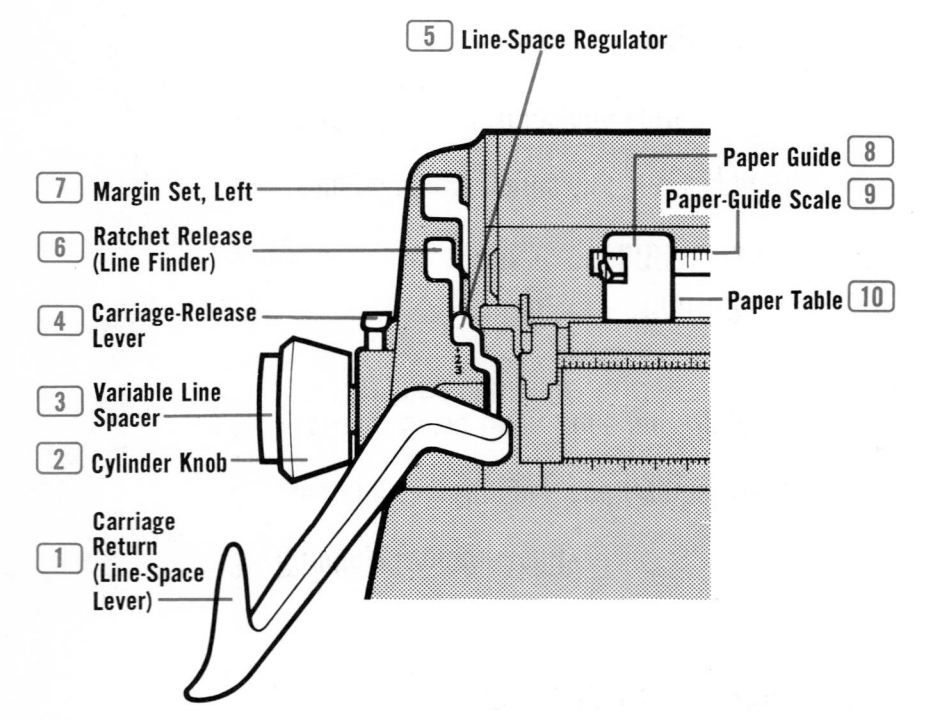

5 Line-Space Regulator

7 Margin Set, Left

6 Ratchet Release (Line Finder)

4 Carriage-Release Lever

3 Variable Line Spacer

2 Cylinder Knob

1 Carriage Return (Line-Space Lever)

8 Paper Guide

9 Paper-Guide Scale

10 Paper Table

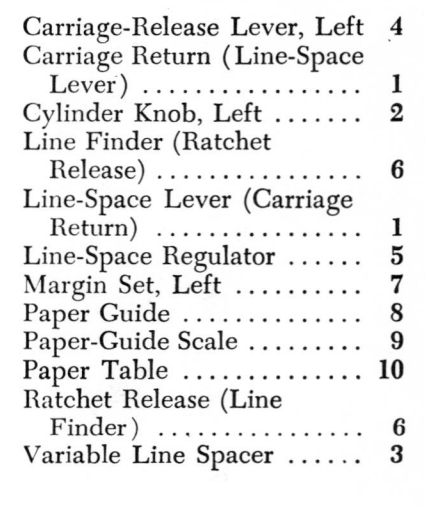

## Top Left Segment of a Typewriter

## Type Right Segment of a Typewriter

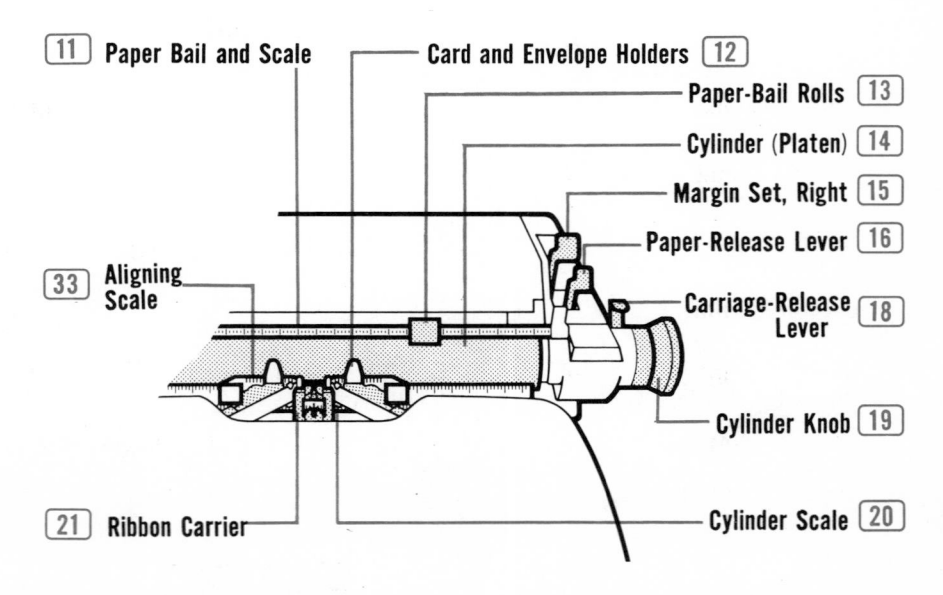

11 Paper Bail and Scale

12 Card and Envelope Holders

13 Paper-Bail Rolls

14 Cylinder (Platen)

15 Margin Set, Right

16 Paper-Release Lever

18 Carriage-Release Lever

19 Cylinder Knob

20 Cylinder Scale

33 Aligning Scale

21 Ribbon Carrier

## Lower Segment of a Manual Typewriter

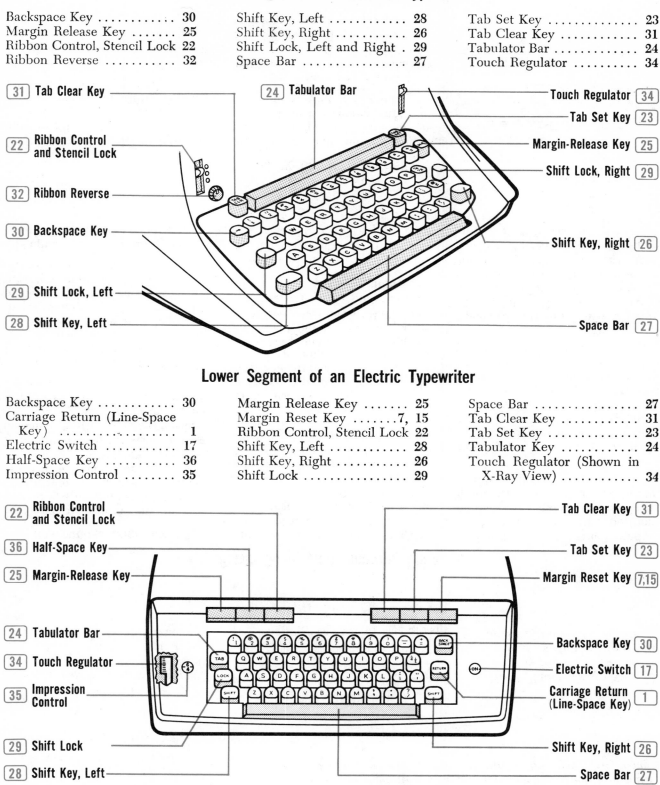

**Lower Segment of a Manual Typewriter (illustration labels)**

31 Tab Clear Key
22 Ribbon Control and Stencil Lock
32 Ribbon Reverse
30 Backspace Key
29 Shift Lock, Left
28 Shift Key, Left
24 Tabulator Bar
Touch Regulator 34
Tab Set Key 23
Margin-Release Key 25
Shift Lock, Right 29
Shift Key, Right 26
Space Bar 27

## Lower Segment of an Electric Typewriter

**Lower Segment of an Electric Typewriter (illustration labels)**

22 Ribbon Control and Stencil Lock
36 Half-Space Key
25 Margin-Release Key
24 Tabulator Bar
34 Touch Regulator
35 Impression Control
29 Shift Lock
28 Shift Key, Left
Tab Clear Key 31
Tab Set Key 23
Margin Reset Key 7,15
Backspace Key 30
Electric Switch 17
Carriage Return (Line-Space Key) 1
Shift Key, Right 26
Space Bar 27

# Machine Adjustments

• *Operating a typewriter involves more than learning to stroke the keys. This page and page vii contain information regarding machine adjustments which you must know for the particular typewriter you are using.*

## Pica and Elite Type

```
Pica:   f j f j f j f j f j       (10 letters)
        |———— 1 inch ————|
Elite:  f j f j f j f j f j f j   (12 letters)
```

• *The cylinder scale (No. 20) range is from 0 to about 90 on pica machines; from 0 to about 110 on elite machines.*

Some typewriters are equipped with pica type; some with elite type. Pica type is larger than elite type. Note the difference.

## Paper Guide and Centering Point

### Standardized Directions

To standardize directions for setting the paper guide and centering paper, your instructor may ask you to insert paper into your machine so that the left edge corresponds to 0 on the scale that is matched to the spacing mechanism on your typewriter. The location of this scale varies on the different typewriters.

When this procedure is followed, the centering point on the scale that is matched to the spacing mechanism will be as follows for paper of standard size (8½ by 11 inches): 42 for machines with pica type and 50 or 51 for machines with elite type.

**Olympia, R. C. Allen, Royal, Smith-Corona.** Set the paper guide so the indicator at the left will point to 0 on the paper guide scale. Insert the paper with the left edge against the guide. Note that the left edge of the paper automatically corresponds to 0 on the scale that is matched to the spacing mechanism of the typewriter.

**IBM.** Insert the paper with the left edge at 0 on the margin scale for a Selector or the lower platen scale for a standard electric. Move the paper guide so that it is alongside the left edge of the paper. Note the position of the paper guide on the paper table; always set the guide in this position.

**Underwood.** Insert the paper with the left edge at 0 on the paper bail scale. Move the paper guide so that it is alongside the left edge of the paper. Note the position of the paper guide scale; always set the guide in this position.

**Remington.** Insert the paper with the left edge at 0 on the bottom carriage scale. Move the paper guide so that it is alongside the left edge of the paper. Note the position of the paper guide on the paper table; always set the guide in this position.

**Special Centering Devices.** Remington, Smith-Corona, and Underwood machines have special centering devices. If your machines have special centering devices, he will give you appropriate instructions.

## Setting the Margin Stops

You may set the margin stops for any length of line desired, such as a 50-, 60-, or 70-space line. To have equal left and right margins, take these two steps:

**Step 1:** Subtract half the line length from the center point of the paper. Set the left margin stop at this point.

**Step 2:** Add half the line length, plus 3 to 7 spaces for the end-of-line bell, to the center point. Set the right stop at this point.

The best margin balance is achieved when the right margin stop is set so the bell will ring about 3 spaces before the point at which you want the line to end.

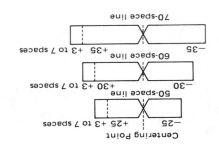

## Royal Electric and Nonelectric

1. Set the left margin stop by placing your left index finger behind the left "Magic" margin control and moving it forward. Move the carriage to the desired point; return the margin control to its original position.
2. Repeat Step 1 for setting the right margin stop, using the right "Magic" margin control.

## Olympia

1. Set the left margin stop by depressing it and moving the carriage to the desired position; then set and release the stop.
2. Use the same operation to set the right margin.

## Smith-Corona Nonelectric

1. Set the left margin stop by pressing the left margin set button to the left. Move the carriage to the desired position and release the button.
2. Use the same operation to set the right margin.

## IBM Selectric

Move the stops to the desired position to get the line length required.

## Smith-Corona Electric

1. Set the left margin stop by depressing the left carriage release button and the left margin button. Move the carriage to the desired location and release the two buttons simultaneously.
2. Use the same operation to set the right margin.

## IBM Nonelectric

1. Set the left margin stop by moving the carriage until it is against the left margin stop; depress and hold down the margin set key as you move the carriage to the desired position; then release the set key.
2. Repeat Step 1 for setting the right margin stop.

## Underwood Electric and Nonelectric

1. Move the left and right margin stops to the desired position on the front scale.
2. The margin indicators on the front scale indicate balanced margin set positions.

## Remington Electric and Nonelectric

Set the left and right margin stops by moving them to the desired positions.

## Clearing and Setting the Tabulator Stops

**Tab Clear** – To clear the tabulator mechanism, depress the tab clear key as you move the carriage to its full width. To remove an individual stop without canceling other stops, tabulate to the stop and operate the tab clear key.

- *On Smith-Corona and Olympia typewriters the total tab clear key clears all stops at one time without moving the carriage.*

**Tab Set** – To set tabulator stops, move the carriage to the desired position; then depress the tab set key. Repeat this operation to set as many tabulator stops as are needed.

## Changing the Ribbon

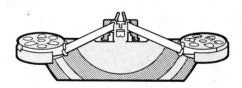

- *In general the instructions given here apply to nonelectric and electric typewriters. Consult the manufacturer's pamphlet accompanying your machine for special instructions.*

1. Wind the used ribbon on one spool. Usually it is best to wind it on the right spool.
2. Study the route of the ribbon as you wind. Note especially how the ribbon winds and unwinds on the two spools. Note, too, how the ribbon is threaded through the ribbon-carrier mechanism.

3. Lift the right spool slightly off its hub to see if both sides are the same. Study both sides of the spool so you will replace it properly.
4. Remove the ribbon from the carrier and remove both spools. Note how the ribbon is attached to the empty spool. The new ribbon must be attached in the same manner.
5. Fasten the new ribbon to the empty spool and wind several inches of the new ribbon on it.
6. Place both spools on their hubs and thread the ribbon through the carrier. *Note: The Selectric typewriter uses a special ribbon cartridge, making the foregoing steps unnecessary.*

# Basic Techniques

## Position of Hands

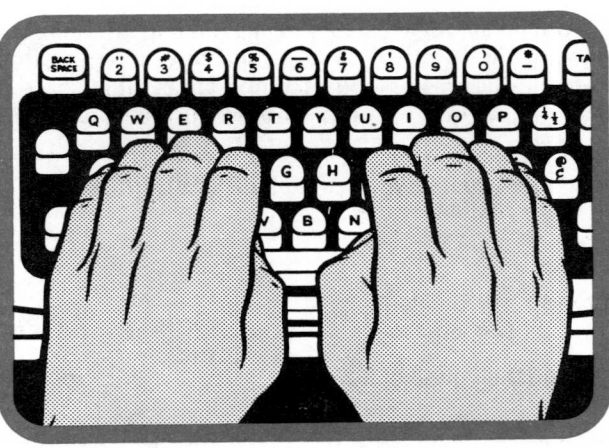

When typing, keep your fingers deeply curved. Girl typists must keep fingernails neatly trimmed. You can't type with long nails.

Do not permit your hands to turn over on the little fingers. Hold the hands directly over the keys. Turn the hands inward slightly to get straight strokes.

Don't buckle your wrists upward. Hold your wrists down near, but not resting on, the front frame of the typewriter. The forearms should form a parallel line with the slope of the keyboard.

Don't rest your fingers heavily on the home keys. Barely touch them with your fingertips. Feel the keys; don't smother them.

When a finger makes a reach from its home position to strike another key, the other fingers remain on or near their home keys. Such reaches are made by the finger without twisting the wrist or moving the arm or elbow.

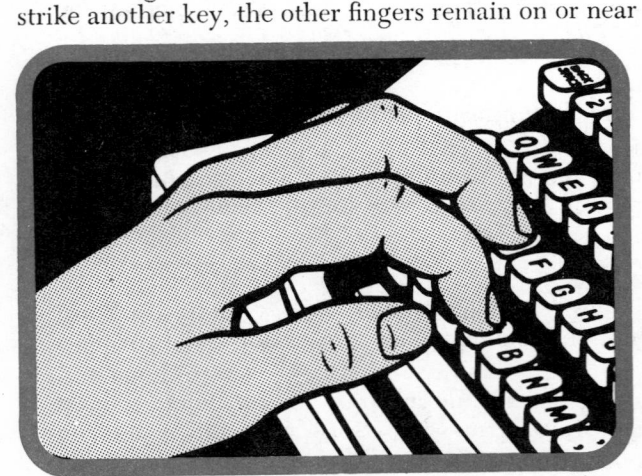

# Posture

Good posture is vital in learning to type well. Given here are 10 guides of good form. Study the guides carefully. Observe them whenever you work at your typewriter.

1. Book at right of machine on bookholder or with something under top for easier reading.

2. Table free of unneeded books and papers.

3. Front frame of the typewriter even with the edge of the desk.

4. Body centered opposite the **h** key, 6 to 8 inches from front frame of typewriter.

5. Sit back in chair. Hold shoulders erect with body leaning forward slightly from waist.

6. Elbows held near the body.

7. Wrists held low with forearms parallel to the slant of the keyboard. Do not rest lower hand on frame of typewriter.

8. Your feet on the floor, one just ahead of the other.

9. Head turned toward book with eyes on copy.

10. Fingers curved and held over second row of keys.

## Typing Rhythm

Strike the keys at a steady pace, without breaks or pauses. At first, you will think each letter as you type it. Later, you will think and type short, easy-to-type words and phrases as a whole. You will type longer, hard-to-type words by letters or syllables. You will combine whole word typing with letter or syllable typing into a smooth, fluent, steady rhythm.

## Stroking

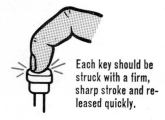

Each key should be struck with a firm, sharp stroke and released quickly.

Center the stroking action in your fingers. Keep elbows, arms, and wrists quiet as you type.

Your fingers should be deeply curved. Use quick, sharp strokes. Release the keys quickly by snapping the fingers toward the palm of the hand.

Hit the keys squarely with short, quick, straight strokes.

The finger is snapped slightly toward the palm of the hand as the key is released.

## Spacing Between Words

Almost one in every five strokes is made with the space bar. To operate the space bar correctly:

1. Hold the right thumb curved under the hand just over the space bar.
2. Strike it with a quick down-and-in motion of the thumb.
3. Keep the right wrist low and quiet as you strike the bar.
4. Keep the left thumb out of the way.

 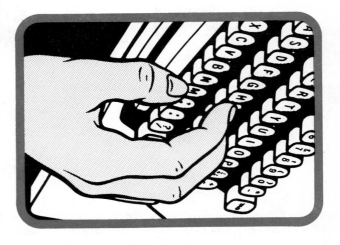

## Paragraph Indentions

You will use the tabulator bar or key (No. 24) to indent for paragraphs. Find this bar or key on your typewriter. Touch lightly the tab bar (right index finger) or tab key (right little finger). Deeply curve the other fingers in making this reach.

# Returning the Carriage

## Manual Typewriter

Return the carriage following these steps:

1. Move the left hand, palm down, to the carriage-return lever (No. 1). Keep your right hand in home position and your eyes on the book.

2. Move the lever forward to take up the slack.

3. With the fingers bracing one another, return the carriage with a flick of the wrist.

4. Quickly return your left hand to its home position and continue typing at once.

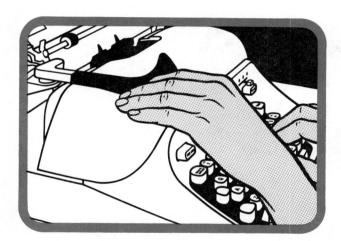 

## Electric Typewriter

1. Reach the little finger of your right hand to the carriage-return key (No. 1).

2. Tap the return key quickly.

3. Quickly return the finger to its home-key position and continue typing at once.

## Shift Keys

Use a one-two count:

**One** – Depress the shift key and hold it down.

**Two** – Strike the capital letter; then quickly release the shift key and return the little finger to its typing position.

## Erasing and Correcting Errors

1. Move the carriage or carrier to the extreme right or left so that eraser crumbs will not fall into the operating parts of the typewriter.

2. To avoid moving the paper out of alignment, turn the cylinder forward if the erasure is to be made on the upper two thirds of the paper; backward, if on the lower third of the paper.

3. To erase on the original sheet, lift the paper bail out of the way and place a 5- by 3-inch card in back of the original copy and in front of the first carbon sheet. Use an eraser shield to protect the letters that are not to be erased. Use a hard typewriter eraser. When you complete the erasure, brush the eraser crumbs away from the typewriter.

4. Move the card in front of the second carbon sheet if more than one copy is being made. Erase the errors on the carbon copy with a soft (or pencil) eraser first, then with the hard typewriter eraser used in erasing on the original copy.

5. When the error has been neatly erased on the original and all the carbon copies, re-move the card, position the carriage to the proper point, and type the correction.

## Typewriter Care

### Do Daily

1. Brush the dust from the typebars or other operating parts of the typewriter.

2. Keep the desk free of dust, especially the area under the machine.

3. Cover the machine when it is not in use.

4. Turn off an electric machine when it is not in use.

### Do Weekly

1. Clean type faces, using approved cleaner.

2. Clean platen, feed rolls, and paper-bail rolls with cloth moistened with cleaning fluid.

3. Read the oiling and special care directions in the operator's manual or guide for your particular typewriter.

# Key-Location Drills for Electric Typewriters

**"at" sign**

Use @ for at in typing bills:  15 pins @ $10 each.
The @ is the shift of 2; type @ with the s finger.
Space before and after @, as follows:  14 @ $9.50.
Buy 437 @ 59.  Sell 703 @ 57.  We sold 49 @ $5.58.

*All typewriters*
*Shift of 2*
*Type with s*
*finger*

**"cent" sign**

¢¢ jj ¢j ¢j ¢j The ¢ sign is the shift of 6:  66¢.
¢¢ ¢j ¢j ¢j¢ Strike ¢ with the right first finger.
Do not space between the ¢ and a figure:  7¢; 85¢.
Use ¢ in typing bills:  38 for 74¢ and 48 for 92¢.

*All typewriters*
*Shift of 6*
*Type with j*
*finger*

**Asterisk**

** kk ** kk k*k k*k The * is the shift of 8:  88*.
** kk *k *k Strike * with the right second finger.
Use * for some footnotes:  I read a book by Hill.*
Use ** for a second footnote:  I liked his poem.**

*All typewriters*
*Shift of 8*
*Type with k*
*finger*

**Underline**

;; ;_; ;_; _; _; The _ is the shift of the hyphen.
_; ;_; Strike the _ with your right fourth finger.
She read Irving Stone's <u>The Agony and the Ecstasy</u>.
Hit all the keys with <u>quick</u>, <u>short</u>, <u>sharp</u> strokes.

*All typewriters*
*Shift of hyphen*
*Type with ;*
*finger*

**Apostrophe**

'; ;'; ;'; The ' is at the right of the semicolon.
Strike ' with the right fourth finger:  It's here.

**Quotation marks**
**(Shift of ')**

The " is the shift of the '.  "I can go," he said.
Use the word "can" often.  "Can't" is a weak word.

*All typewriters*
*Right of ; key*
*Type with ;*
*finger*

**"equals" sign**

;=; ;=; ;=; =; The = is located on the fourth row.
Strike = with the fourth finger.  Two = 2.  Z = 4.

**"plus" sign**
**(Shift of =)**

The + is the shift of =.  22 + 36 + 64 + 98 = 220.
The equals sign:  =; the plus sign:  +; 3 + 4 = 7.

*All typewriters ***
*4th row*
*Type with right*
*4th finger*

**1 key**

ala ala la The 1 key is located on the fourth row.
Strike 1 with the left fourth finger.  Send me 11.

**Exclamation mark**
**(Shift of 1)**

The ! is the shift of 1.  Be quick!  Hurrah!  Run!
Send 121 at once!  Count to 11; then fire!  Hurry!

*All typewriters ****
*4th row*
*Type with left*
*4th finger*

**Bracket**
**([ is shift of ])**

;]; ;]; ;]; The ] key is located on the third row.
In that year [1971], he left for Paris [Illinois].

*Olivetti-Underwood*
*3d row, right*
*4th finger*

a]a a]a ]a The ] key is located on the fourth row.
The [ is the shift of ].  Reach with [4th] finger.

*Selectric ****
*4th row, left*
*4th finger*

**Plus-minus key**
**(Single stroke)**

The ± symbol is used in formulas:  ±1; ±$\frac{1}{2}$; ±.0005.
These motors operate with less than ±5% variation.

*Selectric ****
*4th row, left*
*4th finger*

---

\* Interchangeable key on the Remington.
\*\* Optional key on the Selectric.

# Index

**A**, location of, 3

Abbreviations, ZIP Code, 143
Addresses, large envelope, 147; letters, 83-84; small envelope, 85; ZIP Code, 44
Adjustments, machine, vi
Agenda, of meeting, 75
Aligning scale, iv
Alignment, of paper, 49
Ampersand, location of, 29; spacing before and after, 29, 44; use of, 29
Announcement, on full sheet, 60; on half sheet, 60, 67; on postal card, 100, 101
Apostrophe, location of, 33; spacing before and after, 33, 44
Application letter, 141
Articles, typing titles of, 98
Asterisk ( * ), location of, 37
At (@), location of, 39; spacing before and after, 39
Attention line, 154, 155

**B**, location of, 16

Backspace key, v, 36
Basic techniques, viii-xii; erasing and correcting errors, xii; position of hands, viii; posture, ix; returning the carriage, xi; shift keys, xii; space bar, x; stroking, ix; tabulator bar, key, x; typewriter care, xii; typing rhythm, ix
Bibliography, 116; for formal library report, 119
Bibliography card, 115
Block style letters, business, 150, 151, 155, 167; personal business, 91, 92; personal note, 78-79
Body, of personal business letter, 83-84
Book placement, 1
Book review, how to type, 72-73; how to write, 72
Books, typing titles of, 71
Bound manuscript, directions for typing, 104
Business letters, attention line in, 154, 155; block style, 150, 151, 155, 167; how to type, 143; modified block style, 144, 145, 148, 149, 166; rough draft, 157; postscript, 156, 157; script, 167; subject line, 154, 155
By (x), symbol for, 46

**C**, location of, 8

Capitalization guides, business letter parts, 143
Capital letters, typing of, 23
Carbon copies, 89; of business letters, 143
Card holders, 95
Cards, bibliographical, 115; note, 115; postal, 100-101; with speech notes, 102
Carriage, centering, 4; returning, xi
Carriage-release lever, iv
Carriage return, 3
Cent ( ¢ ), location of, 37; spacing before and after, 37
Centering, carriage, 4; columnar headings, 131; horizontal, 53; shortcut for vertical, 124; vertical, 57

Center point, adjustment of, vi; bound manuscripts, 104; odd-size paper and cards, 100; off-center, 70, 72
Cleaning typewriter, steps in, 93
Colon, location of, 33; spacing before and after, 33, 42
Columnar headings, centering, 131; in table, 132, 133
Columns, typing with leaders, 132
Comma, location of, 14; spacing after, 42
Common proofreaders' marks, 54
Common typing errors, 21
Complimentary close, personal business letter, 83-84; personal note, 80
Composing, creative typing, 53, 59, 100
Cylinder (platen), iv
Cylinder knob, iv
Cylinder scale, iv

**D**, location of, 3

Dash, how to type, 41; spacing before and after, 41, 42
Data sheet, personal, 142
Dateline, modified block style letters, 80; vertical placement of, 143
Degree ( ° ), 48
Diagonal (/), location of, 39; spacing before and after, 39; use in typing fractions, 39
Dictation, basic principles of, 103
Ditto marks ( " ), 46
Division sign ( ÷ ), how to type, 46
Dollar ( $ ), location of, 33; spacing before and after, 33, 44

**E**, location of, 6

Eight (8), location of, 31
Electric typewriters, carriage return, xi, 3; half-space key, v; impression control, v; key-location drills, xiii; switch, v
Elite, center point, 55; type, vi
Enclosure notation, 143
Envelopes, addressing large, 147; folding letters for large, 147; folding letters for small, 85; for business letters, 143; small, 85
Equals sign ( = ), how to type, 46; location of, 39; spacing before and after, 39
Erasing and correcting errors, xii, 66
Errors, correcting by spreading letters, 112; correcting by squeezing letters, 120
Et al., 107
Exclamation mark (!), how to make, 41; location of, 41; spacing before and after, 41
Extra-credit typing, 19, 26, 75, 96, 119, 137, 176

**F**, location of, 3

Feet ( ' ), symbol for, 46
Figures, spacing review, 44
Five (5), location of, 29
Folding letters for large envelope, 147; for small envelope, 85
Footnotes, 108; directions for typing, 107; numbering of, 107; use of *et al.*, *ibid.*, *loc. cit.*, and *op. cit.*, 107

Four (4), location of, 31
Fractions (made), spacing with a whole number, 44

**G**, location of, 5

GWAM (gross words a minute), 13

**H**, location of, 4

Hands, position on keys, viii
Headings, centering of columnar, 131; for a 2-page letter, 158; placement of by judgment, 63
Home keys, 3
Horizontal, alignment of paper, 49; centering, 53; placement, 123
Hyphen, location of, 35; spacing, 42

**I**, location of, 7

*Ibid.*, 107
Impresison control, v, 22
Inches ( " ), symbol for, 46
Indenting for paragraphs, 17
Inferior symbols, 48
Inserting paper, 2
Interoffice memorandums, 160, 162, 163; from script, 174
Itinerary, 168, 170

**J**, location of, 3

Judgment placement of headings, 63

**K**, location of, 3

Key-location drills for electric typewriters, xiii
Keys, backspace, v; location of home, 3; margin-release, v; shift, v, 10, 11; tabulator, v; tabulator clear, v; tabulator set, v

**L**, location of, 3

Leaders, in table, 132; typing with columns, 132
Left parenthesis, 31
Left shift key, 10
Letters, application, 141; block style, 91, 92, 150, 151, 155, 167; business, *see* Business letters; folding for large envelope, 147; heading for second page, 158; how to write, 70; modified block style, 80, 81, 84, 86, 89, 90, 93, 144, 145, 148, 149, 166; personal, *see* Personal letters; second page of, 159
Library report, 117; bibliography for, 119; title page for, 118
Line-space lever, iv
Line-space regulator, 2
Listening for the bell, right margin release, 46, 48, 65
*Loc. cit.*, 107

**M**, location of, 12

Machine adjustments, vi-vii; centering point, vi; changing the ribbon, vii; clearing and setting tabulator stops, vii; paper guide, vi; setting margin stops, vi
Machine parts (illustrated), 1

# Index to Special Drills

# Part 1 ■

## Typewriting Fundamentals

In Part 1 of this book, you will learn how to type by touch. In addition, you will learn how to use the special parts on your typewriter.

In Parts 2 and 3, you will use your typewriter to type reports, outlines, announcements, tables, letters, and other personal and school papers.

## Unit 1 ■

### Learning the Letter Keys

**Preliminary Instructions**

Place this book to the right of your typewriter on a bookholder, or put something under the top of the book. Slant it so that you can read the print easily.

Find each part listed below on your typewriter. Use the illustration as an aid. Learn the names of the parts as they will be used often throughout the book.

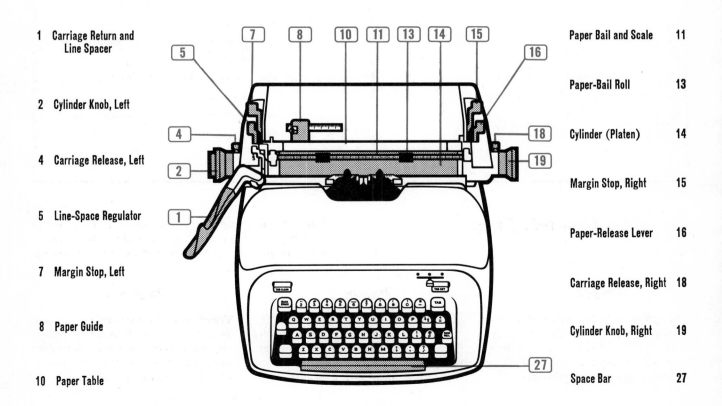

| | |
|---|---|
| 1   Carriage Return and Line Spacer | Paper Bail and Scale   11 |
| 2   Cylinder Knob, Left | Paper-Bail Roll   13 |
| 4   Carriage Release, Left | Cylinder (Platen)   14 |
| 5   Line-Space Regulator | Margin Stop, Right   15 |
| 7   Margin Stop, Left | Paper-Release Lever   16 |
| 8   Paper Guide | Carriage Release, Right   18 |
| 10   Paper Table | Cylinder Knob, Right   19 |
| | Space Bar   27 |

## Problem 2—Program of a Meeting

**Directions – 1.** Fold an 8½- by 11-inch sheet of paper in half. **2.** Insert the folded sheet with the fold at the left. **3.** Arrange the copy for the cover page in an attractive form. **4.** Before typing the inside page, reverse the fold and reinsert the sheet with the fold at the left. **5.** Arrange the copy for the inside page as shown below. Center the copy vertically with ½-inch side margins.

- *For directions on how to center lines on paper of odd size, refer to page 100.*

```
            COMMUNICATING FOR TODAY AND TOMORROW

        American Business Communication Association

             Western Region - Spring Conference




                           * * *

                        * * * * * *

                           * * *




                    Century Plaza Hotel

                    Los Angeles, California

                       May 12, 197-
```

```
                    P R O G R A M

       9:00   Registration              Hotel Lobby

       9:30   Opening Session           Westside Room

              Welcome          James Manos, President

              Address     The Communication Challenge
                           Keith Evans, President
                                  Data Systems, Inc.

      11:00   Group Sessions

              New Techniques in
              Teaching Communications    Encino Room
                    Virginia Lind
                    Clifford Loeb

              New Approaches in          Bel Air Room
              Corporate Communications
                    Donald Kirchner
                    Kathleen Clements

      12:30   Luncheon                   Westside Room

       2:00   Group Sessions

              Communications Media       Encino Room
                    Leo Richman
                    Phyllis Verda

              Research Technology        Bel Air Room
                    Mary Ross
                    James Clark

       3:30   Business Session           Westside Room

       4:00   Adjournment
```

## 80d ■ Extra-Credit Typing

- *For the following problems, prepare your original copy in rough draft form, make your corrections in pencil, and then retype the problem.*

### Problem 1

**Directions –** Write an application letter similar to the one on page 141. Apply for any job in which you might have an interest. Use information about yourself.

### Problem 2

**Directions –** Prepare your résumé to submit with the letter in Problem 1. Use the form shown on page 142. Include references who can give information about you.

### Problem 3

**Directions –** Write a memorandum to the College Bookstore ordering 50 copies of your textbook. Give the title, author, publisher, and date books are needed.

## Adjust Your Typewriter

- *The numbers in parentheses following names of machine parts are those assigned to them on pages iv, v, and 1.*

1. Adjust the paper guide (No. 8). The directions for adjusting it vary from machine to machine. Read those for your typewriter on page vi.

2. Set the line-space regulator (No. 5) at "2" for double spacing (DS).

3. Set the margin stops (Nos. 7 and 15) for a 50-space line, unless this has already been done for you. The directions for setting margin stops vary from machine to machine. Read those for your typewriter on pages vi and vii.

## Insert Paper into the Typewriter

1. Place typing paper to the left of and turned endwise to the typewriter.

2. Pull the paper bail (No. 11) forward.

3. Grasp paper in left hand. Drop the bottom edge of the paper behind the cylinder (No. 14) and against the paper guide (No. 8).

4. Twirl the paper into the machine, using the right cylinder knob (No. 19).

5. If the paper needs straightening after it is inserted, pull the paper release lever (No. 16) toward you. Straighten the paper; push the paper release lever back.

6. Push paper bail back so that it holds the paper against the cylinder. Slide the paper-bail rollers (No. 13) into position. They should be about 2 inches from the left and right edges of the paper.

## Sit Directly in Front of Your Typewriter

- *See page ix for a larger posture illustration.*

1. Have the front of the typewriter even with the edge of the desk. Your body should be centered opposite the **h** key.

2. Your body should be 6 to 8 inches from the front frame of the typewriter.

3. Don't slump; sit erect. Keep your feet on the floor.

4. Hold your elbows near the body.

5. Place your fingers over the second row keys.

**Directions – 1.** Type two 1-minute writings on the first paragraph.

2. Type two 5-minute writings on all paragraphs.

3. Circle the errors and compute the *gwam*. Compare the *gwam* and number of errors for the two writings.

4. Submit the better of the two five-minute timings.

|  | **GWAM** | |
|---|---|---|
|  | **1′** | **5′** |

¶1
79 words
1.4 si

DS From the thousands of occupations listed by the United States | 12 | 2 60

Department of Labor, how does a person go about choosing the correct | 26 | 5 63

one—–the one that will give him self-satisfaction? This is a question | 40 | 8 66

that most people have asked themselves at one time or another. In fact, | 55 | 11 69

quite often a person who has been working at a job for many years may | 69 | 14 72

not even be sure that he has chosen the right one. | 79 | 16 74

¶2
60 words
1.4 si

The difference between choosing a job and choosing the right job | 13 | 18 76

may mean the difference between being a happy person or a frustrated, | 27 | 21 79

discontented bore. The right job for a man is a way of life. It is | 41 | 24 82

a career into which he can throw all of his human resources in order to | 55 | 27 85

reach his highest goals. | 60 | 28 86

¶3
80 words
1.4 si

To find the right job, a person must first decide what he really | 13 | 30 88

wants to do and what he is capable of doing. In other words, one needs | 27 | 33 91

to take a personal inventory. He has to know what kind of training he | 42 | 36 94

will need, and if he can secure that training. He must determine if | 55 | 39 97

he is physically able to do the work. And, of course, it is important | 70 | 42 100

to determine the salary that one can expect to earn. | 80 | 44 102

¶4
71 words
1.4 si

These are all important questions, but there is another one that | 13 | 46 104

probes much more deeply into the thinking of a person. This is the ques- | 28 | 49 107

tion that one must ask himself to determine what his actual purpose is in | 42 | 52 110

life. Only when one knows this purpose can he go about finding the job | 57 | 55 113

that will bring him enjoyment and satisfaction for the rest of his life. | 71 | 58 116

1′ | 1 | 2 | 3 | 4 | 5 | 6 | 7 | 8 | 9 | 10 | 11 | 12 | 13 | 14 |
5′ | 1 | 2 | 3 |

# ▪ Lesson 1

## 1a ▪ Home Keys and Space Bar

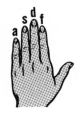

1. Place the fingers of your left hand on **a s d f**.

2. Place the fingers of your right hand on **j k l ;**.

3. Take your fingers off the home keys. Replace them. Say the keys of each hand as you touch them. Repeat several times to get the "feel" of these keys.

4. Curve your right thumb over the middle of the space bar. Strike it with a quick, inward motion of your right thumb. Keep the left thumb out of the way.

5. Curve your fingers. Hold them very lightly over the home keys.

6. Type the line below. Say and think each letter as you strike it.

```
ff jj dd kk ss ll aa ;; fdsa jkl; fdsa jkl; fj fj
```

## 1b ▪ Carriage Return

### Manual Typewriter

2. Keep the fingers of the right hand on their home keys.

3. Move the lever forward to take up the slack.

4. With the fingers bracing one another, return the carriage with a flick of the wrist.

1. Move the left hand, palm down, to the carriage-return lever (No. 1).

5. Return your left hand at once to its home position.

### Electric Typewriter

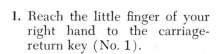

1. Reach the little finger of your right hand to the carriage-return key (No. 1).

2. Tap the return key quickly and return the finger to its home-key position.

## ■ Lesson 80 • *70-space line*

### 80a ■ Keyboard Review • Each line at least three times

5 minutes

Alphabetic SS   I do have a known, qualified girl saxophone player for the jazz combo.

Figure   In English 307A, 41 students made an A, 86 made a B, and 259 made a C.

Flowing, rhythmic stroking

Difficult reach   Breaking abruptly from the brush, Brad's brash brother was breathless.

Easy   Life is a one-way road, and we never have the chance to go back again.

| 1 | 2 | 3 | 4 | 5 | 6 | 7 | 8 | 9 | 10 | 11 | 12 | 13 | 14 |

### 80b ■ Timed Writings

15 minutes

**Directions** – Type the paragraph copy on page 175. Follow the directions given on that page.

### 80c ■ Problem Typing

25 minutes

#### Problem 1—Interoffice Memorandum from Script

Full sheet     60-space line, pica; 70-space line, elite     One carbon copy

Today's date

TO: Faculty Members

FROM: Marilynne Rabinovitch

SUBJECT: Book Orders for Fall Semester

Book orders for the fall semester must be received in my office by June 1. Please include the complete title, author's name, publisher, and number of copies needed.

If we do not receive your order by June 1, books will not be available in the bookstore for your classes at the beginning of the fall semester. It will then be necessary for us to send a special order. Filling this order will take about two weeks.

Please cooperate with us by having your book order to us on time. If you have any questions concerning ordering procedures, please call me at Extension 2463.

XX

### 1c ■ Home-Key Practice • Type each line at least once.

Home keys

DS ff jj ff jj fj fj fj fj dd kk dd kk dk dk dk dk dk

ss ll ss ll sl sl sl sl aa ;; aa ;; a; a; a; a; a;

ffjf ddkd ssls aa;a fj dk sla; fdsa jkl; fdsa jkl;

*Think and say each letter*

### 1d ■ Reach to H

*Type H with the J finger*

Find **h** on the chart and on your machine. Place your fingers over the home keys. Watch your finger as you touch **hj** lightly. Hold the other fingers in position.

*Hold fingers over home keys*

Type this line • jhj jhj jhj had hall hall jhj jhj jhj had had hall

### 1e ■ Location Drill—H

**Directions** – Type each line at least once.          **Technique Goal** – Hold fingers lightly over home keys.

1  DS  jjhj jjhj hj hj hj had had hall hall half half had

2      hj hj all hall hall; a fad; a lash; a dash; a hall

3      a half; a hall; a slash; a flash; a flash; a slash

4      had shad; hall half; ash hash; ash lash; ash slash

5      a lad; a lad had; a lad had a fall; a lad; a fall;

*Type h with the j finger*

### 1f ■ Removing the Paper and Centering the Carriage

2. Depress the paper-release lever (No. 16).

3. Remove the paper with your free hand.

4. Return the lever to its original position.

**Removing the Paper**

1. Pull the paper bail (No. 11) forward.

**Centering the Carriage**

1. Depress the right or left carriage-release lever (No. 4 or No. 18).

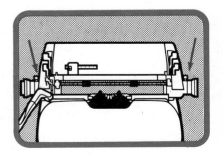

2. Move the carriage to the approximate center of your typewriter.

3. Clear your desk.

## Problem 2—Minutes of a Meeting

**Directions** – Type the minutes of a meeting shown below. Use a 1½-inch left margin, a 1-inch right margin, and a 2-inch top margin. Single-space the copy; double-space between paragraphs. *Remember that the center point will be three spaces to the right of the point normally used.*

- *The minutes of a meeting are an exact record of what happened at a meeting. There is no set form which is used by all companies for recording minutes, but the form shown below is acceptable and is widely used.*

|  | Words |
|---|---|
| Weslaco Steel Products, Inc. | 6 |
| ←———— Double-space | |
| MINUTES OF THE MEETING OF THE BOARD OF DIRECTORS | 16 |

Triple-space ————→

| Date: | May 28, 197- | 19 |
|---|---|---|

Double-space ——→

| Time: | 10 a.m. | 22 |
|---|---|---|
| Place: | Board Room, Corporate Offices | 30 |
| Present: | Albert Fries, Gerald Smith, Robert Kiddoo, George Hawkes, Joseph Buchwald, Paul Blomgren, William Rabe, and Kay Lupul | 42 / 53 / 56 |
| Absent: | Howard Shenson, Fadil Zuwaylif, and James Esmay | 67 |

Triple-space ——→

1. George Hawkes, Chairman of the Board, called the meeting to order. — 79 / 81

2. Minutes of the April meeting were approved as read. — 93

3. A report was presented by Gerald Smith, Chairman of the Long Range Planning Committee.  He made a motion to expand plant facilities to two additional locations within the next two years.  One location would serve Ohio and the other would serve Missouri.  The motion was seconded by Kay Lupul.  After lengthy discussion, the motion was tabled until the next meeting. — 106 / 118 / 130 / 142 / 154 / 166 / 168

4. The only item of new business was a merger proposal from Inland Steel, Inc.  The members of the board voted unanimously to reject this offer.  Chairman Hawkes was instructed to contact the Chairman of the Board of Inland Steel concerning a possible renegotiation of the merger proposal. — 180 / 192 / 204 / 216 / 228

5. The meeting was adjourned at 1 p.m. — 236

Respectfully submitted, — 241

*Robert Kiddoo*

Robert Kiddoo, Secretary — 246

jas — 247

**Minutes of a meeting**

# ■ Lesson 2

## 2a ■ Machine Adjustments

1. Find on your typewriter each part listed in the illustration on page 1.
2. Check the placement of the paper guide.
3. Set the line-space regulator at "2" for double spacing (DS).
4. Check whether your machine is equipped with pica or elite type. Set the margin stops for a 50-space line. If necessary, see pages vi and vii.
5. Insert paper. Adjust the paper-bail rolls.
6. Check your position at the typewriter with each point in the illustration on page ix.

## 2b ■ Keyboard Review

**Directions** – Type each line at least once.          **Spacing Guide** – Space once after a semicolon within a line.

1 Home keys DS `ff jj dd kk ss ll aa ;; ff jj dd kk ss ll aa ;; fj`

2 `fj dk sl a; fj dk sl a; fj dk sl a; fj dk sl a; fj`

3 `add lad add lad all fall all fall add lad add lad;`

4 `jhj jhj hj hj had had half half ash lash lash dash`

5 `a lad; a lad had; a lad had a lash; half had hash;`

Think each key as you strike it

## 2c ■ Reach to G—Reach to U

Type G with the F finger

Find g on the chart and on your machine. Place your fingers over the home keys. Watch your finger as you touch **gf** lightly. Hold the other fingers in position.

Type U with the J finger

Find **u** on the chart and on your machine. Place your fingers over the home keys. Watch your finger as you touch **uj** lightly. Hold the other fingers in position.

`fgf fgf gf gf lag lag lag`   ● Type twice on same line ●   `juj juj uj uj dud dud dud`

## 2d ■ Location Drills—G and U

**Directions** – Type the lines once; then repeat.          **Technique Goal** – Use quick, short, sharp strokes.

g   DS `fgf fgf gf gf fgf lag lag flag flag a lag; a flag;`

`lag lag slag slag glad glad a glad lad; a glad lad`

Type g with the f finger

u   `juj juj uj uj uj dud dud full full us us dusk dusk`

`husk husk; a dud; a dull dud; sulk sulk; fuss fuss`

Type u with the j finger

Walther and Company

Double-space ──────▶

Trial Balance

Double-space ──────▶

December 31, 197-

Triple-space ──────▶

| | | |
|---|---:|---:|
| Cash | $ 25,200 | |
| Notes Receivable | 5,000 | |
| Accounts Receivable | 34,000 | |
| Allowance for Doubtful Accounts | | $ 1,500 |
| Merchandise Inventory | 38,000 | |
| Land | 15,000 | |
| Buildings | 60,000 | |
| Accumulated Depreciation--Buildings | | 9,800 |
| Equipment | 25,000 | |
| Accumulated Depreciation--Equipment | | 6,200 |
| Notes Payable | | 7,200 |
| Accounts Payable | | 15,300 |
| Payroll Taxes Payable | | 555 |
| Capital Stock | | 105,555 |
| Dividends | 6,000 | |
| Sales | | 246,000 |
| Sales Returns and Allowances | 3,200 | |
| Purchases | 120,000 | |
| Purchases Returns and Allowances | | 4,600 |
| Salaries | 42,000 | |
| Advertising | 4,700 | |
| Payroll Taxes | 3,560 | |
| Depreciation of Building | 1,200 | |
| Depreciation of Equipment | 1,750 | |
| Insurance | 3,600 | |
| Other Expenses | 8,100 | |
| | $396,310 | $396,310 |

Trial balance

## 2e ■ Reach to E—Reach to O

Type E with the D finger

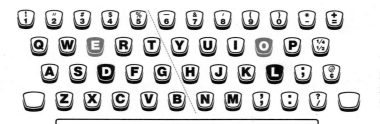

Type O with the L finger

Touch **ed** lightly. Move the **d** finger upward and forward without moving your hand.

Touch **ol** lightly, keeping your **j** and **;** fingers in typing position over the home keys.

ded ded ed ed led led led    • Type twice on same line •    lol lol ol ol log log log

## 2f ■ Location Drills—E and O

**Directions** – Type the lines once; then repeat.    **Technique Goal** – Hold your wrists low and steady.

e    DS  ded ded ed ed ed led led fled fled sled sled fled;    Type e with the d finger

he he she she shed shed he he held held he she she

o    lol lol ol ol ol old old fold fold so so sod sold;    Type o with the l finger

do do go go gold gold hold hold log log fold loss;

## 2g ■ Technique Builder—Stroking

**Directions** – Set the line-space regulator at "1" for single spacing (SS). Type each line twice as shown below, with a double space (DS) after the second typing of a line.

**Technique Goal** – Use quick, short, sharp strokes. Release the keys quickly. Type at a steady, even pace.

*• To double-space between groups of lines, operate the carriage-return lever or key twice.*

1    SS  due duel due duel so sold so sold he held she held
         due duel due duel so sold so sold he held she held    Double-space as you return

2        old fold old fold go goal go goal all shall of off
         old fold old fold go goal go goal all shall of off

3        us dusk us dusk fake lake sake fall full gall gull
         us dusk us dusk fake lake sake fall full gall gull

4        ed led fled sled lead he he do doe doll dole dodge
         ed led fled sled lead he he do doe doll dole dodge    Quick stroke and release

5        he had; he sold; he held; he has; he lead; he fled
         he had; he sold; he held; he has; he lead; he fled

6        she goes; she does; she shall; she sells; she lead
         she goes; she does; she shall; she sells; she lead

## ■ Lesson 79 • *70-space line*

### 79a ■ Keyboard Review • Each line at least three times         *5 minutes*

Alphabetic   SS   Good axles will be quickly broken if the car jumps over a safety zone.

Figure       There were 480 children in the building on May 27, 1965, at 10:00 a.m.    *Wrists and*

pol         A policy that police favor is not always popular with all politicians.    *elbows still*

Easy       If you have to make mistakes, you can try to make a new one each time.

     | 1 | 2 | 3 | 4 | 5 | 6 | 7 | 8 | 9 | 10 | 11 | 12 | 13 | 14 |

### 79b ■ Paragraph Skill Builder—Rough Draft • Four 1-minute writings      *5 minutes*

Words

DS   ¶ The most important things in live should be obscured by the unim-never    13

**70 words** portant. All to often, however, we loose sight of that is truly signi-    27

**1.4 si** ficant. most would agree, for example, that our good health is a gift    42

of us to treasure, and yet so of us take it for granted. We should make    56

an effort to appreciate and greatly prize the many gifts of life all us. about    70

### 79c ■ Proofreading Skill Builder—Consistency in Numbers and Names      *5 minutes*

**Directions** – Type the following paragraph and correct the errors in numbers and names. The accurate name is Palafox and the correct numbers are: for 1960, 10,987,542; for 1970, 14,567,980. Repeat.

DS       Mr. Palafox showed a population figure of 14,567,980 in the 1970

census count but only 10,987,542 in the 1960 count. If Mr. Polofax's    *Eyes*

**50 words** 1970 census figure was correct at 14,675,890, there was a definite    *on*

increase from the 1960 population of 10,897,452.    *copy*

### 79d ■ Typing from Dictation and Spelling Checkup • Type 78b, page 168, from dictation. Retype words in which you made an error.      *5 minutes*

### 79e ■ Problem Typing      *25 minutes*

#### Problem 1—Trial Balance

**Directions** – Type the trial balance shown on page 172. Center it vertically and horizontally on a full sheet of paper, using *reading position*. Leave four spaces between columns. See pages 53 and 57 for a review of centering instructions.

• *To make double lines, use the underline key and type the first of the lines. Then, operate the variable line spacer and move the carriage forward slightly to bring the paper into position. Type the second of the double lines.*

# ■ Lesson 3

## 3a ■ General Directions

1. Adjust your typewriter as explained at the beginning of Lesson 2, page 5. 2. Check your position at the typewriter with each point illustrated on page 2.

3. Double-space after repeating a line even though this reminder will not be restated in directions given for drills. Triple-space between parts of a lesson.

## 3b ■ Keyboard Review

**Directions** – Set the line-space regulator for double spacing (DS). Type once; then repeat.

**Technique Goal** – Keep your fingers curved over the home keys.

Home row    DS  `fdsa jkl; fdsa jkl; gf hj gf hj fall hall glad had`

u               `juj juj uj uj full jug dull dud lugs hug hugs gulf`

e               `ded ded ed ed led fled he held she shed fell shell`    Think the
letters as
you type

o               `lol lol ol ol old sold fold do so gold log loss go`

All letters taught   `keg jug she shall fog half log; he had a dull duel`

## 3c ■ Reach to R—Reach to I

Type R with the F finger

Touch **rf** lightly without moving your hand. Move only the f finger as you reach to the r.

Type I with the K finger

Touch **ik** lightly. Raise the j finger slightly to give the k finger freedom of movement.

`frf frf rf rf for for for`    • Type twice on same line •    `kik kik ik ik kid kid kid`

## 3d ■ Location Drills—R and I

**Directions** – Set the line-space regulator for single spacing (SS). Type each line twice.

**Technique Goal** – Hold your wrists down and quiet as you reach to the new keys.

r    SS  `frf frf rf rf rf fur furl for fork rug rug drug or`    Type r with
the f finger

          `jar jar surf surf rue rue rule rule lark lark roll`

i         `kik kik ik ik ik kid kid did did lid lid slid slid`    Type i with
the k finger

          `dike dike dish dish fill fill if if is is like fig`

~~~

**7th line space**

Words

ITINERARY FOR GEORGE H. BAECHTOLD        7

**Double-space** ————————————▶

June 15-18, 197-        10

◀————————— **Triple-space**

**6 spaces**

Monday, June 15   ↓   San Francisco to Salt Lake City        29

7:30 p.m.        Leave San Francisco International Airport,        40
                 Western Airlines, Flight #321.        46

9:48 p.m.        Arrive Salt Lake City.  Take airport limou-        57
                 sine to Hotel Utah.  Reservation confirmed        66
                 for June 15 and 16.        70

**Double-space** ————————————▶

Tuesday, June 16      Salt Lake City        83

8:30 a.m.        James Esmay of the Salt Lake City office        93
                 will meet you at the hotel.        99

10:00 a.m.       Meeting to discuss merger plans.        108

1:00 p.m.        Tour of Salt Lake City facilities.        117

Wednesday, June 17    Salt Lake City to Denver        135

9:00 a.m.        Leave Salt Lake City Airport, United Air-        145
                 lines, Flight #78.        149

10:10 a.m.       Arrive Denver Airport.  Reservation con-        159
                 firmed for the night, Brown Palace Hotel.        168
                 Howard Shenson of the Denver office will        177
                 meet you for a tour of the Denver facili-        185
                 ties.        187

6:00 p.m.        Dinner with management personnel.  Present        197
                 speech on merger plans.        203

Thursday, June 18     Denver to Chicago to San Francisco        223

8:00 a.m.        Leave Denver Airport, TWA, Flight #71.        234

10:15 a.m.       Arrive Chicago, O'Hare International Air-        244
                 port.  Max Lupul of the Chicago office will        253
                 meet you.        255

1:00 p.m.        Merger negotiations.        262

6:15 p.m.        Leave Chicago, O'Hare International Airport,        273
                 American Airlines, Flight #217.        280

8:25 p.m.        Arrive San Francisco International Airport.        291

~~~

**Itinerary**

## 3e ▪ Reach to C—Reach to N

Type C with the D finger

Touch **cd** lightly with the **d** finger. Hold the **a** finger in typing position, but let the other fingers move with the stroke.

Type N with the J finger

Touch **nj** lightly without moving your hand or wrist. Move only the **j** finger as you make the reach to **n**.

dcd dcd cd cd cod cod cod    • Type twice on same line •    jnj jnj nj nj and and and

## 3f ▪ Location Drills—C and N • Each line twice; DS after repeated lines.

c    SS    dcd dcd cd cd cd cod cod call call calf calf coals      Type c with the d finger
            lick lick sick sick such such cuff cuff luck slack

n          jnj jnj nj nj nj an an and and land land hand hand      Type n with the j finger
            end end lend lend gain gain rain rain fan fan fans

### Proper Stroking

Use a quick, firm sharp stroke.

Release the keys quickly by snapping them toward the palm of the hand.

## 3g ▪ Technique Builder—Stroking

**Directions** – Type each line twice; DS after repeated lines.

**Technique Goal** – Keep your fingers deeply curved. Use quick, firm, direct strokes.

1    SS    fdsa jkl; hj gf ol ed ik rf cd nj fur furl rid ran
2          lid slid slide hid hide ink rink sink sing so song
3          if he is; if she is; if he is here; if she is here      Fingers deeply curved
4          he hid a lid; he did; she had a jade ring; she did
5          end end lend lend send send an and hand land sand;
6          and go; and do; and if; and is; and he; and she is      Quick stroke; quick release
7          for us; do for us; and is for us; and he can do so
8          he is; if he is; if he did; she can; if she can go

Words

FROM:   Tarrant County Community College                                8
            Fort Worth, Texas                                              12

DATE:   August 2, 197-                                                  16

        <u>For Immediate Release</u>                                      25

    COURSE TO BE OFFERED IN NURSERY SCHOOL ADMINISTRATION           35

A course in nursery school administration will be offered           47
for the first time at Tarrant County Community College during       59
the fall semester.  The course, Child Development 41, which is       72
designed to give students the knowledge necessary to run a          84
nursery school, will meet on Monday evenings from 6:45 to 9:45       96
p.m.  Mrs. Gloria Wells, an experienced nursery school admin-        109
istrator, will teach the course.                                    115

Principles and practices of nursery school organization            127
and administration, curriculum development, budgeting, records      139
control techniques, and personnel policies and practices will       152
be covered during the semester.  Relationships with parents,        164
regulatory agencies, and community resources will also be in-       176
cluded.                                                             178

The last day to file an application for fall semester              189
admission to Tarrant County Community College is August 15.         201
Applications are available in the college admissions office         213
at 5800 Fulton Avenue from 8 a.m. to 5 p.m., Monday through         225
Friday.  Additional registration information may be obtained         237
by calling the admissions office at 718-1300, extension 429.        249

                # # #                                       250

**News release**

# ■ Lesson 4

- *Spacing: Double.*
- *Margins: 50-space line. Set the left stop 25 spaces to the left of the center of the paper. Move the right stop to the end of the scale.*

## 4a ■ Keyboard Review

**Directions** – Type the lines once; repeat.

**Technique Goals** – Return the carriage quickly; begin new line without pausing or looking up.

- *Technique goals are given for many of the drills. Keep these goals in mind; be guided by them. Your practice must have a clear, definite goal if it is to be helpful. Technique pointers appear in the margins of many of the drills. Glance at these pointers from time to time; they will help you keep the technique goals of a particular drill in mind.*

| | | |
|---|---|---|
| Home row<br>u, e, o | DS | fdsa jkl; hj gf hj gf uj ed ol jog fled dusk field |
| r | | frf frf rf rf for fork fir fire rid ride rode sure | Eyes on copy |
| i | | kik kik ik ik dike lid disk sir fig fill fail rail |
| c | | dcd dcd cd cd cod code call ice rice dice can lace | Type without pauses |
| n | | jnj jnj nj nj fin find and land end lend snag rang |
| All letters taught | | a large jug; and hold; did shake; and can fill all |

## 4b ■ Reach to T—Reach to . (Period)

Type T with the F finger

Touch **tf** lightly without moving the other fingers from their typing position.

Type . with the L finger

Touch **.1** lightly, lifting the little finger only enough to give freedom of movement.

ftf ftf tf tf fit fit fit • Type twice on same line • 1.1 1.1 .1 .1 full. full.

## 4c ■ Location Drills—T and . (Period)

**Directions** – Type each line twice.

**Technique Goal** – Keep the wrists and arms quiet.

| | | | |
|---|---|---|---|
| t | SS | ftf ftf tf tf tf it it fit fit it lit lift hit fit | Type t with the f finger |
| | | to to ton told told the the then then tan than sit | |
| | | thus thus that that told told late late then these | Type . with the l finger |
| . (period) | | 1.1 1.1 1.1 .1 .1 .1 fill. full. sell. fail. rail. | |

### 78a ■ Keyboard Review • Each line at least three times
*5 minutes*

| | |
|---|---|
| Alphabetic SS | Alex drove the buzzing tan jeep quickly away from the obstacle course. |
| Figure | That international club had 14,750 English and 23,689 Spanish members. |
| Double letters | The shipping office accountant offered to send my baggage immediately. |
| Easy | There is no limit to the height they can go by remaining on the level. |

Type without pauses

| 1 | 2 | 3 | 4 | 5 | 6 | 7 | 8 | 9 | 10 | 11 | 12 | 13 | 14 |

### 78b ■ Spelling Aids • Type each line twice. Study the words as you type.
*5 minutes*

1  SS  perpetuate personnel previously prosecute quaint questionnaire receive

2  reciprocate remarkable routine scientific statistics status sympathize

3  technically technique temporarily tragedy unfortunate unique universal

4  vacancy valid variation vitally waiver warrant writing yielded zealous

Think; spell; type

### 78c ■ Skill Comparison
*5 minutes*

**Directions** – Type a 1-minute writing on each sentence in 78a, above. Compare the *gwam*.

### 78d ■ Problem Typing
*30 minutes*

• *The problems in this lesson and in those that follow are examples of a wide variety of business communications that one encounters in business typing.*

#### Problem 1—News Release

**Directions** – Type the news release shown on the next page. Follow the directions on the illustration.

• *A news release should, if possible, be limited to one page. If multiple pages are required, type*

Full sheet

*"more" in the center of the page a triple space below the last line of copy on all pages except the last one. To indicate the end of the copy in a news release, type # # # in the center of the paper a triple space below the last line of copy.*

60-space line, pica; 70-space line, elite

#### Problem 2—Itinerary

**Directions** – Type the itinerary illustrated on page 170. Follow the directions given on the illustration. Although there are many acceptable formats for an

Full sheet

itinerary, the one illustrated on page 170 is one of the most frequently used. An itinerary should be clearly arranged and easy to follow.

60-space line, pica; 70-space line, elite

## 4d ■ Shifting for Capitals—Left Shift Key

The left shift key (No. 28) is used to type capital letters with the right hand.

USE A
ONE-TWO
COUNT

One – Depress the shift key with the a finger. Hold it down.
Two – Strike the capital letter; then quickly release the shift key and return the a finger to its typing position.

Directions – Each line twice.

Spacing Guide – Space twice after a period that ends a sentence, except when the period comes at the end of the line. When it does, return the carriage without spacing.

1  ss  jJ jJ hH Hal Hal Lee Lee Hal Lee Jake Leed Jo Hill

2  Hal ran.  Jake fell.  Jack hid.  Jo Hall can ride.

3  Hal fell.  He had a hard fall.  He fell near here.

4  I hit it.  Lou hid the lace.  Jane filled the jar.

*Space twice after period*

## 4e ■ Technique Builder—Stroking ● Each line twice

1  ss  to to told told the then then that this this there

2  if it is so; to let; to tell; to go; to do; to the

3  to do this; to do that; to do it; to do the; to us

4  Jack can go.  He can go for an hour.  He can sail.

5  Karl can sell the gun.  He can sell it to Hal Lee.

6  Jake Hale can go to Long Lake.  He can sail there.

7  Jane Knight led the girls in a song in Lange Hall.

*Hold arms, wrists, and elbows steady*

## 4f ■ Typing from Dictation

Directions – Type the words as your teacher dictates them.

Technique Goal – Think the whole word as you type it. Say each word to yourself as you type.

1  DS  if if if is is is he he he if he if he is if he is

2  he he she she is is his his did did he had she had

3  or of of or or for for go go so so he did if he is

4  for us for us if he is go for us he had us she did

*Think the whole word*

## Problem 2—Business Letter from Script

**Directions** – Type the following letter in modified block style with blocked paragraphs. For review, refer to the illustration of this style on page 148.

Full sheet — 60-space line — Open punctuation — Small envelope — Carbon copy — Address on 7th line space from date

Current date / Mr. William Self / 486 East Rose Lane / Tulsa, Oklahoma 74101 / Dear Mr. Self / We are pleased that you have retained our office to represent you in connection with your recent accident. (¶) All information which you have, including the names of your doctors, is confidential and should not be given out. Refer everyone to this office for information. (¶) We know from experience that in many instances complications arise in days, weeks, or months after an accident; and because of this we cannot attempt to settle your case until such time as we know whether or not your injury will be of a permanent nature. (¶) Our office will investigate this matter and keep you informed concerning all facets of your case. / Cordially yours / MARTIN, LOWE, AND WISELY / John C. Martin, Attorney / xx

## Problem 3—Business Letter in Block Style

**Directions** – Type the following letter in block style. For review, refer to the illustration of a letter in this style on page 151. In a two-column tabulation a short-cut method may be used. Set a tab stop for the first column 5 to 15 spaces to the right of the left margin. For the second column, backspace 5 to 15 spaces for the indention from the right margin and then one space for each letter in the longest columnar entry. Set a tab stop for the right column at this point.

Full sheet — 60-space line — Open punctuation — Address on the 3d line space from date

*Current date* / Mrs. Marian Gray / 16943 West Orange Avenue / Trenton, N. J.  80609 / Dear Mrs. Gray / We appreciate the excellent manner in which you have paid your account. Even though it is paid in full, please do not feel that your account is closed. It remains open in our file ready to serve you. (¶) You may wish to take advantage of the big sale on home furnishings we now have in progress. You will find big savings on the following items:

| | | | |
|---|---|---|---|
| Sofas | Chairs | Dinettes | Bookcases |
| Tables | Table Lamps | Television Sets | Stereo Sets |
| Floor Lamps | Beds | Mattresses | Draperies |
| Dressers | Mirrors | Carpeting | Vacuum Cleaners |
| | | Area Rugs | Rug Shampooers |
| | | Ranges | Refrigerators |
| | | Washers | Dryers |
| | | Dishwashers | Small Appliances |

Remember, any item may be purchased on our easy payment plan with no money down. The sale is for a limited time only, so why not come in now and take advantage of these many outstanding values. / Very sincerely yours / D. A. Standifer / Credit Manager / xx

# ■ Lesson 5

- *Spacing: Double.*
- *Margins: 50-space line.*

## 5a ■ Keyboard Review

**Directions** – Type each line once; then repeat.     **Technique Goal** – Type only as fast as you can type well.

| | | |
|---|---|---|
| u, e, o | DS | uj ed ol dusk led fold due rule sold fork four hoe |
| r, i | | rf ik rf ik for fork fir fire door dire risk share |
| n | | jnj jnj nj nj tan than hen then den dent send sent |
| t | | ftf ftf tf tf to told the then their hat late this |
| . (period) | | jJ hH lL Hal led.  Joe ran.  Lee fell.  Jack rode. |
| All letters taught | | Lou can take the old flag.  Jill ran as he called. |

*Space twice after period*

## 5b ■ Shifting for Capitals—Right Shift Key

The right shift key (No. 26) is used to type capital letters with the left hand.

USE A
ONE-TWO
COUNT

**One** – Depress the shift key with the **;** **finger.** Hold it down.

**Two** – Strike the capital letter; then quickly release the shift key and return the **;** **finger** to its typing position.

**Directions** – Each line twice.     **Spacing Guide** – Remember to space twice after a period that ends a sentence (except at the end of a line).

1  SS  fF fF gG gG Flo Flo Gus Gus dD dD Dick Sue Al Ross
2      Flo left.  Dick can ride.  Al can go.  Rod hid it.
3      Sue and Fern lent it to Ed.  Ted and Rose sold it.

*Quick, firm reach to the shift key*

## 5c ■ Technique Builder—Stroking • Each line twice

1  SS  as has; do does; so sold; he held; to told; it fit
2      go good; so song; the then; is this; led lend land
3      an and; the their there; it fit; us just; is list;
4      Kirk can go to the class.  The girl can go for it.
5      Chuck and Frank took Jane.  She is in their class.
6      Ken said that he and Karl lent the old gun to Joe.

*Quick, short, sharp strokes*

### 77a ■ Keyboard Review • Each line at least three times

Alphabetic SS  A young bank executive in High Falls was amazed at John's quick reply.

Figure  All 24 people agreed that 35 of the 167 books added should be fiction.

*Eyes on copy
as you return
the carriage*

Weak fingers  An awareness of probable political opinions will aid our public cause.

Easy  A problem is something you view when you take your eyes off your goal.

| 1 | 2 | 3 | 4 | 5 | 6 | 7 | 8 | 9 | 10 | 11 | 12 | 13 | 14 |

### 77b ■ Paragraph Guided Writings

**Directions** – 1. Set goals of 40, 50, and 60 words a minute. Type two 1-minute writings at each rate. Try to type your goal word just as time is called. Your teacher may call the quarter or half minutes to guide you. 2. Type additional writings at the 50- and 60-word rates as time permits.

DS  People gain success in a variety of ways. Some men feel that they are successful if they are rich. Others feel that fame indicates success. The truly successful man, however, may merely be one who has found contentment and happiness in what he is doing. He may be rich or poor, famous or obscure.

60 words
1.4 si

*Quick
carriage
return*

### 77c ■ Problem Typing

#### Problem 1—Business Letter in Modified Block Style, Indented Paragraphs

**Directions** – Type in modified block style with indented paragraphs. For review, refer to the illustration on page 145.

• *The problems in this lesson review the basic letter styles presented in this unit.*

Full sheet    50-space line    Mixed punctuation    Small envelope    Carbon copy    Address on 9th line space from date

*Current date* / Mr. James Gage, Attorney / 756 Commerce Street, Suite 465 / Honolulu, Hawaii 96813 / Dear Mr. Gage / I have examined your client, Mr. Ronald Dewitt. He suffers from a chronic lumbo-sacral strain of a rather mild degree. There is no indication for further formal treatment to his back. However, since the patient has never worn a lumbar brace, I recommend that he be fitted with one which will immobilize the lower thoracic cage. After wearing this back support for four months, his symptoms should completely disappear and the back support can be gradually discarded. (¶) Permanent physical impairment resulting from the alleged injury of May 15 is not anticipated. A detailed report of my examination of Mr. Dewitt is available. / Yours truly / Robert A. Peterson, M. D. / xx

### 5d ■ Typing from Dictation • Type these words as your teacher dictates them.

1  DS  he he the the he he the the an an and and an an an

2      is is his his go go got got it it fit fit he is it

3      an and he the go got it fit is his go got do go so

4      to to to do if if if he did and he and she and the

Think and type words

# ■ Lesson 6

- Spacing: Double.
- Margins: 50-space line.

### 6a ■ Keyboard Review • Type each line once; repeat.

t  DS  ftf ftf tf tf to told it lit fit hit the then lift

n      jnj jnj nj nj den dent and land send nail ran gain

Left shift      I hid the ring.  I hid it in a jar.  Jan found it.

Right shift      Rod and Sue can go.  Fran can go too.  Ted hit it.

All letters taught      Don Ross can find the sign that is near June Lake.

Eyes on copy

### 6b ■ Reach to W—Reach to M

Type W with the S finger

Touch ws lightly, lifting the a finger slightly to give freedom of movement.

Type M with the J finger

Touch **mj** lightly, without twisting your hand or moving the other fingers from position.

sws sws ws ws ws wish who   • Type twice on same line •   jmj jmj mj mj mj jam jam

### 6c ■ Location Drills—W and M • Each line twice

w  SS  sws sws ws ws ws wish wish when when will low well

      won won work work show show wall wall glow row how

Type w with the s finger

m      jmj jmj mj mj jam jam mad made make mail main whom

      came came come come much mist mild male lame shame

      more more melt melt meld meld form farm miss smash

Type m with the j finger

## 76d ■ Sustained Skill Building

**Directions** – 1. Type a 5-minute writing; compute *gwam*.
2. Type two 1-minute writings on each paragraph, the first for speed, the second for control. 3. Type another 5-minute writing on all the paragraphs. Compute *gwam*; compare *gwam* and number of errors for both 5-minute writings. Submit the better of the two.

● Contains all letters

|  |  | GWAM 1'  5' |
|--|--|-------------|

**¶1**
**69 words**
**1.4 si**

DS

A man or woman who can write a good letter is an asset to any com- | 13 | 3 | 59
pany. Since American business spends billions of dollars each year on | 27 | 5 | 61
letters, some companies are trying to build better writing skills in | 41 | 8 | 64
their employees. They feel that this will not only cut down on the | 55 | 11 | 67
costs involved, but a much better public relations job can also be done. | 69 | 14 | 70

**¶2**
**62 words**
**1.4 si**

Any good business letter needs certain basic qualities. It must | 13 | 16 | 72
be clear, coherent, and concise. A letter is clear if the reader can | 27 | 19 | 75
tell exactly what the writer is trying to say. It is coherent if it | 41 | 22 | 78
is logical in thought as well as in construction. It is concise, also, | 55 | 25 | 81
if efficient use is made of words. | 62 | 26 | 82

**¶3**
**68 words**
**1.4 si**

In order to construct a letter with these qualities, the writer | 13 | 29 | 85
must look at the problem very closely. He must know exactly what he | 27 | 32 | 88
hopes to accomplish and know something about the person to whom | 39 | 34 | 90
the letter will be sent. With this insight into the problem, the writer | 54 | 37 | 93
has a much better chance of achieving the desired purpose of the letter. | 68 | 40 | 96

**¶4**
**82 words**
**1.4 si**

Writing good letters is not easy. This skill, however, can be | 13 | 42 | 98
learned. Above all else, the writer should remember to make the let- | 26 | 45 | 101
ter easy to read and to understand. If he keeps this in mind, words | 40 | 48 | 104
that are not clear, references that are hazy, and sentence structure | 54 | 51 | 107
that is difficult to follow will not be used. By avoiding these weak- | 68 | 54 | 110
nesses, the writer will be much more likely to have an effective letter. | 82 | 56 | 112

1' | 1 | 2 | 3 | 4 | 5 | 6 | 7 | 8 | 9 | 10 | 11 | 12 | 13 | 14 |
5' | 1 | 2 | 3 |

## 6d ■ Technique Builder—Stroking

**Directions** – Type each line twice.

**Technique Goals** – Avoid sidewise stroking; hold the hands directly over the keys.

1  SS  win won word work works will with how show row low

2  am same aim lame flame come dome mad made mar mark

3  Kirk will go to the late show.  I can go with him.

4  Al can lead our team.  Jo and Rod will go with us.        Quick, sharp strokes

5  We shall go with them.  The four men will go also.

6  Hal leads the drill team.  Our team will go there.

7  Don saw the game with Gale and Joe.  Al took Jane.

## 6e ■ Sentence Skill Builder

**Directions** – Type two 1-minute writings on each sentence. Compute your gross words a minute (*gwam*).

**Technique Goals** – Eliminate waste motions in the arms and wrists. Return the carriage quickly; type steadily.

- *In typewriting, 5 strokes are counted as one word. Each line below has 50 strokes, or 10 words. Each complete line typed gives you a score of 10 words. For a partially typed line, note the scale. Add the figure nearest the last word or letter typed to your complete sentence score. This is your gross words a minute (gwam).*

1  DS  Ken said that he saw the two girls go to the show.

2  Fern and Karl will take the left road to the lake.
   |  1  |  2  |  3  |  4  |  5  |  6  |  7  |  8  |  9  |  10  |

# ■ Lesson 7

- *Spacing: Double.*
- *Margins: 50-space line.*

## 7a ■ Keyboard Review

**Directions** – Type each line once; repeat.

**Posture Goal** – Sit back in your chair; body erect.

Home row  DS  fdsa jkl; fdsa jkl; gf hj gf hj lad glad shad half

w  sws sws ws ws wish win wind well will low slow how

m  jmj jmj mj mj jam jam fame same lame mad made make        Eyes on copy

t, n  tf nj tf nj tide lift fit end lend an and tan than

All letters taught  Jack Dodge will sign the forms to run in the race.
   |  1  |  2  |  3  |  4  |  5  |  6  |  7  |  8  |  9  |  10  |

### 76a ■ **Keyboard Review** • Each line at least three times                                    *5 minutes*

| | | |
|---|---|---|
| Alphabetic ss | The big fall journal will itemize stock quotes and explain key events. | |
| Figure | On December 17, 1903, Orville Wright flew his airplane for 12 seconds. | Quick sharp stroking |
| Shift | The article, "How to Write Letters," appeared in the Writer's Journal. | |
| Easy | Men are not able to take it with them if they spend it before they go. | |

| 1 | 2 | 3 | 4 | 5 | 6 | 7 | 8 | 9 | 10 | 11 | 12 | 13 | 14 |

### 76b ■ **Proofreading Skill Builder—Reading for Meaning**                                    *10 minutes*

**Directions** – Type the following paragraphs, filling in the blank spaces with the appropriate words selected from those given in the right margin. Use double spacing and a 60-space line. Repeat.

DS      Plans and _____ for the Lincoln School are now _____.

We should _____ your coming to _____ office at 3 p.m. on

June 12 so that we might go over the details for this _____.

     After our discussion, you may _____ to take the plans

with you for _____ study. It will be _____ for us to

have your bid not _____ than August 1.

     If it will not be _____ for you to meet on _____ 12,

please let us _____. Any day that _____ will be satis-

factory. We hope to begin construction on this project no later

than _____ 1.

necessary
wish
complete
week
June
convenient
later
know
appreciate
job
specifications
our
further
very
October

### 76c ■ **Technique Builder—Stroking** • Each line three times                                    *5 minutes*

| | | |
|---|---|---|
| Difficult reach | ss | Numbers of uniformed men were unanimously united to fight the unknown. |
| Weak fingers | | Polite political opponents shouldn't publicly oppose popular opinions. |
| Weak fingers | | We were unaware that the puzzled quorum would not award a quick prize. |
| Double letters | | That bookkeeper had an occasion to correct the errors in the accounts. |

Type steadily

| 1 | 2 | 3 | 4 | 5 | 6 | 7 | 8 | 9 | 10 | 11 | 12 | 13 | 14 |

### 7b ■ Reach to V—Reach to , (Comma)

Type V with the F finger

Touch **vf** lightly without moving your hand. Keep the other fingers over their home keys.

Type , with the K finger

Touch **,k** lightly, lifting the **j** finger slightly to give freedom of movement.

```
fvf fvf vf five five dive   • Type twice on same line •   k,k k,k ,k ,k work, work,
```

### 7c ■ Location Drills—V and , (Comma)

**Directions** – Type each line twice.

**Spacing Guide** – Space once after a comma.

v  ss
```
fvf fvf vf vf vf five five drive drove lived loves
```
Type v with the f finger
```
have have move move give give view views void void
```

, (comma)
```
k,k k,k ,k ,k ,k work, work, dark, mark, the work,
```
Type , with the k finger
```
and the, and then, for this, for that, if he will,
```

### 7d ■ Reach to Y

#### Straight, Direct Stroking

Type Y with the J finger

Touch **yj** lightly without moving the other fingers from their typing position.

```
• Type twice on same line •
jyj jyj jyj yj yj jay jay
```

Do not turn hands sidewise

Hold hands upright, directly over keys

### 7e ■ Location Drill—Y

**Directions** – Each line twice.

**Technique Goal** – Curve your fingers deeply to make the long reach to y without moving the hand.

y  ss
```
jyj jyj yj yj yj jay jay lay lay fly fly slay slay
```
Type y with the j finger
```
yes yes yet yet yell yell dry dry try try sly they
```
```
slay jay say they ray gray year year fly flay flay
```

## Problem 2—Interoffice Memorandum

Half sheet        60-space line, pica; 70-space line, elite        One carbon copy

Words

May 28, 197–

3

TO: Clifford Loeb, Agent

8

FROM: Gail Stegelmann, Accounting Department

17

SUBJECT: Cancellation of Policy #584–295

25

Mr. Larry Glenn called today and cancelled his policy with us. He was quite unhappy about the way in which his last claim was settled.

40
53

Since you are his agent, I thought you might want to contact him today and try to discuss the problem. The claim was handled by George Wilson, who is no longer with our company. Perhaps you can convince Mr. Glenn to retain his policy with us.

67
81
96
102

xx

102

## Problem 3—Memorandum from Rough Draft

Full sheet      60-space line, pica; 70-space line, elite      Two carbon copies      Make all necessary corrections

May 15, 197– ← *10th line space*

↓ *4th line space*

# → TO: Clifton Conrad
From: Doyle Evans, Vice President

SUBJECT: Sales *for April* at Gulfgate Branch

TS → The *total* sales for the months of March and april at *three* ~~two~~ branch

SS → stores are as follows:

*Center the table horizontally.*

| | DS → March | April |
|---|---|---|
| Mission hills ← 8 spaces → | $628,421.82 | $784,961.29 |
| Gulfgate | 837,364.10 | 642,831.15 |
| Eastside | 529,832.71 | 676,933.84 |

Please contact Mr. ~~Brown~~ *Thomas*, Manager at Gulf gate, concerning

SS → the decrease in sales. Per haps there are problems about which we are not aware. May I hear from you before the Board meeting *on Monday.*

X X

## 7f ■ Technique Builder—Stroking ● Each line twice

1  SS  vow vow live love live give gives move moved glove

2      the they ray tray stray sly lay slay gray ray gray

3      to try, and they, to have, if they, and yet, if my

4      the view, to live, can move, will try, if they try

5      Dan sold the old mask.  He sold it to Steve Young.

6      Ray will go.  He will go with Fay.  Mel can drive.

7      Al can go.  He may ride with Rod, as he has a car.
    | 1 | 2 | 3 | 4 | 5 | 6 | 7 | 8 | 9 | 10 |

*Hands directly over the keys*

## 7g ■ Sentence Skill Builder

**Directions** – Type two 1-minute writings on each sentence. Compute your gross words a minute (*gwam*).

**Technique Goals** – Hold the hands directly over the keys. Strike the keys with straight, direct strokes.

1  SS  The men worked at the lake for the first two days.

2      She went to the old school with her aunt that day.

3      Try to do this work just as well as you can do it.
    | 1 | 2 | 3 | 4 | 5 | 6 | 7 | 8 | 9 | 10 |

*Wrists and elbows still*

When you reach from home position to strike another key, keep the other fingers on or near their home keys. Make the reach with the finger without twisting the wrist or moving the arm or elbow.

# ■ Lesson 8

● *Spacing: Double.*
● *Margins: 50-space line.*

## 8a ■ Keyboard Review ● Type each line once; repeat.

v           DS  fvf fvf vf vf five live strive move love have give

, (comma)       k,k k,k ,k ,k work, rack, trick, to give, to rock,

y               jyj jyj yj yj yet yell year sly they lay flay gray

All letters taught   Merv Rhoades may take the main road to Fort Wayne.

                Ray Locke wore a light grey suit to the late show.
    | 1 | 2 | 3 | 4 | 5 | 6 | 7 | 8 | 9 | 10 |

*Sit erect with eyes on copy*

10th line space

May 20, 197-

DS

TO:  Doyle Evans

FROM:  James West, President  *J. W.*

SUBJECT:  Goals for Effective Management Consulting

TS

It is my pleasure to welcome you as a new consultant with
West and Associates, Inc.  Our company has been able to attain
its high standard of excellence in our field by following
several goals.  These goals are:

1.  Always prepare a written statement which outlines the
aim and scope of your work, your plan of procedure, the results you expect to achieve, and the terms of your contract.

2.  Submit periodic reports of your progress to the appropriate executives in the company for which you are doing the
consulting.

3.  Always work constructively with the employees in your
client's company.  Try to teach them new principles, methods,
skills, or techniques which will help them to carry out the
improvements you suggest once you have left.

4.  Keep close contact with your client as he considers, then
implements, your recommendations.  You may need to make a
post-installation review of the changes or improvements that
you recommend.

5.  And finally, always leave your client with the feeling
that he will want to retain you again if he needs the kind of
services you can provide.

If you try to achieve these goals, you will do a good job for
your client.  This, in turn, will enable you to help us maintain our high standards in management consulting.

DS

xx

Reference initials

**Interoffice memorandum**

## 8b ■ Reach to B—Reach to P

Type B with the F finger

Type P with the ; finger

Touch **bf** lightly, allowing your **d** and **s** fingers to move slightly to give freedom of movement.

Touch **p;** lightly, keeping your elbow quiet. Keep your right wrist low and steady.

```
fbf  fbf  bf  bf  bf  buf  buff      • Type twice on same line •      ;p;  ;p;  p;  p;  p;  lap flap
```

## 8c ■ Location Drills—B and P

**Directions** – Type each line twice.

**Technique Goal** – Type with wrists and arms in position.

b      SS
```
fbf  fbf  bf  bf  bf  buff  buff  bluff  bluff  job  job  mob

bug  bug  but  but  both  both  rob  rob  bold  bold  by  buy

bold  bold  ball  ball  sob  sob  rub  rub  scrub  scrub  by
```
Type b with the f finger

p
```
;p;  ;p;  p;  p;  p;  lap  lap  rip  rip  trip  trip  rap  rap

trap  trap  plan  plan  play  play  slip  slip  slap  plain
```
Type p with the ; finger

## 8d ■ Reach to Z

Type Z with the A finger

Touch **za** lightly, keeping the other fingers in typing position.

• Type twice on same line •

```
aza  aza  za  za  za  haze  haze
```

Don't buckle or twist your wrists

Keep the wrists low and steady

## 8e ■ Location Drill—Z

**Directions** – Type each line twice.

**Technique Goal** – Keep the wrists low and steady as you type.

z      SS
```
aza  aza  aza  za  za  za  haze  haze  maze  maze  zeal  zeal

zone  zone  haze  maze  zeal  zone  fuzz  fuzz  froze  size

froze  size  zoo  zones  maze  zeal  size  doze  dozen  zoo
```
Type z with the a finger

**Directions – 1.** Type two 1-minute writings on the first paragraph.

**2.** Type two 5-minute writings on all paragraphs.

**3.** Circle the errors and compute the *gwam*. Compare the *gwam* and number of errors for the two writings.

**4.** Submit the better of the two five-minute timings.

● Contains all letters

|  | GWAM |
|--|--|
|  | 1'  5' |

**¶1**
**73 words**
**1.4 si**

DS

Students who have wanted to work their way through college have | 13  3  57

always been able to do so. But with more students attending school now | 27  5  59

than ever before, there is a greater demand for part-time jobs. On the | 42  8  62

other hand, there are also more jobs available. The result is that most | 56  11  65

students can still find many chances to earn a large part of their col- | 70  14  68

lege expenses. | 73  15  69

**¶2**
**55 words**
**1.4 si**

If a person plans to work his way through college, he should ac- | 13  17  71

quire a skill. There are many skills that one could acquire, but stu- | 27  20  74

dents with skills in the clerical areas of typing, shorthand, and book- | 41  23  77

keeping seem to be among the most successful in obtaining part-time jobs. | 55  26  80

**¶3**
**70 words**
**1.4 si**

Surveys have shown that the most popular part-time jobs for col- | 13  28  82

lege students have been as clerk-typists. Many colleges report that | 27  31  85

there are more jobs in this group than there are students to fill them. | 41  34  88

When a student acquires skill in typewriting for his own personal use, | 55  37  91

he should realize that he can put this skill to work in a variety of | 69  40  94

ways. | 70  40  94

**¶4**
**72 words**
**1.4 si**

College officials predict that the number of students seeking part- | 13  42  96

time jobs will increase steadily, but so will the number of jobs. Place- | 28  45  99

ment officers feel that any student who has a skill and who keeps his | 42  48  102

grades up so that he can devote enough time and effort to his job should | 57  51  105

have no trouble finding a part-time position to help pay his college | 70  54  108

expenses. | 72  54  108

1' | 1 | 2 | 3 | 4 | 5 | 6 | 7 | 8 | 9 | 10 | 11 | 12 | 13 | 14 |
5' | 1 | 2 | 3 |

### 8f ■ Indenting for Paragraphs

You will use the tabulator bar or key (No. 24) to indent for paragraphs. Find this bar or key on your typewriter. Touch lightly the tab bar (right index finger) or tab key (right little finger). Deeply curve the other fingers in making this reach.

Next, turn to page vii and read how to use the tab clear key (No. 31) and the tab set key (No. 23).

### 8g ■ Paragraph Typing

**Directions** – Set the machine for a 5-space paragraph indention and double spacing. Type once. Repeat if time permits.

**Technique Goal (Manual)** – Hold the tab bar or key down until the carriage stops.

**(Electric)** – Tap the tab key lightly and immediately return to home position.

|  |  |  | Words in ¶ | Total Words |
|---|---|---|---|---|
| ¶1 26 words | DS | Bob will go to the zoo.  It may be near your | 9 | 9 |
|  |  | store.  If he stops there to see you, please have | 19 | 19 |
|  |  | him call me.  I wish to talk to him. | 26 | 26 |
| ¶2 26 words |  | In the long run, it is the way you work that | 9 | 35 |
|  |  | counts.  If you strike the keys with short, sharp | 19 | 45 |
|  |  | strokes, you will learn to type well. | 26 | 52 |

| 1 | 2 | 3 | 4 | 5 | 6 | 7 | 8 | 9 | 10 |

## ■ Lesson 9

- *Spacing: Double.*
- *Margins: 50-space line.*

### 9a ■ Keyboard Review • Type each line once; repeat.

| b | DS | fbf fbf bf bf bud bus bluff bold bring rub rib rob |
|---|---|---|
| p |  | ;p; ;p; p; p; pled pledge plain help gulp rip trip |
| z |  | aza aza za za zone zones zeal size maze doze dozed |
| y, v |  | yj vf yj vf live five yet they sly move love stray |

Hold wrists low and steady

Van Trent can leave Buz Gray a check for the work.

**All letters taught**

John might pay for the work that needs to be done.

| 1 | 2 | 3 | 4 | 5 | 6 | 7 | 8 | 9 | 10 |

# ■ Lesson 75 • *70-space line*

Alphabetic SS Bob's zest for speeding was quickly dimmed after his extensive injury.

Figure    There were 185 people from Texas, 396 from Maine, and 2,470 from Iowa.    Quick, sharp strokes

Hyphen    John, my brother-in-law, is teaching four on-the-job training classes.

Easy    The map was left on the desk for him to see before he drove to Boston.
| 1 | 2 | 3 | 4 | 5 | 6 | 7 | 8 | 9 | 10 | 11 | 12 | 13 | 14 |

## 75b ■ Timed Writings
15 minutes

**Directions** – Type the material on page 161, following the instructions given at the top of that page.

---

### INTEROFFICE MEMORANDUMS

• *The interoffice memorandum is used for correspondence between offices or departments within a company. Its chief advantage is that it can be set up very quickly.*

1. Interoffice correspondence is usually typed on a special company form labeled "Interoffice Memorandum." Printed headings are used for opening lines.

2. When printed headings are not used, however, the date is typed on the 7th line space from the top for a half-page memorandum and on the 10th line space for a full-page memorandum. The additional lines in the heading are each double-spaced with the first line typed on the 4th line space following the date. A triple space should be left between the subject line and the first line of the message.

3. Block style should be used for typing the message.

4. A 60-space line is used for pica type, a 70-space line for elite type.

5. The body of a memorandum is usually single-spaced, but a double space should be left between paragraphs. A very short memorandum, however, may be double-spaced if the typist prefers.

6. In a memorandum personal titles (Mr., Mrs., Dr., etc.) are usually omitted. The salutation, complimentary close, and signature are also omitted. Some dictators prefer, however, to sign their initials following their name in the opening lines. This indicates final approval after the memo has been typed.

7. Reference initials are typed a double space below the message. All notations (enclosure, carbon copy, etc.) are typed in the same position as they are in regular correspondence.

---

## 75c ■ Problem Typing
25 minutes

### Problem 1—Interoffice Memorandum

**Directions** – Type the memorandum illustrated on page 162. Refer to the instructions given above.

Full sheet                          One carbon copy                          Use your own reference initials

## Page 1—Second Page of a Two-Page Letter

**Directions** – Assume that you have completed the first page of a two-page letter. Type the following copy as though it is the second page of this letter. Use the first illustration on page 158 for the heading for the second page. Make an original and one carbon copy. Use modified block style, blocked paragraphs.

Full sheet          70-space line, elite; 60-space line, pica          Mixed punctuation          Large envelope

Words

Mr. Clarence Knutson                 2                 May 3, 197–          7

Triple-space——→

The following plans are still available in Unit II:          18

| Plan Number | Size (Sq. Ft.) | Price |  |
|---|---|---|---|
| | | | 24 |
| 201 | 1,754 | $32,950 | 28 |
| 202 | 1,979 | 34,950 | 31 |
| 202A | 2,054 | 36,800 | 35 |

Both first and second trust deeds are available. First trust deeds are          49
at 7 percent for 29 years, and second trust deeds are at 8 percent for          63
10 years. The loans are fully amortized with no balloon payments.          77

After you have had an opportunity to look over this information, please          91
call me if you have additional questions. I will be happy to show you          105
through any of the houses that you might like to see.          116

Yours truly,          119

Donna Halverson          122
Sales Representative          126

## Problem 2—Second Page of a Two-Page Letter

**Directions** – Type in modified block style with indented paragraphs. Follow the second illustration shown on page 158.

Full sheet          70-space line, elite; 60-space line, pica          Mixed punctuation          Carbon copy          Large envelope

Mr. G. R. Killion / Page 2 / May 3, 197– (¶) All utilities are underground so that nothing will mar your enjoyment of this hillside setting. Each floor plan, with its variations and wide choice of elevations, offers a unique opportunity for individuality of design and adaptation to the special needs of your family. (¶) The first section of houses will be ready for occupancy in approximately five weeks. Model homes are open every day from 10 a.m. to 6 p.m. Why not come out this weekend and let me show you through the models. Now is an excellent time to buy while you still have a wide choice of both locations and styles. (¶) I am enclosing a brochure which will give you more detailed information on prices and financial arrangements. We will look forward to seeing you soon at Western Hills and to helping you choose the home of your choice. Sincerely yours, / WESTERN HILLS DEVELOPMENT COMPANY / Thomas E. Murrah, Vice President, Sales / Enclosure

## 9b ■ Reach to Q—Reach to ?

Type Q with the A finger

Touch **qa** lightly without moving the wrist and elbow in or out. Hold them steady.

Type ? with the ; finger

As you touch **?;** lightly two or three times, remember to depress the left shift key.

aqa aqa qa qa aqa qa quit     • Type twice on same line •     ;?; ;?; ?; ?; Why?  When?

## 9c ■ Location Drills—Q and ?

**Directions** – Type each line twice.          **Spacing Guide** – Space twice after ? at the end of a sentence.

q          SS aqa aqa aqa qa qa qa quit quit quip quip quay quay          Type q with
                                                                         the a finger

              quit quite square square squire squire quote quote

?              ;?; ;?; ;?; ?; ?; ?; Can she dance or sing a song?        Type ? with
                                                                         the ; finger

              Will Al drive?  Can Bob swim?  Can they play ball?

## 9d ■ Reach to X

Type X with the S finger

Touch **xs** lightly, lifting the a finger slightly to give freedom of movement.

• Type twice on same line •

sxs sxs xs xs six six fix

Curve right thumb over
space bar

Strike with quick down, up,
and in motion

## 9e ■ Location Drill—X

**Directions** – Type each line twice.          **Technique Goal** – Keep the fingers deeply curved
                                                and the wrists low and steady.

x          SS sxs sxs sxs xs xs xs six six fix fix fox hoax hoax          Type x with
                                                                         the s finger

              lax coax flax flax next next flex flex mixed mixed

              fix your tax forms, mixed the next, the sixth hoax

## 9f ■ Technique Builder—Stroking

Directions – Type each line once.

Technique Goal – Hold your wrists and arms steady; reach to the keys with your fingers.

1   DS   qa quit quite quiet quote quotes quest queen quire

2       xs ox oxen lax flax mix mixed fix fox next box six

3       quite sure, and quit, will quote, your quiet quest

4       and mix, can fix, my next, his box, our tax, an ox

5       the prize, my size, any zone, with zeal, and seize

6       Will Keith go?  Is that road good?  How far is it?

7       Drive right.  The life that you save may be yours.

| 1 | 2 | 3 | 4 | 5 | 6 | 7 | 8 | 9 | 10 |

*Wrists and elbows still*

*Finger-action stroking*

## Adjusting the Ribbon-Control Lever

1. Your typewriter has a ribbon-control lever (No. 22). Find it on your machine.
2. Set the ribbon-control lever to type on the upper portion of the ribbon.

3. Note the position of the ribbon-control lever.

4. At the beginning of a lesson, check the ribbon-control lever to see that it is in this position.

## 9g ■ Typing from Dictation

Directions – Type these words as your teacher dictates them.

Technique Goals – Think the word; type it. Space quickly after each word.

1   DS   to to do do to do to do if if he he if he if he if

2       he he the the they they then then them them he the

3       an an and and and he and the and he and the and he

4       go go got got if he got if he got if they got they

*Think the word as you type it*

## 9h ■ Extra-Credit Typing • Each line twice

1   SS   This is the kind of job I like.  I can do it well.

2       Use your head on a task; then try your hand at it.

3       I will gain high skill all right if I work for it.

4       Good form will aid them to do this work with ease.

| 1 | 2 | 3 | 4 | 5 | 6 | 7 | 8 | 9 | 10 |

*Quick strokes with instant release*

## ■ Lesson 74 • *70-space line*

### 74a ■ Keyboard Review • Each line at least three times

5 minutes

Alphabetic SS  Julian may have paid for the exquisite zigzag sewing machine by check.

Figure  I got 280 crates of eggs, 159 pounds of ham, and 3,647 gallons of tea.

Keep your
eyes on
the copy

Shift  Mr. George W. Carter will speak at the Wichita Booster Club on Monday.

Easy  That winding road led to a tiny village high in the snow-covered Alps.

| 1 | 2 | 3 | 4 | 5 | 6 | 7 | 8 | 9 | 10 | 11 | 12 | 13 | 14 |

### 74b ■ Sustained Skill Building

10 minutes

Directions – 1. Type a 1-minute writing. The last word you type will be your goal word.
2. Type a 5-minute writing on the same material. At the end of each minute, your teacher will call the carriage return. Try to reach the goal word at each 1-minute goal signal.

DS      By setting goals when learning typewriting, one has something for

which to aim. When a person reaches a certain speed, he must establish a

62 words
1.4 si

goal for a higher rate. If he keeps setting new goals, he will keep try-

Type
steadily

ing to reach them. There is practically no limit to achievement when the

goal is set high enough.

### 74c ■ Typing from Dictation and Spelling Checkup • Type 73c, page 156, from dictation. Retype words in which you made an error.

5 minutes

---

**TWO-PAGE LETTER**

When typing a two-page letter, use plain paper for the second page. Begin the heading on the 7th line space from the top. The heading can either be typed at the left margin in block style or in horizontal form as shown in the illustrations at the right. Triple-space between the heading and the resumed letter. Use the same margins as the first page, and leave approximately a 1-inch bottom margin on all pages.

• *Include at least two lines of a paragraph on each page when a paragraph is broken. Never divide a word at the end of a page.*

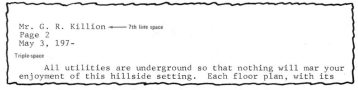

```
Mr. G. R. Killion  ◄——— 7th line space
Page 2
May 3, 197-
Triple-space
        All utilities are underground so that nothing will mar your
enjoyment of this hillside setting.  Each floor plan, with its
```

**Block style heading for second page**

```
Mr. Clarence Knutson          2  ◄— 7th line space       May 3, 197-
Triple-space
The following plans are still available in Unit II:

    Plan Number          Size (Sq. Ft.)          Price
        201                 1754                $32,950
```

**One-line heading for second page**

### General Directions ■ Lessons 10-13

Single-space (SS) drill lines and sentences, but double-space (DS) between repeated groups of lines. Double-space (DS) and indent paragraphs. Triple-space between sections of a lesson.

**Time Schedule:** Beginning with this unit, practice time is given for each section of a lesson. If it seems best to vary the schedule, do so with the approval of your instructor.

## ■ Lesson 10

• *Use a 50 space line for all lessons in this unit.*

### 10a ■ Keyboard Review • Each line twice
*7 minutes*

| | | |
|---|---|---|
| q | SS | aqa aqa qa qa quit quip square squid squash squint |
| x | | sxs sxs xs xs six fix next mixed flax box hoax lax |
| ? | | When?  Where?  Which one?  Can he go to the store? |
| p, b | | p; bf p; bf plea bring trip blot gulp bold rip rob |
| Alphabetic | | Quick, Jay, fix my two big zinc valves which drip. |

Type with sure reaches

|   1   |   2   |   3   |   4   |   5   |   6   |   7   |   8   |   9   |   10   |

### 10b ■ Technique Builder—Word-Response Typing • Each line twice
*5 minutes*

| | | |
|---|---|---|
| 1 | SS | go go got got he he she she he got she got for the |
| 2 | | for the for us he did he did the work did the work |
| 3 | | and the and they and then to the to them to go for |
| 4 | | so this so this is the so this is the work so that |

Read words
Think words
Type words

### 10c ■ Sentence Guided Writings
*20 minutes*

**Directions – 1.** Type each line twice for practice. **2.** Type each line for one minute with the call of the guide. Try to type each line as the guide is called.

**3.** Type 1-minute writings on the last two sentences without the call of the guide. *Note: Your instructor will tell you how the guide will be called.*

| | | | Words in Line | GWAM 30″ Guide |
|---|---|---|---|---|
| | | • Contains all letters | | |
| 1 | SS | Sit up straight when you type. | 6 | 12 |
| 2 | | You must think right to type right. | 7 | 14 |
| 3 | | Fix your eyes on the book when you type. | 8 | 16 |
| 4 | | As you hit the keys, do not move your wrists. | 9 | 18 |
| 5 | | Hold your thumb close to the space bar, not on it. | 10 | 20 |
| 6 | | Just put some zip in your work; use quick strokes. | 10 | 20 |

|   1   |   2   |   3   |   4   |   5   |   6   |   7   |   8   |   9   |   10   |

## Problem 1—Business Letter with Postscript

**Directions** – Type the following letter in modified block style. Place the address on the 9th line space from the date. Make an original and one carbon copy.

● *Refer to page 89 for instructions concerning the preparation of carbon copies of letters.*

Full sheet          60-space line          Mixed punctuation          Blocked paragraphs          Small envelope

*Today's date* / Mr. Paul Roe / 15678 West Hillview Road / Corvallis, Oregon 97331 / Dear Mr. Roe: / It was a pleasure talking with you concerning the prospect of planning and building your new home. I have analyzed your wishes and feel that I can now estimate the cost for the type of construction you desire. I do not feel, however, that it would be feasible to build a one-story house with the number of square feet you wish on the lot you presently own. I would suggest that you either secure a larger lot or consider building a two-story house on your present lot. (¶) If you will call my secretary, she will make an appointment for you to come in again and discuss these building plans. I feel certain that I can stay within your cost specifications. / Sincerely yours, / J. F. Covington / Architect / xx / If you are interested in seeing about a larger lot, there are a number of reputable real estate agents to whom I can refer you.

## Problem 2—Business Letter with Postscript, Rough Draft

**Directions** – Type the following letter, making all necessary corrections. Type the address on the 9th line space from the date.

April 12, 197-

Mr. Ronald Anderson, *Credit Department*
The Fashion ~~Store~~ *Center*
6101 Clifton Road
Atlanta, GA 30333
Dear Mr. Anderson,

I am pleased to give you a reference for Mr. Martin M. Ryan who has filed an application with you for an account. He ~~had~~ *has* an excellent credit rating with our company. During the ~~last~~ *past* eight years he purchased merchandise from us on a regular basis and had balances on his account as high as $750. His payments ~~was~~ *were* always made regularly and he reduced his balance to 0 *zero* before moving to your ~~city.~~ *locality.*

We enjoyed doing business with Mr. Ryan. I am sure that he should prove to be an excellent credit customer for your company.

Yours truly, THE GLASSMAN CO.

Ronald Clemore, Credit Department

XX

*P.S. Mr. Ryan's account with us also included credit privileges for his teenage daughter.*

# Proofreading Your Copy

You must learn to find and mark your typing errors. Some common typing errors are shown below.

1. A cut-off capital letter is an error.

2. Failure to space between words is an error.

3. An omitted letter or an extra letter is an error.

4. The wrong letter or a strikeover is an error.

5. An omitted or an added word is an error.

6. A missed or wrong punctuation mark is an error.

7. An extra space is an error.

8. A transposed letter is an error.

**Rule:** *Count only one error to a word. Circle the whole word containing an error.*

(ne) of the points to keep in m

is (thatyou) must think well to wri

A (cler) thought (iss) the prime need

You (musy) know, too, how to (use)

right (word) in the (the) right place. Wo

tools used by those who write() A

to (u se) them() well,

We (muts) all learn to write wel

## 10d ■ Paragraph Typing

*13 minutes*

Directions – 1. Set the machine for a 5-space paragraph indention and double spacing.
2. Type the paragraphs once. Circle your errors. Repeat if time permits. Try to make fewer errors.

• *The syllable intensity (si) is given for the paragraphs below. It is a guide to the difficulty of the material. Copy of average difficulty is said to have an si of 1.4. The following copy is thus quite easy.*

| | | | Words in ¶ | Total Words |
|---|---|---|---|---|
| ¶ 1 22 words 1.0 si | DS | One of the points to keep in mind is that we | 9 | 9 |
| | | must think well to write well; a clear thought is | 19 | 19 |
| | | the prime need. | 22 | 22 |
| ¶ 2 25 words 1.0 si | | We must know, too, how to use the right word | 9 | 31 |
| | | in the right spot. Words are tools used by those | 19 | 41 |
| | | who write. Learn to use them. | 25 | 47 |
| ¶ 3 28 words 1.0 si | | We must all learn to write well. This skill | 9 | 56 |
| | | is so high on the list of the things all men need | 19 | 66 |
| | | to have that we should work for it with zeal. | 28 | 75 |

| 1 | 2 | 3 | 4 | 5 | 6 | 7 | 8 | 9 | 10 |

# ■ Lesson 73 • *70-space line*

## 73a ■ Keyboard Review • Each line at least three times

*5 minutes*

Alphabetic SS Philip quoted lengthy excerpts from over ten books written about jazz.

Figure    There were 59 blue, 204 red, 37 green, and 168 yellow shirts for sale.

ex    The exiled executive was not exempt from the excessive executor's fee.

Easy    Howard felt that all the men in the glee club sang well enough to win.

| 1 | 2 | 3 | 4 | 5 | 6 | 7 | 8 | 9 | 10 | 11 | 12 | 13 | 14 |

*Wrists low and still*

## 73b ■ Proofreading Skill Builder—Errors in Meaning

*5 minutes*

Directions – Find the error in each of these sentences; then type
each sentence correctly.  Repeat.

1    SS She should being the accounting job just as soon as she arrives today.

2    A total of seven yours were required for James to complete the degree.

3    The company will try to sent the statements to George in fifteen days.

4    Please read the application from to see if all questions are answered.

| 1 | 2 | 3 | 4 | 5 | 6 | 7 | 8 | 9 | 10 | 11 | 12 | 13 | 14 |

*Read carefully*

## 73c ■ Spelling Aids • Type each line twice. Study the words carefully as you type them.

*5 minutes*

1    SS grateful grievance handicapped height illegible improvise inconsistent

2    incomparable insubordinate injurious indispensable inferior initiative

3    judiciary khaki lease lenient liabilities linoleum maintenance maximum

4    management mileage negotiations neither nuisance optimistic proprietor

*Think; spell; type*

## 73d ■ Skill Comparison

*5 minutes*

Directions – Type a 1-minute writing on each sentence in 73a,
above.  Type the easy sentence first and then try
to type all the other sentences at the same rate.

---

**BUSINESS LETTER WITH POSTSCRIPT.** A postscript is typed a double space below the reference initials. It need not be preceded by the letters P. S. Indent or block the postscript according to the style of the other paragraphs of the letter.

bd
◄——Double-space
If you are interested in seeing about a larger
a number of reputable real estate agents to wh
refer you.

## ■ Lesson 11 • *50-space line*

### 11a ■ Keyboard Review • Each line twice

| | | |
|---|---|---|
| y | SS | jyj jyj yj yj yes they may say lay day fly fry dry |
| z | | aza aza za za zone zeal size blaze haze doze froze |
| br reach | | br br bright brake broke bronze brain brief brands |
| pl reach | | plan plane planer plat plate play place plot plead |
| Alphabetic | | Knox Duque saw my large zebra jump over his craft. |

Sure,
deliberate
strokes

|   1   |   2   |   3   |   4   |   5   |   6   |   7   |   8   |   9   |   10   |

---

### TOUCH REGULATOR

• *Refer to page v for aid in locating the touch regulator (No. 34) on your machine.*

The touch regulator permits you to adapt the tension of the keys to the natural striking force of your fingers. Decrease the tension if you have a light touch; increase the tension if you have a heavy touch. On machines having a dial, the lower numbers give the lighter tension.

---

### 11b ■ Technique Builder—Word-Response Typing • Each line twice

*5 minutes*

| | | |
|---|---|---|
| 1 | SS | he \| he \| did \| he did \| he did \| he did it \| he did the |
| 2 | | and \| and he \| and he \| and the \| and if he \| and if he |
| 3 | | do \| go \| do go \| and do \| and do go \| and go \| to go to |
| 4 | | for \| for \| it \| for it \| for it is \| is the \| it is the |

Think the
words as
you type

### 11c ■ Sentence Guided Writings • As directed in 10c, page 20

*20 minutes*

• Contains all letters

| | | | Words in Line | GWAM 30" Guide |
|---|---|---|---|---|
| 1 | SS | Dave and John won first prize. | 6 | 12 |
| 2 | | The goal is to type what you write. | 7 | 14 |
| 3 | | Skill is the right mix of mind and hand. | 8 | 16 |
| 4 | | Yes, words are tools used by those who write. | 9 | 18 |
| 5 | | They must learn how to use these tools quite well. | 10 | 20 |
| 6 | | *Your aim is to type each line with the time guide.* | 10 | 20 |

|   1   |   2   |   3   |   4   |   5   |   6   |   7   |   8   |   9   |   10   |

## Problem 1—Business Letter with Attention Line

Block          Full sheet          60-space line          Mixed punctuation          Small envelope          Address on 8th line space from date

July 3, 197– / Apache Ski Equipment Ltd. / 316 Oakwood Drive / Montreal 1, Quebec / Attention Mr. William Ryan / Gentlemen: / Since the ski areas in this section of Canada are becoming more popular every year, I feel that there is an available market for your equipment in Regina. I am interested in the possibility of becoming your dealer in this area. (¶) I own and manage one of the largest sports equipment stores in Regina. We have a wide variety of ski equipment, and we would like to add your merchandise to our selection. We would like to make Apache ski equipment available for the new ski season beginning in November. Our volume of business is great enough to enable us to purchase a large initial stock of merchandise from you. (¶) Will you please send me some information regarding your local dealership policies. Perhaps it would be possible for me to talk this matter over with your sales representative the next time that he is in this area. / Sincerely yours, / Alfred Stockard / xx

## Problem 2—Business Letter with Subject Line

Block          Full sheet          60-space line          Mixed punctuation          Large envelope          Address on 8th line space from date

August 17, 197– / Mr. Michael Harms, Attorney / 333 Elm Street, Suite 305 / Waycross, Georgia 31501 / Dear Mr. Harms: / SUBJECT: Medical Examination for Grace Lane / Will you please have your client, Mrs. Grace Lane, contact Dr. J. E. Johnson, 427 Pine Street, for an appointment for a medical examination as provided in her policy with us. I am sending Dr. Johnson a copy of this letter which will authorize him to perform the examination. (¶) Please be sure that Mrs. Lane takes with her any X-rays that were made by doctors who have treated her previously. Dr. Johnson will need to review these as part of his examination. (¶) Since we know that Mrs. Lane is interested in settling her case as quickly as possible, we hope that she will schedule her appointment with Dr. Johnson by the end of this month. With the co-operaton of you and your client, we should be able to proceed toward a settlement very soon. We think that it should be possible to set a hearing date when the final report of Dr. Johnson is available. / Very truly yours, / WESTERN INSURANCE COMPANY / Gene Genson, Claims Department / xx

## Problem 3—Business Letter in Block Style

**Directions** – Type the letter in Problem 1 again. This time, however, address it to:

Des Jardines Sporting Goods Ltd.
478 Calgary Avenue
Vancouver 1, British Columbia

Use the name of Timothy Dallinger for the attention line. In the body of the letter substitute the new company name whenever it is needed.

## 11d ■ Paragraph Typing

13 minutes

**Directions – 1.** Set the machine for a 5-space paragraph indention and double spacing.

**2.** Type the paragraphs once. Circle your errors. Repeat. Try to make fewer errors.

|  |  |  | Words in ¶ | Total Words |
|---|---|---|---|---|

**¶ 1**
**24 words**
**1.0 si**

DS    As a rule, we can do much more than we think    9    9

we can.  Most of the time, though, we all do much    19    19

less than we think we do.    24    24

**¶ 2**
**27 words**
**1.0 si**

The key to a job well done is to be found in    9    33

the way we start.  We must first set a goal; then    19    43

go to work.  We win when the job is done.    27    51

**¶ 3**
**31 words**
**1.0 si**

All of us know at least one man who just sits    9    60

and waits for his ship to come in.  This man waits    19    70

in vain, for ships come to a port in which the men    30    81

work.    31    82

| 1 | 2 | 3 | 4 | 5 | 6 | 7 | 8 | 9 | 10 |

## ■ Lesson 12 • *50-space line*

### 12a ■ Keyboard Review • Each line twice

7 minutes

Alphabetic    SS    Jack Benz played the sax with vim for Gilda Quinn.

b        fbf fbf bf bf bug but bit burn blind blur bail buy

po reach      pod post poke point poach port pole pour pond pork

Third row     quip quit writ top you we rope ripe wire trip were

Easy          You are quite right, and I shall do this work now.

| 1 | 2 | 3 | 4 | 5 | 6 | 7 | 8 | 9 | 10 |

Eyes on this copy

### 12b ■ Typing in All Capital Letters • Each line twice

5 minutes

• *To capitalize a whole word, several words, or an entire line, depress the shift lock (No. 29) and type. To release the shift lock, depress either the right or the left shift key.*

1    SS    Please send the NEWS LETTER to all of our members.

2        The book, SONS OF LIBERTY, is on the reading list.

3        We saw the colorful film, HAWAII, THE ALOHA STATE.

Use shift lock

# ■ Lesson 72 • *70-space line*

### 72a ■ Keyboard Review • Each line at least three times

Alphabetic SS  Melvin, an expert, quickly fed the wild jungle animals at the big zoo.

Figure  Of the 10,273 houses in the tract, 584 were brick and 690 were stucco.

Shift  London, Paris, Rome, Milan, and Nice are very popular European cities.

Quick
carriage
return

Easy  If a person never finishes anything he starts, his goal was not clear.

| 1 | 2 | 3 | 4 | 5 | 6 | 7 | 8 | 9 | 10 | 11 | 12 | 13 | 14 |

### 72b ■ Paragraph Skill Builder—Straight Copy • Type four 1-minute writings.

*5 minutes*

DS  There are many jobs for which one may prepare himself. Some of these jobs demand a college degree, but for others a high school education is enough. It is certainly true, however, that more training is required today for success than was needed many years ago. This trend seems likely to continue.

60 words
1.4 si

Concentrate
as you type

### 72c ■ Building Skill on Figures and Symbols • Each line three times

*5 minutes*

1  SS  The balance of your account is $16.73, and it was overdue on March 25.

2  "Watch your step!" he said as we were walking down the slippery steps.

3  An up-to-date price list showed an increase of 8% in less than a year.

4  We will not be able to get the suit (Style #5903) on 2/10, n/30 terms.

| 1 | 2 | 3 | 4 | 5 | 6 | 7 | 8 | 9 | 10 | 11 | 12 | 13 | 14 |

Do not look
at your hands

---

BUSINESS LETTER WITH ATTENTION LINE. An attention line is used to direct a letter to a particular person. It is usually typed on the second line below the address, as illustrated at the right. (In addressing the envelope, type the attention line in the lower left corner.) Gentlemen is the proper salutation to use in a letter with an attention line.

Apache Ski Equipment Ltd.
316 Oakwood Drive
Montreal 1, Quebec  —— Double-space

Attention Mr. William Ryan

Gentlemen:  —— Double-space

BUSINESS LETTER WITH SUBJECT LINE. When a subject line is used in a letter, it may be typed on the second line below the salutation and centered; or it may be typed at the left margin as illustrated at the right.

Mr. Michael Harms, Attorney
333 Elm Street, Suite 305
Waycross, Georgia   31501

Dear Mr. Harms:  > Double-space

SUBJECT:  Medical Examination for

## 12c ■ Sentence Guided Writings

**Directions** – 1. Type each line twice for practice.
2. Type each line for a 1-minute writing with the call of the guide each 20 seconds.

3. Type the last two sentences for additional 1-minute writings as time permits without the call of the guide.

| | | | Words in Line | GWAM 20'' Guide |
|---|---|---|---|---|
| | | • Contains all letters | | |
| 1 | SS | He can see the old maps there. | 6 | 18 |
| 2 | | Send the bronze box to Quail Falls. | 7 | 21 |
| 3 | | Jack passed this quiz with a high score. | 8 | 24 |
| 4 | | A dense haze blocked the scene from our view. | 9 | 27 |
| 5 | | This tour takes you by the old homes in the South. | 10 | 30 |
| 6 | | *Speed is gained when you use quick, sharp strokes.* | 10 | 30 |

| 1 | 2 | 3 | 4 | 5 | 6 | 7 | 8 | 9 | 10 |

## 12d ■ Paragraph Typing • As directed in 11d, page 23.

| | | | Words in ¶ | Total Words |
|---|---|---|---|---|
| | | • Contains all letters | | |
| ¶1 27 words 1.0 si | DS | Do not let a pause slow you down if you want | 9 | 9 |
| | | to type fast.  In great part, your speed will be | 19 | 19 |
| | | based on the way you can make time count. | 27 | 27 |
| ¶2 30 words 1.0 si | | Size up the way you strike all the keys. | 8 | 35 |
| | | Your strokes should be quick, crisp, and sharp. | 18 | 45 |
| | | Just keep in mind that the time you lose is a tax | 28 | 55 |
| | | on speed. | 30 | 57 |
| ¶3 32 words 1.0 si | | Place the book on the desk so that you can | 9 | 66 |
| | | see it with ease.  Keep your eyes on the book. | 18 | 75 |
| | | Each false move you make has its price, and that | 28 | 85 |
| | | price is a low rate. | 32 | 89 |

| 1 | 2 | 3 | 4 | 5 | 6 | 7 | 8 | 9 | 10 |

## 12e ■ Fluency Practice • Each line three times; circle errors.

| 1 | SS | Type with a fixed goal in mind; use quick strokes. | |
|---|---|---|---|
| 2 | | Time is on the side of the man who plans his work. | Type without pauses |
| 3 | | As a rule, the men who sling mud must give ground. | |

| 1 | 2 | 3 | 4 | 5 | 6 | 7 | 8 | 9 | 10 |

## 71d ■ Speed Ladder Paragraphs

**Directions – 1.** Type five 1-minute writings on the following paragraphs starting with the first paragraph. When you can type the first paragraph at the specified rate, type the next one. Try to reach the 60-word rate.

2. Type five more 1-minute writings starting with ¶1. Move from one paragraph to the next only when you type at the rate specified *without error.*

3. Type a 5-minute writing on all ¶'s. Compute *gwam.*

| | | | | GWAM | |
|---|---|---|---|---|---|
| | | | | 1' | 5' |

**¶1**
**44 words**
**1.4 si**

DS   If a person has been taking typing for a semester, he should have | 13 | 3 55

developed perfect techniques. This is not always the case, however. | 27 | 5 57

That is why it helps to check frequently to see what improvements can | 41 | 8 60

still be made. | 44 | 9 61

**¶2**
**48 words**
**1.4 si**

A person frequently needs improvement in stroking techniques. The | 13 | 11 63

stroking action should be centered in the fingers. Elbows, arms, and | 27 | 14 66

wrists should be held quiet. Each key should be struck with a firm, | 41 | 17 69

sharp stroke and released quickly. | 48 | 18 70

**¶3**
**52 words**
**1.4 si**

Also for stroking properly, the finger needs to be kept deeply | 13 | 21 73

curved. It should be snapped slightly toward the palm of the hand as | 27 | 24 76

the key is released. Fingernails should be kept trimmed in order to | 40 | 26 78

enable a person to have this correct curve of the fingers. | 52 | 29 81

**¶4**
**56 words**
**1.4 si**

One should also check to see if the correct finger is being used to | 14 | 32 84

strike each key. It is easy to fall into habits of improper stroking. | 28 | 34 86

Only by taking a personal inventory of stroking patterns can one see if | 42 | 37 89

his techniques are correct. If they are not, skill may be hampered. | 56 | 40 92

**¶5**
**60 words**
**1.4 si**

In addition to checking for stroking problems, a person should make | 14 | 43 95

sure that he is keeping his eyes on the copy and is sitting up straight | 28 | 46 98

with both feet on the floor. Proper techniques in these respects, along | 43 | 49 101

with correct stroking, will help one develop a higher speed rate with | 57 | 51 103

greater accuracy. | 60 | 52 104

1' | 1 | 2 | 3 | 4 | 5 | 6 | 7 | 8 | 9 | 10 | 11 | 12 | 13 | 14 |
5' | 1 | 2 | 3 |

### 13a ■ Keyboard Review • Each line at least twice

*7 minutes*

| | | |
|---|---|---|
| Alphabetic | SS | Every exam with puzzling questions baffled Jackie. |
| b | | fbf fbf bf bf bus build but bake bone board by buy |
| po | | pole pod point poor pore pour pop pork pound pouch |
| nu | | nut nudge nurse null numb nun nut nurse numb nudge |
| Easy | | It will pay to do a job as well as it can be done. |

| 1 | 2 | 3 | 4 | 5 | 6 | 7 | 8 | 9 | 10 |

*Type without pauses*

### 13b ■ Technique Builder—Word-Response Typing • Each line twice

*5 minutes*

1 SS to do | to do it | to go | it is | it is the | it is to

2    if it | if it is | if the | and go | and do | and if it

3    and the | and if the | and did it | and do | and do it

4    and he | and if he | if he | if he is | for it | for me

*Think and type word groups*

### 13c ■ Technique Builder—Space Bar and Shift Keys • Each line twice

*5 minutes*

• Contains all letters

1 SS Karl, Vern, and Dwayne may go to New York in June.

2    Liz Knox wrote a book on quaint homes in the East.

3    Type this.  Read it.  Go there.  Count the chairs.

4    Sue saw Ann and Ruth at the art show in Fern Park.

| 1 | 2 | 3 | 4 | 5 | 6 | 7 | 8 | 9 | 10 |

*Shift firmly*

*Space quickly*

### 13d ■ Fluency Practice

*5 minutes*

**Directions** – Type each line at least three times.    **Technique Goal** – Type smoothly and continuously.

1 SS All roads to the top are paved with grief and joy.

2    Learn to type well; keep your eyes on these lines.

3    *This is the kind of book that will make you think.*

4    *One can judge a man by the books he likes to read.*

| 1 | 2 | 3 | 4 | 5 | 6 | 7 | 8 | 9 | 10 |

*Type without pauses*

*Eyes on this copy*

## Problem 3—Business Letter in Block Style

**Directions** – Type the letter in Problem 2, page 150, with the following changes: **1.** Address the letter to Mr. Charles Miles / 15975 Overhill Road / Boston, Mass.  02143.
**2.** Change the amount in the second paragraph to $100.

3. Use the company name, FILENE'S, in the closing lines of the letter.

• *The inside address illustrates the abbreviation of a state name in order to avoid a last line which is much longer than the other lines.*

Full sheet                    50-space line                    Open punctuation                    Small envelope

# ■ Lesson 71 • *70-space line*

### 71a ■ Keyboard Review • Each line at least three times                                    5 minutes

| | |
|---|---|
| Alphabetic  SS | Grady and Jill must take the quiz, but very few of us expect to do so. |
| Figure | A total of 20,971 students had grade point averages from 1.45 to 3.86. |
| Figure-Symbol | Please order 150 #6 cans @ 25¢ each with a 2% discount within 15 days. |
| Easy | Almost any man could make better use of his time if he would just try. |

Quick, sharp strokes

| 1 | 2 | 3 | 4 | 5 | 6 | 7 | 8 | 9 | 10 | 11 | 12 | 13 | 14 |

### 71b ■ Technique Builder—Balanced-Hand Words                                    10 minutes

**Directions** – Type each line three times. Take two 1-minute writings on each of the last two lines.

**Technique Goal** – Try to increase your speed on balanced-hand words.

| | |
|---|---|
| Phrases  SS | for the \| to the land \| with the \| by us \| they may do \| with them \| and she |
| Phrases | may wish \| for the right \| for the girl \| for if \| if she may \| to fight if |
| Sentence | The proxy fight by the neurotic man is to blame for the rigid penalty. |
| Sentence | The chairman may wish to fight for the right of clemency for the girl. |

Think words as you type

| 1 | 2 | 3 | 4 | 5 | 6 | 7 | 8 | 9 | 10 | 11 | 12 | 13 | 14 |

### 71c ■ Skill Comparison • Type two 1-minute writings on each sentence. Compare your rates on the different types of copy.                                    10 minutes

| | |
|---|---|
| Straight copy  SS | A wise man is one who worries only about the important things in life. |
| Figures | The 1965 team won 37 games and tied 20 out of the 84 that they played. |
| Rough draft | If one person thinks of himself only he may find that life is boring. |
| Script | A person reveals much by the value that he attaches to certain things. |

Type steadily

| 1 | 2 | 3 | 4 | 5 | 6 | 7 | 8 | 9 | 10 | 11 | 12 | 13 | 14 |

## 13e ■ Timed Writings

**Directions – 1.** Type the paragraphs once for practice; then type a 1-minute writing on each one.
**2.** Finally, type a 2-minute writing on both paragraphs. Circle errors. Compute *gwam* on all writings.

● *In figuring your gwam for the writings on the paragraphs, use the 1-minute column at the right and the 1-minute scale underneath the paragraph to figure your 1-minute rate. Use the 2-minute column and scale to figure your 2-minute rate.*

|  | | GWAM | | |
|--|--|--|--|--|
|  | | 1' | 2' | |

¶1
38 words
1.0 si

DS    You can learn to type well all right.  To do     9   5   44
so, you must train your mind to think as you type     19  10  49
and your hands to do the things they should.  You     29  15  54
must have a clear goal before you as you work.        38  19  58

¶2
39 words
1.1 si

Keep your fingers well curved, and hold them     9   24  63
just over the home keys.  Use quick, short, sharp     19  29  68
strokes.  Hold your wrists down and steady.  Keep     29  34  73
your eyes on this book if you wish to type well.      39  39  78

1'| 1 | 2 | 3 | 4 | 5 | 6 | 7 | 8 | 9 | 10 |
2'| 1 | 2 | 3 | 4 | 5 |

## 13f ■ Sentence Guided Writings ● As directed in 12c, page 24

● Contains all letters

|  |  | Words in Line | GWAM 30" Guide |
|--|--|--|--|
| 1 | SS Quinn will fix the zinc plate. | 6 | 12 |
| 2 | Print the blank forms in black ink. | 7 | 14 |
| 3 | My road turns to the east at that point. | 8 | 16 |
| 4 | Bells of this size come packed five to a box. | 9 | 18 |
| 5 | You can type these lines as the guides are called. | 10 | 20 |
| 6 | *Jeff may be the guide on our trip through the zoo.* | 10 | 20 |

| 1 | 2 | 3 | 4 | 5 | 6 | 7 | 8 | 9 | 10 |

## 13g ■ Extra-Credit Typing ● Each line three times; circle errors.

1    SS He is quick, smart, and strong; he can do the job.
2       I know that the more I know the more I must learn.
3       He can do the job now all right if he is to do it.
4       Men are thus judged by the things they do and say.

Type steadily

| 1 | 2 | 3 | 4 | 5 | 6 | 7 | 8 | 9 | 10 |

**Communications
Consultants, Inc.**
1742 Massachusetts Avenue     Boston, Massachusetts  02138     (617) 339-4822

April 15, 197-  ← Dateline typed 2 spaces
below letterhead or on
the 12th line space

3

8th line space

Address →
Mrs. Edna Hofer, Office Manager          9
Great Northern Insurance Company        16
922 Briarhill Avenue                    20
Toronto 5, Ontario                      24

Salutation → Dear Mrs. Hofer             27

Body →
The block style in which this letter is typed is     37
becoming quite popular with many companies because   47
of its simplicity.                                   51

Many typists prefer the block style since they can   61
type it more rapidly.  The date, inside address,     71
salutation, and closing all begin at the left mar-   81
gin.  The paragraphs are not indented.  There are    91
no problems of special placement.                    98

In the open punctuation style used in this letter,  108
no mark follows the salutation or the complimentary 119
close.  Although it would be equally correct to use 129
the mixed punctuation style, the block letter is    139
most often typed with open punctuation.             147

Please let us help you with any of your business    157
communications problems.                            162

Complimentary close →
Very cordially yours   → Double-space              166

COMMUNICATIONS CONSULTANTS, INC. ← Company name in closing   173

4th line space →
*Mark C. Halverson*

Typed name and title →
Mark C. Halverson, President                        179

Reference initials →
xx   → Double-space                                 179

When open punctuation is used, marks are omitted after the
lines of the date, address, salutation, and complimentary
close unless an abbreviation is used, in which case the
period is typed as part of the abbreviation.

When a company name is used in the closing, it is typed in
all capital letters double-spaced below the complimentary
close.  The dictator's name is then typed on the 4th line
space below the company name.

**Business letter in block style**

# Unit 3 ■

## Learning the Number and Symbol Keys

### General Directions ■ Lessons 14-20

1. Single-space repeated sentences and drill lines. Double-space between repeated groups of lines.

2. Double-space sentences typed only once.

3. Double-space paragraph copy. Set a tabulator stop for a 5-space paragraph indention.

• *Use a 50-space line for all lessons in this unit.*

## ■ Lesson 14

### 14a ■ Keyboard Review • Each line twice                    *5 minutes*

**Alphabetic**    ss    The quick brown fox jumped over all the lazy dogs.

**gr**     grind grain grill grow groom gray grape green grub

**Easy**     Keep your fingers well curved as you hit the keys.

*Keep fingers deeply curved*

**Easy**     He said that tact fails the instant it is noticed.

| 1 | 2 | 3 | 4 | 5 | 6 | 7 | 8 | 9 | 10 |

### 14b ■ Location of Figure 1                    *2 minutes*

• *On all electric and some manual typewriters, the figure 1 appears on the top row. Strike it with the a finger. On some manual typewriters, the figure 1 is made with the letter l. Type the appropriate line two times.*

**Figure 1**    ss   ala ala ala la la la 11 aims, 11 altars, 11 armies

*Type 1 with the a finger*

**Letter l as 1**    Sell 11 aprons.  State 11 aims.  See the 111 apes.

*Letter l as 1*

### 14c ■ Reach to 3—Reach to 7                    *5 minutes*

Type 3 with the D finger                                                  Type 7 with the J finger

**Touch d3d** lightly two or three times. Lift the first finger slightly to make the reach easily and naturally.

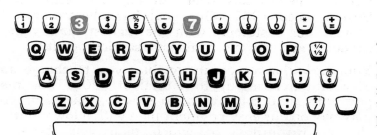

Touch **j7j** lightly two or three times. Make the reach without arching your wrist. Hold the other fingers in position.

d3d  d3d  d3d  d3d  3d  3d  d3d    • Type twice on same line •    j7j  j7j  j7j  j7j  7j  7j  j7j

# ■ Lesson 70 • *70-space line*

## 70a ■ Keyboard Review • Each line at least three times

| | |
|---|---|
| Alphabetic SS | The two key firm executives quibbled over major property zone changes. |
| Figure | There were 59 blue, 204 red, 37 green, and 168 yellow shirts for sale. |
| Underline | <u>Hawaii</u>, <u>Caravans</u>, and <u>The Source</u> are novels written by James Michener. |
| Easy | If a person has never made a mistake, he has never tried anything new. |

Watch your copy

| 1 | 2 | 3 | 4 | 5 | 6 | 7 | 8 | 9 | 10 | 11 | 12 | 13 | 14 |

## 70b ■ Timed Writings • Type two 1-minute and one 5-minute writing on 66d, page 139. Compute gwam.

10 minutes

## 70c ■ Typing from Dictation and Spelling Checkup • Type 69c, page 146, from dictation. Retype words in which you made an error.

5 minutes

## 70d ■ Problem Typing

25 minutes

### Problem 1—Business Letter in Block Style

**Directions** – Type the model letter on page 151. Follow the directions given on the illustration. *When a company name is used in the closing, it is typed in* *all capital letters a double space below the complimentary close. The dictator's name is then typed on the 4th line space below the company name.*

Full sheet          50-space line          Open punctuation          Small envelope

### Problem 2—Business Letter in Block Style

**Directions** – Type the following letter as illustrated on page 151. Type the address on the 11th line space *from the date. Choose a complimentary close, sign your own name, and use the title, Credit Manager.*

Today's date     Full sheet     Open punctuation     50-space line     Small envelope     Omit reference initials

Words

| | |
|---|---|
| Mr. William Self | 3 |
| 486 East River Drive | 6 |
| Boston, Mass.   02174 | 11 |
| | 15 |
| Dear Mr. Self | 18 |

We are pleased to welcome you as a new charge cus- 28
tomer. Filene's has been serving the residents of 38
Boston since 1907. Our goal has always been to 48
provide our customers with the highest quality mer- 58
chandise and the most efficient service possible. 68

Your new charge account enables you to charge any 78
of your purchases up to a total of $200. You may 88
pay within 30 days with no service charge, or you 98
may pay on our easy payment plan with a low monthly 109
charge. Regardless of which plan you choose, I 118
think you'll find a Filene's charge account a most 128
convenient way to shop. 133

## 14d ■ Location Drills—3 and 7 • Each line twice

6 minutes

**3**  SS  d3d d3d d3d 3d 3d 3d 33 days, 33 dikes, 33 for 333

Take 33 feet.  Take 33 gallons.  Give us 333 jars.

*Type 3 with the d finger*

**7**  j7j j7j j7j 7j 7j 7j 77 jets, 77 jars, 777 and 777

Send 77 jars.  Order 777 jets.  List the 777 jobs.

*Type 7 with the j finger*

## 14e ■ Key-Location Practice • Each line twice

10 minutes

**1**  SS  We made 313 jars in 17 days.  We sold 331 of them.

**2**  We bought 13 in 17 hours.  He ate 313 in 17 hours.

*Reach for the top row*

**3**  She read 73 pages in 37 minutes.  I read 31 pages.

**4**  John moved 373 sets to 731 Main Street on June 13.

*Wrists low and steady*

**5**  Al worked 37 hours last week and sold 713 tickets.

**6**  *Read pages 13, 17, 113, 117, and 317 in this book.*

**7**  *The 37 men took Flight 31 to Boston on January 17.*

*Eyes on the book*

| 1 | 2 | 3 | 4 | 5 | 6 | 7 | 8 | 9 | 10 |

## 14f ■ Continuity Practice

17 minutes

**Directions** – Type once; circle errors. Repeat.          **Technique Goal** – Type steadily with eyes on book.

• Contains all letters

|  |  | GWAM |  |
|---|---|---|---|
|  | 1' | | 3' |

**¶ 1**  DS  You must read to stay in the race.  Events    9  3  34

45 words
1.2 si

are occurring at such a dizzy pace that unless    18  6  37

you read you will quickly be out of touch with    27  9  40

the world.  You must do something more, though,    37  12  43

than expose yourself to the printed page.    45  15  46

**¶ 2**  Look upon reading as a search for meaning.    54  18  49

47 words
1.2 si

One who reads well seeks.  That is the basic    63  21  52

technique of reading.  You cannot get meaning out    73  24  55

of words simply by looking at them any more than    83  28  59

you can wear jewels that are locked in a case.    92  31  62

| 1' | 1 | 2 | 3 | 4 | 5 | 6 | 7 | 8 | 9 | 10 |
| 3' | | 1 | | 2 | | 3 | | 4 | | |

## Problem 2—Business Letter in Modified Block Style, Blocked Paragraphs

**Directions** – Type this letter according to the directions on page 148. Type the address on the 7th line space from the date.

- *Center the three lines in the body of the letter by the longest line.*

Full sheet     60-space line     Mixed punctuation     Large envelope

Words

February 12, 197–    4

Mr. Michael Dunn    7
14578 Willow Lane    11
Houston, Texas    77004    15

Dear Mr. Dunn:    18

We are pleased to know that you are interested in our new    30
Thousand Oaks Subdivision. This new housing development is    42
a unique combination of advantages you've sought in a loca-    54
tion for a home. Thousand Oaks is convenient to schools,    65
shopping areas, and churches and there is easy access to the    78
major expressways.    82

Not only is the location exceptional for a new housing devel-    84
opment, but every home, regardless of price, has the follow-    106
ing outstanding features:    112

                        Cedar shake roof    115
                        Brick or stone fireplace    120
                        Built-in range and oven    125

The homes are in the finishing stages and should be ready for    137
occupancy in three weeks. The enclosed brochure will give you    150
more detailed information. Why don't you come out today and    162
let me show you through the models. I believe that you will    174
find a home at Thousand Oaks which will meet the needs of you    187
and your family.    190

                              Sincerely yours,    194

                              Janice Wilde    196

197

xx

Enclosure    199

## Problem 3—Business Letter in Modified Block Style, Blocked Paragraphs

**Directions** – Type the model letter on page 148 but address it to Mr. John Ruppanner / 23591 Wilton Avenue / Covington, Kentucky 51011.

Full sheet     50-space line     Mixed punctuation     Large envelope

## ■ Lesson 15 · *50-space line*

### 15a ■ Keyboard Review · Each line twice

7 minutes

Alphabetic   SS  Jovial Felix dances mazurkas badly with quiet Peg.

3        d3d d3d 3d 3d 33 days, 333 decks, 33 caps, 31 elms

7        j7j j7j 7j 7j 77 jugs, 77 jars, 777 urns, 717 jets

br       bring brief brim broke brain break brow brush bray

Easy     You must stay awake to make your dreams come true.
         | 1 | 2 | 3 | 4 | 5 | 6 | 7 | 8 | 9 | 10 |

*Observe good posture rules*

### 15b ■ Reach to #—Reach to & · Each line twice

*6 minutes*

• *The reaches to the 3 and 7 keys were presented in Lesson 14. The symbols appearing on these two keys are presented in this lesson. This is the pattern followed in introducing all figure and symbol keys in this unit.*

On all typewriters, # is the shift of 3.

Before a figure, # stands for number. After a figure, # stands for pounds. There is no space between the sign and the number.

On all typewriters, & is the shift of 7.

The & (ampersand) is a substitute for the word *and*. When using the ampersand, place a space before and after it.

#    SS  d3d d#d d3d d#d #d #d #133, #13 and #173 and #3137

         I sent Draft #1731.   I used 331#.   Buy 17# of #73.

*# is the shift of 3*

&        j7j j&j j7j j&j &j &j Jones & Goode, Knight & Gray

         Write to Stone & Lark.   King & Lee sold 717 dozen.

*& is the shift of 7*

### 15c ■ Reach to 5—Reach to 9

*5 minutes*

Type 5 with the F finger

Touch **f5f** lightly two or three times. Keep your left wrist low as you make the reach. Avoid moving your hand forward.

Type 9 with the L finger

Touch **191** lightly two or three times. Lift the first and second fingers slightly to give you freedom of action.

f5f  f5f  f5f  f5f  5f  5f  f5f    • Type twice on same line •    191 191 191 191 91 91 191

## Overland Camping Trailers, Inc.

701 Garfield Avenue  Detroit, Michigan 48201  313/722-8401

Words

Center point ——————→ December 12, 197-    4

Dateline typed 2 spaces
below letterhead or on
the 12th line space

14th line space

Mr. Charles Briggs    7
Address ——————→ 17503 East Riverview Road    13
Covington, Kentucky  51011    18

Salutation ——————→ Dear Mr. Briggs:    22

We are pleased to know that you are interested in    32
Overland Camping Trailers.  I am enclosing the    41
brochure that you requested. It will give you a    51
very comprehensive picture of the many different    61
Body ——————→ models of trailers that we manufacture to make    70
your camping easier and more enjoyable.    78

The dealer in your city who handles our product is    88

ROE TRAILER SALES, INC.    93

I know that this dealer will be happy to meet you    103
and show you the model in which you are interested.    114

Complimentary close ——————— Center point ——————→ Sincerely yours,    117

4th line space    *Ray Wills*

Typed name and title ——————————————→ Ray Wills, Sales Manager    122

Reference
initials ——→ xx  〉 Double-space    123

Enclosure
notation ——→ Enclosure    125

**Business letter in modified block style, blocked paragraphs**

### 15d ■ Location Drills—5 and 9 • Each line twice

5    ss  f5f f5f f5f 5f 5f 5f 55 fires, 555 feet, 55 floors

          Sell 555 feet.  Mail 155 files.  Order 55 and 515.

*Type 5 with the f finger*

9      191 191 191 91 91 91 99 lids, 99 lights, 999 lakes

          Buy 99 lids.  Sell 1,919 lamps.  Pay for 9 and 19.

*Type 9 with the l finger*

### 15e ■ Key-Location Practice • Each line twice

*10 minutes*

      • Review of all figure and symbol keys covered

1    ss  Please send 71 in May, 93 in June, and 57 in July.

2      Lock & Strand can ship 519# of grass seed at once.

3      I want 17 feet of #93 pipe; I have 35 feet of #19.

4      Can you send 95 sets?  Please reply by January 17.

5      3 and 5 and 7 and 9 and 13 and 151 and 171 and 191

*Quick, firm reach to the shift key*

6      *Check #3957 was sent to Glass & Payne on March 19.*

7      *Land & Lee sold 195 sets of forms to Book & Paige.*

      | 1 | 2 | 3 | 4 | 5 | 6 | 7 | 8 | 9 | 10 |

### 15f ■ Sustained Skill Building

*11 minutes*

**Directions** – Type 1-, 2-, and 3-minute writings on the paragraphs in 14f, page 28. Compute *gwam*. Try to equal your 1-minute rate on the longer writings. For the 2-minute rate, use the 1-minute column and scale to get total words; then divide by 2.

## ■ Lesson 16 • *50-space line*

### 16a ■ Keyboard Review • Each line twice

*7 minutes*

Alphabetic  ss  Haze just blocked my sixth quest to view Fern Gap.

5      f5f f5f 5f 5f 55 fins, 515 feet, 55 forms, 55 furs

9      191 191 91 91 99 lines, 191 lots, 99 loads, 99 men

*Eyes on this copy*

& #    j7j j&j d3d d#d send 737# on Bill #3519; Lee & Son

Easy    The supply of cheap talk often exceeds the demand.

      | 1 | 2 | 3 | 4 | 5 | 6 | 7 | 8 | 9 | 10 |

## Problem 1—Business Letter in Modified Block Style, Blocked Paragraphs

**Directions** – Type the letter on page 148, following the directions on the illustration. Refer to the directions below for addressing a large envelope. If a large envelope is not available, cut paper to large envelope size (9½″ x 4⅛″).

• *An enclosure notation is used when a paper (or papers) is sent with the letter. Type the notation a double space below the reference initials. Use the plural, Enclosures, if two or more items will be enclosed.*

Full sheet                Mixed punctuation                50-space line                Large envelope

## ADDRESSING LARGE ENVELOPES AND FOLDING LETTERS

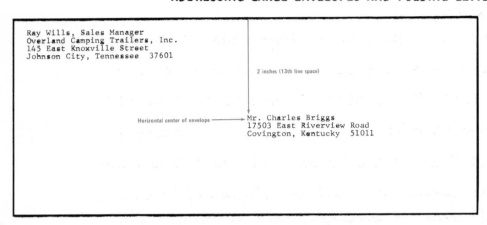

Ray Wills, Sales Manager
Overland Camping Trailers, Inc.
145 East Knoxville Street
Johnson City, Tennessee  37601

2 inches (13th line space)

Horizontal center of envelope ⟶ Mr. Charles Briggs
17503 East Riverview Road
Covington, Kentucky  51011

A large envelope (9½″ by 4⅛″) is usually typed for business letters with enclosures, or for letters of more than one page. Type the address 2 inches from the top and at the horizontal center of the envelope. The state name may be typed in full, in the standard abbreviation, or in the 2-letter ZIP Code abbreviation. Type the ZIP Code two spaces after the state name.

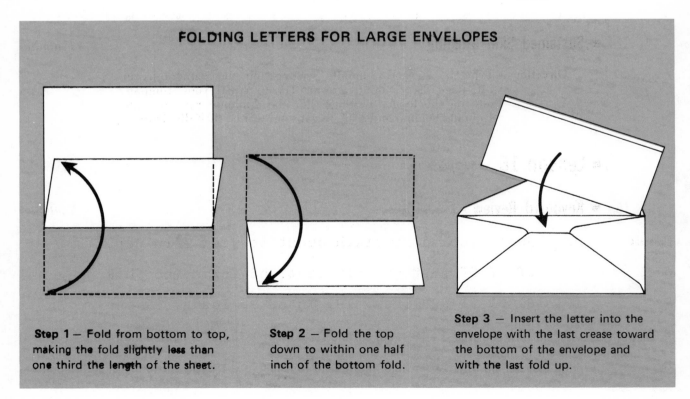

## FOLDING LETTERS FOR LARGE ENVELOPES

**Step 1** – Fold from bottom to top, making the fold slightly less than one third the length of the sheet.

**Step 2** – Fold the top down to within one half inch of the bottom fold.

**Step 3** – Insert the letter into the envelope with the last crease toward the bottom of the envelope and with the last fold up.

## 16b ■ Reach to %—Reach to ( • Each line twice

*6 minutes*

On all typewriters, % is the shift of 5.

Do not space between the number and the percent sign that follows it.

On all typewriters, ( is the shift of 9.

Do not space between the left parenthesis and the material it encloses.

%    SS   f5f f%f f5f f%f %f %f% 55%, 99% and 3% and 19% f%f    % is the shift of 5

Al got a discount of 5%.   Ed got 15% and I got 7%.

(      191 1(1 191 1(1 To type (, shift and strike the 9.    ( is the shift of 9

The ( is the left parenthesis.   Strike 9; then (9.

## 16c ■ Reach to 4—Reach to 8

*5 minutes*

Type 4 with the F finger

Touch f4f lightly two or three times. Keep your wrist low and quiet. Do not move your hand forward.

Type 8 with the K finger

Touch k8k lightly two or three times. Make reaches to the top row by extending your fingers. Hold the wrist low and steady.

f4f f4f f4f f4f 4f 4f f4f    • Type twice on same line •    k8k k8k k8k k8k 8k 8k k8k

## 16d ■ Location Drills—4 and 8 • Each line twice

*6 minutes*

4    SS   f4f f4f f4f 4f 4f 4f 44 feet, 444 firs, 44 and 414    Type 4 with the f finger

Send 44 forms.   We need 144 feet.   Get us 44 furs.

8      k8k k8k k8k 8k 8k 8k 88 kits, 888 knives, 8 for 88    Type 8 with the k finger

Buy 88 kites.   Sell 18 kits.   Fix 18 and 88 knobs.

## 16e ■ Key-Location Practice • Each line once; then repeat.

*10 minutes*

1    DS   Drive 188 miles in 13 hours.   She is 41 years old.

2      The ( is the shift of 9.   The interest rate is 5%.

3      The # is the shift of 3.   Please send Form #94751.    All figures and symbols taught

4      The & is the shift of 7.   Call Hall & Stone today.

5      *The percent is the shift of 5. Add the sales tax of 3%.*

6      *Zenda & Crosby sold 371 of the 489 sets on Friday.*    Wrists low and steady

7      *They may get Forms #88 and #99 from Johns & Queen.*

| 1 | 2 | 3 | 4 | 5 | 6 | 7 | 8 | 9 | 10 |

**Problem 3—Business Letter in Modified Block Style, Indented Paragraphs**

**Directions** – Type the letter on page 145 but address it to Mr. Lyle Clark, Manager /
Atlantic Savings and Loan / 4391 Salem Avenue / Portland, Maine 04101.

Full sheet      60-space line      Mixed punctuation      Small envelope

# ■ Lesson 69 • *70-space line*

## 69a ■ Keyboard Review • Each line at least three times

5 minutes

| | | |
|---|---|---|
| Alphabetic | SS | A sharp young executive quickly amazed overjoyed bankers from Wichita. |
| Figure | | If a person adds 15, 23, 64, 90, and 78, he will get an answer of 270. |
| Hyphen | | His father-in-law, a well-to-do millionaire, is truly a self-made man. |
| Easy | | The man who is proud of his country will never be afraid to defend it. |

| 1 | 2 | 3 | 4 | 5 | 6 | 7 | 8 | 9 | 10 | 11 | 12 | 13 | 14 |

Quick, sharp strokes

## 69b ■ Proofreading Skill Builder—Letter Transposition Errors

5 minutes

**Directions** – Find the errors in these sentences,
then type them correctly. Repeat.

1   SS   The typing book shuold be elevated for ease in raeding.

2     Your feet should be falt on the floor when you sit proprely.

3     For the best results keep the fingres curved and the wrsits down.

4     You will be a much better typsit if you will follow these suggestoins.

| 1 | 2 | 3 | 4 | 5 | 6 | 7 | 8 | 9 | 10 | 11 | 12 | 13 | 14 |

Wrists and elbows still

## 69c ■ Spelling Aids

5 minutes

**Directions** – Type each line twice. Throughout this unit you will be given words
that are frequently misspelled in business letters. Study the words
carefully as you type them.

1   SS   abbreviated accompanying accountant additional agenda arrears assemble

2     bankruptcy beneficiary brief calendar carburetor caution circumstances

3     debtor deceive directory distinguished economy edition expedite enable

4     efficiency exhausted facilities faculty fraudulent fundamental genuine

Type by letter response

## 16f ■ Continuity Practice from Script

*11 minutes*

**Directions** – Type once; circle errors. Repeat. **Technique Goal** – Type steadily with eyes on book.

All letters
90 words
1.2 si

| | | Words |
|---|---|---|
| DS | Teddy Roosevelt said many years ago that by | 9 |
| | far the best prize that life has to offer is the | 19 |
| | chance to work hard at a job worth doing. One can | 29 |
| | hardly question this point of view, nor need one | 39 |
| | add much to it. Look upon a job as a chance to | 48 |
| | create a way of life for yourself. Choose a | 57 |
| | calling that lets you develop the talents and | 66 |
| | interests you have. Join those who derive joy | 76 |
| | from their work because they like it and because | 86 |
| | they are expert in it. | 90 |

## ■ Lesson 17 • *50-space line*

### 17a ■ Keyboard Review • Each line twice

*7 minutes*

| | | |
|---|---|---|
| Alphabetic | SS | Expert judges vehemently quiz four wicked bandits. |
| 4 | | f4f f4f 4f 4f 44 frames, 414 feet, 14 and 14 and 4 |
| 8 | | k8k k8k 8k 8k 88 kinds, 818 keys, 18 and 88 and 81 |
| % ( | | f5f f%f l9l l(l for 13% and 15%, ( is on the 9 key |
| Easy | | If you know of any way to do a job better, use it. |

| 1 | 2 | 3 | 4 | 5 | 6 | 7 | 8 | 9 | 10 |

Elbows in

### 17b ■ Sustained Skill Building

*10 minutes*

**Directions** – Type a 1-, 2-, and 3-minute writing on the paragraph in 16f above. Compute *gwam.* Try to equal your 1-minute rate on the longer writings. For the 2-minute rate, use the 1-minute column and scale to get total words; then divide by 2.

**Communications
Consultants, Inc.**
1742 Massachusetts Avenue    Boston, Massachusetts  02138    (617) 339-4822

Words

Center point ⟶ November 28, 197- ← Dateline typed 2 spaces
below letterhead or on
the 12th line space    4

9th line space

Address ⟶
Mr. John Ray, Vice President                                    9
New England Imports, Inc.                                      15
65 Commercial Wharf                                            19
Boston, Massachusetts   02110                                  24

Salutation ⟶ Dear Mr. Ray:                                     27

        The modified block style in which this letter is typed   38
is a style that I recommend for you to consider using in your    51
company correspondence.  This style is widely used by both       63
liberal and conservative business letter writers, and I be-      74
lieve that you might find it very effective for your letters.    87

        When the date was typed on this letter it was begun at   98
the horizontal center of the page.  You may prefer to type      110
Body ⟶ it elsewhere.  The choice depends on the arrangement of your  122
letterhead.  The date should be placed so that it gives bal-    134
ance to the letter.                                             138

        You will notice that the paragraphs are indented and that  150
mixed punctuation is used.  It would be equally correct, how-   162
ever, to block the paragraphs or to use open punctuation.       174

        If I can give you additional information about this or   185
other letter styles, please contact me.                         193

Complimentary close ⟶ ——— Center point ——— ⟶ Very truly yours,   197

4th line space    *Paul Walker*

Typed name and title ⟶ ——————————————— ⟶ Paul Walker, Consultant   201

Reference
initials ⟶ jh  ⟵ Double-space                                    202

In mixed punctuation a colon follows the salutation and a
comma follows the complimentary close.

Reference initials are used for identification and are typed
in the lower left corner.  The initials shown here are those
of the typist.  When the dictator's name is typed as part of
the closing lines, it is recommended that his initials or name
be omitted from the reference line.

## Business letter in modified block style, indented paragraphs

### 17c ■ Reach to $—Control of : (Colon) • Each line twice      *5 minutes*

On all machines $ is the shift of 4.

Type $ with the f finger. Do not space between the $ sign and the number that follows it.

On all machines : is the shift of ;.

Type : with the ; finger. Do not space after : which separates hours and minutes. Space twice after : in other uses.

| | | |
|---|---|---|
| $ | SS | f4f f$f f4f f$f $f $f $44, $444, $4.38, $14 and $8 |
| | | Pay $45.  We owe $54.  Spend $14.71.  He sent $47. |

*$ is the shift of 4*

| | |
|---|---|
| : | ;:; ;:; by 3:14, at 9:35, not until 11:15 or 11:38 |
| | Please send these items:  books, pens, and stamps. |

*: is the shift of ;*

### 17d ■ Reach to ' (Apostrophe) • Each line twice      *3 minutes*

On manual machines, ' is the shift of 8. Type ' with the k finger.

On electric machines, ' is to the right of the semicolon. Type the ' with the right fourth finger.

The apostrophe does not have a space before or after it.

| | | |
|---|---|---|
| Manual | SS | k8k k'k k8k k'k 'k 'k don't, can't, didn't, Jane's |
| Electric | | ;'; ;'; '; '; can't, didn't, isn't, wasn't, hasn't |
| Both | | Al can't go.  I can't drive.  It's in Fred's desk. |

*' is the shift of 8*

*Type ' with the ; finger*

### 17e ■ Reach to 2—Reach to 0      *5 minutes*

Type 2 with the S finger

Type 0 with the ; finger

Touch s2s lightly two or three times. Lift the little finger slightly to give freedom of action.

Touch ;0; lightly two or three times. Keep your elbow quiet and hold the other fingers in typing position.

s2s s2s s2s s2s 2s 2s s2s   • Type twice on same line •   ;0; ;0; ;0; ;0; 0; 0; ;0;

### 17f ■ Location Drills—2 and 0 • Each line twice      *6 minutes*

| | | |
|---|---|---|
| 2 | SS | s2s s2s s2s 2s 2s 2s 22 suits, 122 sets, 212 ships |
| | | He set 12 records in 22 days.  Take 21 or 22 sets. |

*Type 2 with the s finger*

| | |
|---|---|
| 0 | ;0; ;0; ;0; 0; 0; 0; 100 pets, 110 pelts, 50 pints |
| | Hal may take 20, 30, 40, or 50 of the white cards. |

*Type 0 with the ; finger*

### Problem 1—Business Letter in Modified Block Style, Indented Paragraphs

**Directions** – Type the letter shown on page 145. Follow the directions given on the illustration. Refer to the directions for addressing a small envelope on page 85. If you do not have a small envelope, cut paper to the small envelope size, 6½″ x 3⅝″.

Full sheet　　　　　　　60-space line　　　　　　　Mixed punctuation　　　　　　　Small envelope

### Problem 2—Business Letter in Modified Block Style, Indented Paragraphs

**Directions** – Type the following letter in the modified block style illustrated on page 145. Type the address on the 7th line space from the date.

● *For this letter and for the remaining letters in the book, use your own initials as reference initials.*

| | Words |
|---|---|
| March 21, 197– | 3 |
| | |
| Mr. Donald Carrington | 7 |
| 678 West Yukon Street | 12 |
| Anchorage, Alaska    99501 | 17 |
| | |
| Dear Mr. Carrington: | 21 |

We are pleased to know that you plan to spend your summer — 33 vacation in Alberta. I am happy to give you the information — 45 that you requested regarding fishing and hunting. — 55

There is no closed season on trout, grayling, and rocky — 66 mountain whitefish. Angling permit fees are $2 for residents — 79 as well as nonresidents. Permits are valid from April 1 to the — 92 following March 31, and are required of all fishermen except — 104 children under 16 years of age. — 110

A fishing license is required in all parks in the Canadian — 122 Rockies, and is good for any of these parks for the season. In- — 135 formation about open waters, seasons, and creel limits is pro- — 147 vided when the park fishing license is purchased. — 158

Nonresident game hunters must be accompanied by a licensed — 169 guide or outfitter. Guides are not required for bird hunting, — 182 however. No hunting is permitted in Alberta's provincial or — 194 national parks. — 198

If I can be of further help, please let me know. — 208

　　　　　　　Very truly yours,　　　　211

　　　　　　　Robert Peterson　　　　214
　　　　　　　Travel Consultant　　　　218

xx　　　　　　　　　　　　　218

## 17g ■ Key-Location Practice • Each line twice

1    SS   Take 44 or 45 quarts.   Pay $20.   I may collect 5%.

2         His car weighs 3,470 pounds.   Return Form #20 now.

3         Strike ( with the 9 finger.   Type 94, 37, and 502.      *Wrists low and steady*

4         This is Clay's schedule:   He will arrive at 10:15.

5         *Jim O'Neil can't call on Brush & Thorne on May 27.*

|   1   |   2   |   3   |   4   |   5   |   6   |   7   |   8   |   9   |   10  |

## ■ Lesson 18 • *50-space line*

### 18a ■ Keyboard Review • Each line twice

*7 minutes*

Alphabetic   SS   Jack bought six pounds of quartz to pave my walks.

2         s2s s2s 2s 2s 22 sets, 21 sacks, 212 and 22 and 21

0         0;0 0;0 0; 0; 100 pints, 110 pelts, 10 pets, 1,000       *Type surely and steadily*

$ '       Don't send $20; send $22.   I can't pay $20 for it.

Easy      It takes more than hot air to keep breezing along.

|   1   |   2   |   3   |   4   |   5   |   6   |   7   |   8   |   9   |   10  |

### 18b ■ Sentence Guided Writings

*11 minutes*

**Directions – 1.** Type each sentence for a 1-minute writing with the call of the guide each 20 seconds. Try to complete each sentence as the guide is called.

**2.** Type the last two sentences for additional 1-minute writings as time permits, without the call of the guide.

| | | Words in Line | GWAM 20″ Guide |
|---|---|---|---|
| 1 SS | There is a high price on lost time. | 7 | 21 |
| 2 | *Reduce time loss; add to your rate.* | 7 | 21 |
| 3 | Hold your wrists down; keep them steady. | 8 | 24 |
| 4 | *Make your fingers reach to all the keys.* | 8 | 24 |
| 5 | To type well, observe the rules of good form. | 9 | 27 |
| 6 | *Keep your feet on the floor for good balance.* | 9 | 27 |
| 7 | One rule of good form is to sit erect as you type. | 10 | 30 |
| 8 | *You should hold your eyes on the copy in the book.* | 10 | 30 |

|   1   |   2   |   3   |   4   |   5   |   6   |   7   |   8   |   9   |   10  |

**68c** ■ **Capitalization Guides—Business Letter Parts** • Read the explanations; then type each line three times.                    *5 minutes*

**Line 1** – In business letters, capitalize the first and last words, all titles, and all proper names used in the salutation.

**Line 2** – Capitalize only the first word of the complimentary close.

**Line 3** – All titles appearing in the address should be capitalized.

**Line 4** – If a title follows the name of the dictator in the closing lines of a letter, it must always be capitalized.

1    ss    Sir: My dear Sir: Dear Sir: Gentlemen: Dear Mr. Brown: Dear Susan

2         Sincerely yours, Yours very truly, Respectfully yours, Cordially yours

3         Miss Sue Myers, Director; Mr. Don Floyd, Chairman; Lt. Ron Lewis, USMC

4         Cathy White, President; David Walther, Principal; Tom Martin, Attorney

Hold the shift key down firmly

---

## INFORMATION ABOUT BUSINESS LETTERS

**Stationery Size** – Most business letters are typed on 8½- by 11-inch stationery that is imprinted with the name and address of the company.

**Envelopes** – Use small envelopes (6½″ x 3⅝″) for one-page letters and large envelopes (9½″ x 4⅛″) for two-page letters or for letters with enclosures.

**Vertical Placement of Dateline** – When using letterhead paper, the dateline should be typed two lines below the letterhead. If plain paper is used, the date should be on the 12th line space from the top.

**Carbon Copies** – One or more carbon copies are usually made of business letters. Follow the directions on page 89 for preparing carbon copies.

**Letter Styles** – The three most widely used styles are:

*Modified block with indented paragraphs* (shown on page 145).

*Modified block with blocked paragraphs* (shown on page 148).

*Block*, in which all elements are blocked at the left margin (shown on page 151).

**Punctuation Styles** – Two commonly used punctuation styles are open and mixed. In *open* punctuation, no punctuation marks are used after the salutation or the complimentary close. In *mixed* punctuation a colon is placed after the salutation and a comma after the complimentary close.

**Reference Initials** – The typist should always type his initials at the left margin two line spaces below the typed name of the dictator of the letter. When the dictator's name is typed as part of the closing line, it is recommended that his initials or name be omitted from the reference line.

**Enclosure Notation** – An enclosure notation is used when an item (or items) is sent with the letter. Type the notation a double space below the reference initials. Use the plural, *Enclosures*, if two or more items are enclosed.

**Abbreviations** – Although excessive abbreviations should be avoided, it is acceptable to abbreviate state names in an address in order to maintain uniformity of line length. However, the two-letter ZIP Code abbreviations (see Problem 2, Lesson 62, page 132) should be used only with a ZIP Code. Leave two spaces between the state name and the ZIP Code.

## 18c ■ Reach to )—Reach to "

6 minutes

**Directions** – Type each line twice.

On all machines, ) is the shift of 0.

On manual machines, " is the shift of 2.

On electric machines, " is the shift of '.

Do not space between the right parenthesis and the material it encloses.

On all electric machines, " is to the right of the semicolon. Type it with the right fourth finger.

Type " without a space between it and the word it encloses. A double space follows " when it ends a sentence.

● *Turn to p. xiii for additional drills.*

```
)  All machines SS  ;0;  ;);  ;0;  ;);  );  );  type 0;  then type );  think )        ) is the
                                                                                        shift of 0

"  Manual         s2s  s"s  s2s  s"s  "s  "s  "column"  for  "column"  "gigi"           " is the
                                                                                        shift of 2
                  Type "forty," not "fourty."   Read "Bridging Gaps."

"  Electric       ;";  ;";  ;';  ;";  Use "can" often.   "Can't" is weak.               " is the
                                                                                        shift of '
                  The " is the shift of the '.   "They won," he said.
```

## 18d ■ Reach to 6—Reach to Hyphen

5 minutes

.Type 6 with the J finger

Type — with the ; finger

Touch **j6j** lightly two or three times. Make the reach without arching your wrist. Hold the other fingers in typing position.

Touch **;-;** lightly two or three times without moving the other fingers from their typing position.

```
j6j  j6j  j6j  j6j  6j  6j  j6j    ● Type twice on same line ●    ;-;  ;-;  ;-;  ;-;  -;  -;  ;-;
```

## 18e ■ Location Drills—6 and Hyphen

6 minutes

**Directions** – Each line twice.

**Technique Goals** – Reach with your fingers for the top row. Keep wrists and elbows in.

```
6     SS  j6j  j6j  j6j  6j  6j  6j  66 jets,  6616 jacks,  66 jumps      Type 6 with
                                                                          the j finger
          He made 66 jumps.   Take 16 jets.   Add 166 and 616.

-         ;-;  ;-;  ;-;  -;  -;  -;  set-to, send-off, know-it-all        Type — with
                                                                          the ; finger
          Her son-in-law had the right-of-way on the street.
```

RESUME

Mary Ann Walter

Address

17330 Bronte Place
Granada Hills, California  91344
Telephone Number:  368-5791

Personal Information

Age:  20                    Height:  5 feet 5 inches
Weight:  121 pounds          Health:  Excellent

Education

Graduate, Granada Hills High School, Granada Hills, California, June, 197-.

Associate of Arts Degree, Valley Community College, Northridge, California, June, 197-.
Major:  Secretarial Administration.

Work Experience

General clerk, Chase Manufacturing Company, Northridge,
California, summer of 197-.  Duties:  Typing sales
orders and filing invoices.

Secretary, Meyers Machine Tool Products Company, Granada
Hills, California, summer of 197-.  Duties:  Taking
dictation and typing letters and reports.

References

Dr. G. J. Christensen, Chairman, Business Education Department, Valley Community College, Northridge, California.

Mr. Harold Finn, Chairman, Business Education Department,
Granada Hills High School, Granada Hills, California.

Mr. Newton Meyers, President, Meyers Machine Tool Products
Company, Granada Hills, California.

**Personal résumé**

## 18f ■ Key-Location Practice

10 minutes

**Directions** – Each line twice.

**Technique Goal** – Keep your eyes on the copy.

• Review of all figure and symbol keys covered

1 SS  He read pages 21, 39, 48, and 75, as she directed.

2  Send Bill #379 to Good & Deed.  My discount is 7%.  *Sit erect*

3  The record (206.9 miles per hour) is held by #295.

4  The "Elizabethan" covers 392 miles in 390 minutes.  *Feet on the floor*

5  The largest check ever drawn was for $642,600,000.

6  *Al's record for this term is four B's and two A's.*  *Eyes on this copy*

7  *This 7,560-ounce gold nugget is the largest found.*

```
| 1 | 2 | 3 | 4 | 5 | 6 | 7 | 8 | 9 | 10 |
```

## ■ Lesson 19 • *50-space line*

### 19a ■ Keyboard Review • Each line twice

7 minutes

Alphabetic  SS  The gray fox jumped quickly over lazy brown ducks.

6  j6j j6j 6j 6j 66 jokes, 616 jumps, 156 Jones Drive  *Elbows in*

-  ;-; ;-; -; -; well-to-do, right-of-way, flare-back

" )  "Really," not "realy."  Type ) with your ; finger.  *Wrists low and quiet*

Easy  Read with great care the copy from which you type.

```
| 1 | 2 | 3 | 4 | 5 | 6 | 7 | 8 | 9 | 10 |
```

---

### BACKSPACING

• *The backspace key assists you in positioning the carriage. Later you will learn how the backspace key assists you in underlining words.*

**Manual Machines** – The backspace key on manual machines is located at the extreme left of the fourth row. Depress the key with the little finger as you keep the f finger in its proper position and the d and s fingers on or near their home row positions.

**Alternate Suggestion** – If your little finger is weak, operate the backspace key with one of the other fingers. To use a finger other than your little finger, move your entire hand to the fourth row and return it to the home keys after backspacing.

• *On some portable and electric machines the backspace key is at the extreme right of the fourth row of keys. In this case use the little finger of the right hand for controlling the backspace key.*

### Problem 1—Application Letter

**Directions – 1.** Type the application letter given below. Use a personal letter style such as that illustrated in Lesson 40, page 84.

**2.** Type the address on the 8th line space from the date for elite and on the 6th line space for pica. *The symbol (¶) indicates a new paragraph.*

Full sheet                70-space line, elite; 60-space-line, pica                Mixed punctuation                Blocked paragraphs

17330 Bronte Place / Granada Hills, California   91344 / May 18, 19––

Mr. Marshall Keyser, Vice President / Mission Manufacturing Company / 14358 Chasen Street / Northridge, California   91324

Dear Mr. Keyser:

Mr. James Manos, Placement Director at Valley Community College, has informed me that you will soon need a secretary. I believe that my college education and my two summers of experience working in manufacturing companies similar to yours should qualify me for your consideration. (¶) My major field of study in college has given me extensive training for a position as an executive secretary. Besides the fundamental secretarial skills of shorthand, typing, and office machines, I have had classes in accounting, business law, and business English. (¶) During my last two summer vacations, I have worked for manufacturing companies filling in for secretaries who were on vacation. This work has given me a variety of experiences in all phases of secretarial work which I believe would be of value to you. (¶) The enclosed résumé gives more detailed information about my education and personal qualifications. It also gives the names and addresses of several people who have given me permission to use them as references. (¶) May I come for an interview at your convenience? You may reach me at the address or telephone number given on the top of my résumé.

Sincerely yours,

Mary Ann Walter

### Problem 2—Personal Résumé

**Directions –** Type the résumé that is illustrated on the following page. Use a 1½-inch top margin, a 60-space line for pica type, and a 70-space line for elite.

- *Usually an applicant for a position should include a personal résumé with his letter of application. Such a résumé is given in this problem.*

## ■ Lesson 68 • *70-space line*

**68a ■ Keyboard Review** • Each line at least three times                                      *5 minutes*

Alphabetic SS   Rex jumped up and ran quickly over the hills away from a grizzly bear.

Figure   The total enrollment in 1960 was only 34, but in 1972 it was up to 85.   Quick carriage return

Double letters   He offered a suggestion of immediate necessity for the beginning cook.

Easy   The best things in life do not always come to those who wait and hope.

| 1 | 2 | 3 | 4 | 5 | 6 | 7 | 8 | 9 | 10 | 11 | 12 | 13 | 14 |

## 19b ■ Reach to Underline—Reach to *

6 minutes

**Directions** – Type each line twice.

### Manual

The underline is the shift of the 6.
The asterisk is the shift of the hyphen.

To underline, backspace (or move by hand) to the first letter of the word; then type the underline once for each letter in the word. If several words are to be underlined, use the shift lock.

### Electric

The underline is the shift of the hyphen.
The asterisk is the shift of the 8.

Use the right fourth finger to type the underline. Use the right second finger to type the asterisk. *Turn to p. xiii for additional drills on electric typewriters.*

| | | |
|---|---|---|
| _ Manual | SS j6j j_j j6j j_j _j _j right, lowest price, at once | Type _ with the j finger |
| * | ;-; ;*; ;-; ;*; *; *; the * is the shift of the -. | Type * with the ; finger |
| _ Electric | ;_; ;_; _; _; _; The _ is the shift of the hyphen. | Type _ with the ; finger |
| * | k8k k*k k8k k*k The * is the shift of 8.   *k *k *k | Type * with the k finger |

## 19c ■ Reach to ¢—Reach to ½ and ¼

5 minutes

On manual machines, type ¢ with the ; finger.

On electric machines, ¢ is the shift of 6. Type it with the j finger.

There is no space between the number and the ¢ sign.

←Manual—Electric→

• Type twice on same line •

On all machines, ½ and ¼ are to the right of the letter p.

Type ½ with the ; finger; ¼ is the shift of ½.

There is no space between a figure and ½ or ¼.

;¢; ;¢; ¢; ¢; 12¢ and 15¢     j¢j j¢j ¢j ¢j 26¢ and 67¢

;½; ;½; ½; ½; 14½ and 15½     ;¼; ;¼; ¼; ¼; 7¼ ¼; ;¼ ¼;

## 19d ■ Location Drills—¢, ½, and ¼

6 minutes

**Directions** – Type each line twice.

**Technique Goal** – Keep elbows in and quiet.

| | | | |
|---|---|---|---|
| ¢ | Manual | SS ;¢; ;¢; ;¢; ¢; ¢; ¢; 73¢, 25¢ for 12, 93¢ for them | Type ¢ with the ; finger |
| ¢ | Electric | j6j j¢j j6j j¢j The ¢ sign is the shift of 6.   66¢ | Type ¢ with the j finger |
| ½ | | ;½; ;½; ;½; ½; ½; ½ pint, ½ cord, ½ ton, 15½ miles | Type ½ with the ; finger |
| ¼ | All machines | ;¼; ;¼; ;¼; ;¼; ¼; ¼; 27½ miles, 7¼ and 7¼ are 14½ | ¼ is the shift of ½ |

### 67a ■ Keyboard Review • Each line at least three times

Alphabetic SS  Jim had very quickly put labels on six coils of wire going to the zoo.

Figure  This year 205 men will work on Maui, 437 on Oahu, and 1,689 on Hawaii.

oi, io  An ointment or a lotion could be used to moisten the lion's sore paws.

Easy  He bought the land by the lake to build a cabin for his fishing trips.

| 1 | 2 | 3 | 4 | 5 | 6 | 7 | 8 | 9 | 10 | 11 | 12 | 13 | 14 |

*Type without pauses*

---

## PROOFREADING TECHNIQUES

Proofreading is a very important element in the correct typing of business communications. Every piece of work should be carefully proofread before it is distributed.

A typist must look closely for a variety of possible errors. These include typographical errors, spelling errors, punctuation and grammatical errors, transposition of letters and lines, errors in page numbers, errors in meaning, errors in uniformity of names and numbers, exactness in names and addresses, and inconsistency of style.

The proofreading may be done by the person who types the material or it may be done by someone else. For some types of copy, particularly statistical copy, two people may be engaged in the proofreading operation. One person can read the copy aloud from the draft manuscript while someone else checks the accuracy of the copy that was typed.

---

### 67b ■ Proofreading Skill Builder—Spelling Errors

**Directions** – Find the incorrectly spelled word in each sentence. Type the sentence, spelling the word correctly. Type the sentences again.

1  SS  All carbon copies of eleven letters were sealed in seperate envelopes.

2  A person can drive completely accros this country in only eight hours.

3  Only too of the picture post cards that were mailed ever reached home.

4  There is a strong beleif that Marilyn does have the skill for the job.

5  His use of grammer is so poor that he is very difficult to understand.

6  The clerical interview was to be held in the company personal office.

7  Please do not dissapoint Charlene with a poor performance on your job.

8  The discription for the new job was not listed in the training manual.

---

### 67c ■ Skill Comparison • Type a 1-minute writing on each sentence of 66a, page 138. Compare your rates on these sentences.

## 19e ■ Key-Location Practice

**Directions** – Type once; circle errors; repeat.

**Technique Goal** – Type slowly and surely.

|  | Words |
|---|---|
| DS    Let's call this report "World Records".  The | 9 |
| lowest score on an 18-hole golf course is 55 (15 | 19 |
| under par).  A ½¢ stamp was issued in the United | 29 |
| States in 1922.  The highest selling phonograph | 38 |
| record of all time is White Christmas, which up to | 48 |
| 1962 sold 34,681,857 copies.  The Dutch are the | 58 |
| most severely taxed people in the world.  A single | 68 |
| man who earns $5,600 has 40% taken by taxes. | 77 |

| 1 | 2 | 3 | 4 | 5 | 6 | 7 | 8 | 9 | 10 |

## 19f ■ Timed Writings

*11 minutes*

**Directions** – Type the paragraphs once for practice; then type two 1-minute writings on each one.

● Contains all letters

|  | | GWAM | |
|---|---|---|---|
|  | | 1' | 3' |
| ¶1 32 words 1.2 si | DS    The experts all tell us that we should learn | 9 | 3 37 |
|  | from the mistakes of others.  No one has the time | 19 | 6 40 |
|  | to make them all himself.  We gain when we listen | 29 | 10 44 |
|  | to this advice. | 32 | 11 45 |
| ¶2 34 words 1.2 si | Know that failure is the only prize we will | 9 | 14 48 |
|  | acquire in this world without hard work.  We must | 19 | 17 51 |
|  | be willing to work for those things that most of | 29 | 20 54 |
|  | us need and desire to have. | 34 | 22 56 |
| ¶3 36 words 1.2 si | A speaker talking about jobs said that if one | 9 | 25 59 |
|  | but had the right key, he could sing in any flat. | 19 | 28 62 |
|  | He implied, of course, that a man with a useful | 29 | 32 66 |
|  | skill would always have a good job. | 36 | 34 68 |

| 1' | 1 | 2 | 3 | 4 | 5 | 6 | 7 | 8 | 9 | 10 |
| 3' | | 1 | | 2 | | 3 | | 4 | |

**Directions** – 1. Type a 5-minute writing. Compute your *gwam*. 2. Type two 1-minute writings on each of the paragraphs. Type the first writing for speed and the second for control.

3. Finally, type another 5-minute writing on all the paragraphs. Compute your *gwam*. Compare the *gwam* and the number of errors for the two 5-minute writings. Submit the better of the two.

|  |  | GWAM |
|  |  | 1' | 5' |

¶1
66 words
1.4 si

DS

Spelling correctly is a problem for some people. A word may be    13  3  60
spelled wrong because a person doesn't see or hear the word properly.    27  5  62
When a person misspells a word mentally, he may misspell it on paper.    41  8  65
Anyone can, however, acquire good spelling habits that will help him    55  11  68
overcome errors he may have been making for many years.    66  13  70

¶2
78 words
1.4 si

One habit a person can develop is to compile a list of words that    13  16  73
he frequently misspells. As he becomes confident of the correct spell-    27  19  76
ing, he can check the word off the list. As the list becomes shorter,    42  22  79
his spelling should improve. Another habit is to spell new words aloud.    56  24  81
Say the word aloud; write it down. This effort with new words will help    71  27  84
one to become a much better speller.    78  29  86

¶3
79 words
1.4 si

The "dictionary habit" is one that also can be developed. With it    13  32  89
a person can be sure that he will never be guilty of misspelling a word.    28  34  91
All one has to do is look up a word if he is not sure of the spelling.    43  37  94
This habit not only insures correct spelling, it also helps a person    56  40  97
learn to spell difficult words. If one looks up a word often enough,    70  43  100
he may eventually remember how to spell it.    79  45  102

¶4
60 words
1.4 si

Correct spelling is needed in all writing. A misspelled word jumps    14  47  104
out at a reader and gives an impression of ignorance and carelessness.    28  50  107
There is no excuse that is good enough. We must all learn to spell    42  53  110
correctly; if this seems to be impossible, we must be willing to be    55  56  113
chained to a dictionary.    60  57  114

1' | 1 | 2 | 3 | 4 | 5 | 6 | 7 | 8 | 9 | 10 | 11 | 12 | 13 | 14 |
5' |         1         |         2         |         3         |

### 20a ■ Keyboard Review • Each line twice

Alphabetic  ss  Brad Jay gave me six tickets for an L-P Quiz Show.

¢  She has 28¢.  Send her 19¢.  Pay 37¢.  Deduct 39¢.  *Wrists low*

½  ;½; ;½; ½; ½; We sold 37½ pints.  Take 28½ quarts.  *Reach with your fingers*

– *  She may see this design in a copy of Chinese Art.*

Easy  Keep your mind on your work as you type this copy.

| 1 | 2 | 3 | 4 | 5 | 6 | 7 | 8 | 9 | 10 |

### 20b ■ Reach to @ and / • Each line twice

*6 minutes*

On manual machines, @ (symbol for at) is the shift of ¢. Type @ with the ; finger. There is a space before and after the @.

On electric machines, @ is the shift of **2**. Type it with the left third finger.

On all machines, the / is the lower case of ?. Type / with the ; finger. Do not space before or after the diagonal.

- *The diagonal is used in typing fractions for which there is no special keyboard symbol, as 3/8. Note in Line 3 below how a whole number and a fraction that is not on the keyboard are spaced.*

@  Manual  ss  ;@; ;@; ;@; @; @; @; buy 217 @ 45¢, sell 574 @ 39¢  *@ is the shift of ¢*

@  Electric  s2s s@s s2s s@s s@s ship 132 @ 27¢, sell 295 @ 30¢  *@ is the shift of 2*

/  All machines  ;/; ;/; ;/; /; /; /; 2/3, 13 3/4, up 18 1/8 points  */ is lower case of ?*

Be uniform in typing fractions; thus, 1/2 and 5/8.

### 20c ■ Reach to = and + • Each line twice

*4 minutes*

Some typewriters have an = and + key at the right end of the top row. Type = and + with the ; finger.

- *A space precedes and follows both the = and the + symbols.*

=  ss  ;=; ;=; ;=; =; =; Three = 3.  In this case, X = 8.  *Type = with the ; finger*

+  The + is the shift of =.  53 + 21 + 41 + 17 = 132.  *+ is the shift of =*

### 20d ■ Typing from Dictation • Each line twice

*4 minutes*

1  ss  99 88 77 66 55 44 33 22 11 12 23 34 45 56 76 82 90  *Reach with your fingers*

2  50 450 39 390 73 84 26 230 110 40 36 96 101 22 780

# Unit 9 ■

# Typing Business Communications

## General Directions ■ Lessons 66-80

Use a 70-space line length for all drills and timed writings in this unit. Single-space sentences and drill lines. Double-space between groups of repeated lines. Double-space paragraph copy. Directions for each problem will indicate the correct line length to use. Your teacher will tell you whether or not you are to erase and correct errors in the problems of this unit.

## ■ Lesson 66

### 66a ■ Keyboard Review • Each line at least three times for all lessons in this unit.
*5 minutes*

Alphabetic SS   Jack, a grave explorer, found quality zinc by making that wide search.

Figure   The building had 1,560 desks, 2,837 file cabinets, and 49 work tables.   Quick, sharp strokes

Shift   Leon Wilson and John Walter were UCLA fans but Dick Perry favored USC.

Easy   The glass dish fell from the table and broke into a million tiny bits.

| 1 | 2 | 3 | 4 | 5 | 6 | 7 | 8 | 9 | 10 | 11 | 12 | 13 | 14 |

### 66b ■ Paragraph Skill Builder—Figure Copy • Type four 1-minute writings.
*5 minutes*

DS   Your order for 12 dozen turkeys was filled today. The shipment should reach you by December 14, in time for your Christmas shoppers.

60 words
1.4 si
We will be happy to give you a standard 5% discount if you pay the balance within 8 days. The total amount of the invoice, after deducting the discount, is $760.39.

Keep your eyes on the copy

### 66c ■ Technique Builder—One-Hand Words
*10 minutes*

**Directions** – Type each line three times. Take two 1-minute timings on each of the last two lines.

**Technique Goal** – Try to increase your speed on one-hand words.

Phrases   SS   as my | as we see | as you join | at a | see him | we see | as we see | saw a

Phrases   as he sees | we were only | we were aware | as you look | you see him only   Fingers deeply curved

Sentence   As you know, Johnny T. Edwards saw a savage lion nip at a brave puppy.

Sentence   We were aware of few exaggerated opinions given on the phony monopoly.

| 1 | 2 | 3 | 4 | 5 | 6 | 7 | 8 | 9 | 10 | 11 | 12 | 13 | 14 |

## 20e ■ Key-Location Practice

**Directions** – Type once; circle errors; repeat.          **Technique Goal** – Think as you type.

1  DS  Send 3 1/3 feet @ 72¢ a foot.  Call Simpson & Son.

2      I quote Emerson:  "Each mind has its own method."*

3      Send 40¼ pounds to O'Dell; send 3½ pounds to Frye.                *Eyes on this copy*

4      The world's deepest water well is 7,009 feet deep.

5      Will Kurt's sales plans be adopted by Station KBG?               *Quick, sure strokes*

6      *His Bill #1589 (dated May 26) is due in one month.*

7      *I can buy a copy of Master Spy for $5.17, less 5%.*


## 20f ■ Timed Writings

**Directions** – Type the paragraphs once for practice; then type two 3-minute writings. Compute *gwam*. Submit the better writing.

● Contains all letters

| | | GWAM 1' | 3' |
|---|---|---|---|

¶1
32 words
1.2 si

DS    All of us make mistakes, but some of us give          9    3  37
them too much aid.  Genius is the ability to evade         19    6  40
work by doing a job right the very first time it           29   10  44
has to be done.                                            32   11  45

¶2
34 words
1.2 si

      The mistakes you should avoid at this point          41   14  48
in your typing are mistakes in technique.  Just be         51   17  51
exact in the way you type.  You can gain good              60   20  54
skill only if you type right.                              66   22  56

¶3
36 words
1.2 si

      Of all the faults one can have in typing,            74   25  59
those he has in stroking the keys are by far the           84   28  62
most costly.  You must know that even a small flaw         94   31  65
here will be repeated dozens of times.                    102   34  68

1' | 1 | 2 | 3 | 4 | 5 | 6 | 7 | 8 | 9 | 10 |
3' |   1   |   2   |   3   |   4   |

**Directions – 1.** Type this table on a full sheet of paper and center it in *reading* position.

**2.** Leave 6 blank spaces between the columns and double-space the items in each column.

## PERSONAL CONSUMPTION EXPENDITURES FOR THE U.S.

### (In Millions of Dollars)

| Item | 1960 | 1970 |
|---|---|---|
| Food and tobacco | 87,510 | 142,915 |
| Clothing, accessories, and jewelry | 33,032 | 62,278 |
| Personal care | 5,324 | 10,101 |
| Housing | 46,305 | 91,224 |
| Household operation | 46,906 | 85,618 |
| Medical care | 19,116 | 47,268 |
| Personal business | 14,974 | 35,497 |
| Transportation | 43,134 | 77,871 |
| Recreation | 18,295 | 39,049 |
| Private education and research | 3,718 | 10,353 |
| Religious and welfare activities | 4,748 | 8,826 |
| Foreign travel and remittances -- net | 2,179 | 4,810 |

Source: Office of Business Economics, U.S. Department of Commerce, The World Almanac and Book of Facts, 1972, p. 411.

## 65d ■ Extra-Credit Typing

### Problem 1

**Directions** – Type the names of as many states and their capitols as you can recall. Provide the main, secondary, and columnar headings. Arrange the table on a full sheet of paper and determine the number of blank spaces that you wish to leave between the two columns.

### Problem 2

**Directions** – List the names of ten people prominent in the entertainment world and indicate the medium in which each is best known. Choose main, secondary, and columnar headings. Type the table on a half sheet of paper with adequate spacing between columns.

### Problem 3

**Directions** – Retype the table in Problem 2, above. This time, take out the subheading and add three 0's to all of your figures to indicate millions of dollars. Use your own judgment concerning the vertical placement and the spacing between the columns.

# Unit 4 ■

## Learning Basic Operations and Building Typing Continuity

### General Directions ■ Lessons 21-25

**Line length** – Beginning with this lesson, set margin stops for a 60-space line. Make this adjustment at the start of each lesson.

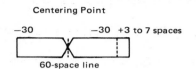

Centering Point

−30        −30  +3 to 7 spaces

60-space line

**Spacing** – Single-space lines of words and sentences; double-space between repeated groups of lines. Double-space paragraph copy.

## ■ Lesson 21

### 21a ■ Keyboard Review

5 minutes

**Directions** – Type each line at least twice.    **Technique Goals** – Type the first three lines slowly and exactly. Increase your stroking rate on the last line.

| | | |
|---|---|---|
| Alphabetic | SS | Liz Howe can mix five quarts of gray paint for Bud and Jack. |
| Figure-Symbol | | Why hasn't Order #462-10 been shipped?  (It amounts to $37.) |
| Balanced hand | | to the, for them, to do, with their, for us, to cut, so they |
| Easy | | When you write papers, be brief; there is no weight to wind. |

Feet on floor

| 1 | 2 | 3 | 4 | 5 | 6 | 7 | 8 | 9 | 10 | 11 | 12 |

### 21b ■ Reach to ! and —— (Dash)

5 minutes

**Directions** – Type each line at least twice.

**Exclamation point** – If your machine has a key for !, shift, and type it with the a finger. Space twice after the !.

**Dash** – Type the dash with two hyphens. Do not space before or after the dash.

- *On those machines not having a key for the !, type the apostrophe; backspace and type the period. Do not space between the word and the exclamation point.*

1    SS Attention!  Act now!  Save!  Save!  Bargains galore!  Hurry!

Sit erect!  Be alert!  Type right!  Use quick, sure strokes!

--    Your character--not wealth or position--is of supreme worth.

The law and the stage--both are clearly forms of exhibition.

# ■ Lesson 65 • *70-space line*

## 65a ■ Keyboard Review • Each line three times                    *5 minutes*

Alphabetic SS  Major Quigley's proxy voted to finalize the Big Lake Company's bylaws.

One hand  Fred Hunt will trace the crates of plums that were sent to my address.

One hand  People check the time at least 50 times a day, or 18,250 times a year.

Easy  Men know they are sure to be wrong if they are so sure they are right.

| 1 | 2 | 3 | 4 | 5 | 6 | 7 | 8 | 9 | 10 | 11 | 12 | 13 | 14 |

Think
as you
type

## 65b ■ Timed Writings                    *15 minutes*

**Directions** – Type two 1-minute and two 5-minute writings on 61d, page 130. Compute *gwam*. Submit the better of the two 5-minute writings.

## 65c ■ Problem Typing                    *25 minutes*

### Problem 1—Table with Multiple-Line Columnar Headings and Footnotes

**Directions** – 1. Type this table on a full sheet of paper and center it in *reading position.*

2. Leave 8 blank spaces between columns. Double-space the items in each column.

• Set the tab stop at the space where the most frequently occurring item in the column appears.

### WORLD'S HIGHEST DAMS *

| Maximum Height (Feet) | Name | Country | Year Completed ** |
|---|---|---|---|
| 1,017 | Nurek | U.S.S.R. | UC |
| 932 | Grande Dixence | Switzerland | 1962 |
| 892 | Inguri | U.S.S.R. | UC |
| 858 | Vaiont | Italy | 1961 |
| 800 | Mica | Canada | UC |
| 777 | Mauvoisin | France | 1958 |
| 774 | Sayansk | U.S.S.R. | UC |
| 770 | Oroville | U.S.A. | 1968 |
| 764 | Chirkey | U.S.S.R. | UC |
| 752 | Contra | Switzerland | 1965 |

* Dan Golenpaul (ed.), Information Please Almanac, Atlas, and Yearbook (New York: Simon and Schuster, 1970), p. 471.

** UC means under construction.

## 21c ■ Spacing after Punctuation Marks—Review

*10 minutes*

**Directions** – Type each line twice. Read the explanation for a line before you type it.

### EXPLANATIONS

**Line 1** – Space twice after end-of-sentence punctuation.

**Line 2** – Do not space after a period within an abbreviation. Space once after a period that ends an abbreviation; twice if that period ends a sentence.

**Line 3** – Space once after a comma.

**Line 4** – Space twice after a colon. Exception: Do not space before or after a colon in stating time.

**Line 5** – Type the dash with two hyphens, without spacing before or after.

**Line 6** – Do not space before or after the hyphen in a hyphenated word.

### SENTENCES

1   SS   Can she type? Great! She can start tomorrow. Please call.

2   I saw her at 10 a.m. Jerry will leave on the 9 p.m. flight.

3   She brought jewelry, dishes, clothes, and linens from Spain.

4   I checked these sizes: 8, 10, and 12. He left at 5:17 p.m.

5   These traits--courtesy and poise--should never be forgotten.

6   John bought a hand-carved frame for the well-known painting.

| 1 | 2 | 3 | 4 | 5 | 6 | 7 | 8 | 9 | 10 | 11 | 12 |

*Read the explanations; then type*

## 21d ■ Technique Builder—Word-Response Typing ● Each line three times

*5 minutes*

1   SS   to do | to do it | to do the | and he | and the | and if | and she

2   if he | and if he | and if the | and if she | and if it | and the

3   if it | if he | if the | if it is | if it is the | if it is to do

4   to do | to do it | to do the | to form | to work | to do the work

*Think the words; type them*

## 21e ■ Sentence Skill Builder ● Type two 1-minute writings on each sentence. Compute gwam.

*5 minutes*

1   SS   If he is to do the job that is to be done, he can do it now.

2   She is to do the work if she can do it as it should be done.

| 1 | 2 | 3 | 4 | 5 | 6 | 7 | 8 | 9 | 10 | 11 | 12 |

*Type whole words*

## 21f ■ Speed Ladder Paragraphs

*15 minutes*

**Directions** – Type 1-minute writings on the paragraphs that follow. When you can complete the first paragraph in one minute, type the second; then the third, fourth, and fifth. Your teacher may call the half minutes to guide you.

● *The rate increases four words a minute with each succeeding paragraph. All letters are used in the paragraphs.*

## 64d ■ Problem Typing

### Problem 1—Table with Columnar Headings and Footnote

**Directions** – 1. Type this table on a half sheet of paper, centering it in *exact vertical center*.
2. Single-space the entries in each column, leaving 6 blank spaces between the columns.

● *Footnotes in tables are typed in the same way as footnotes in manuscripts. As shown in the table below, however, they are usually typed immediately below the table even though the table consumes only a partial page.*

### LOWEST POINTS IN SELECTED STATES

| State | Lowest Point | Elevation in Feet |
|-------|--------------|-------------------|
| California | Death Valley | 282* |
| Colorado | Arkansas River | 3,350 |
| Louisiana | New Orleans | 5* |
| Maine | Atlantic Ocean | Sea Level |
| Montana | Kootenai River | 1,800 |
| New Mexico | Red Bluff Reservoir | 2,817 |
| Oregon | Pacific Ocean | Sea Level |
| Pennsylvania | Delaware River | Sea Level |
| Utah | Beaverdam Creek | 2,000 |
| Wyoming | Belle Fourche River | 3,100 |

Single-space ——▶
Double-space ——▶

*Below sea level

### Problem 2—Table with Columnar Headings and Footnote in Rough Draft

**Directions** – 1. Type this table on a half sheet of paper and center it in *exact vertical center*.
2. Single-space the entries in each column and leave 8 blank spaces between columns.

● *Tab stops should always be set at that space where the most frequently occurring item in the column appears. Also, figures should always be aligned at the right.*

### HIGHEST POINTS in SELECTED STATES

| State | Highest Point | Height * |
|-------|---------------|----------|
| Alaska | Mount McKinley | 20,320 |
| California | Mount Whitney | 14,495 |
| Colorado | Mount Elbert | 14,423 |
| Delaware | Elbright Road | 442 |
| Mississippi | Woodall Mountain | 806 |
| Rhode Island | Jerimoth Hill | 812 |
| Florida | In Walton County | 345 |
| Hawaii | Mauna Kea | 13,796 |
| Louisiana | Diskill Mountain | 538 |
| Washington | Mount Rainier | 14,410 |

* In feet

¶1
20 words
1.2 si

DS  Fantasy is more fun than logic, but we must be willing | 11 | 4 | 65
to face the truth when we need to do so, too. | 20 | 7 | 67

¶2
24 words
1.2 si

You will not do well in typing until you analyze the | 11 | 10 | 70
way you type. Check an item; improve it. Move on to the | 22 | 14 | 74
next one. | 24 | 15 | 75

¶3
28 words
1.2 si

Begin with the way you strike the space bar. Does the | 11 | 18 | 78
thumb move downward and inward when you space between | 23 | 22 | 82
words? It should, but does it? | 28 | 24 | 84

¶4
32 words
1.2 si

Check the way you return the carriage. Do you return | 11 | 28 | 88
it with a very quick flick of the wrist when you reach the | 23 | 31 | 91
end of the line; then resume typing at once? | 31 | 34 | 94

¶5
36 words
1.2 si

Look next at the way you handle the job of shifting for | 11 | 38 | 98
capital letters. Split-second timing is needed. Do you | 23 | 42 | 102
make the reach to the shift keys with hinge motions of your | 35 | 46 | 106
wrists? | 36 | 46 | 106

¶6
40 words
1.2 si

Finally, give some thought to your posture. Are your | 11 | 50 | 110
fingers well curved and your wrists held low and steady? Do | 23 | 54 | 114
you sit back in the chair, with body erect? Do you keep | 34 | 58 | 118
your feet flat on the floor? | 40 | 60 | 120

```
1' |  1  |  2  |  3  |  4  |  5  |  6  |  7  |  8  |  9  |  10 |  11 |  12 |
3' |     1     |     2     |     3     |     4     |
```

# ■ Lesson 22 • *60-space line*

## 22a ■ Keyboard Review • Each line at least twice          *5 minutes*

Alphabetic      SS  Vale swam back with extra zest in quest of a judge's trophy.

Figure-Symbol       The longest opera is "Parsifal" by W. R. Wagner (1813-1883).

One hand            up we my as on be in at him was you red ill saw oil few pull          Think as
                                                                                          you type
Easy                Our goal must be to make the most of the talents we possess.

```
|  1  |  2  |  3  |  4  |  5  |  6  |  7  |  8  |  9  |  10 |  11 |  12 |
```

## Problem 2—Four-Column Table with Multiple-Line Columnar Headings

**Directions – 1.** Type this table on a full sheet of paper in *reading position*. **2.** Double-space the columnar items and leave 8 blank spaces between columns.

● As illustrated below, columnar headings with a differing number of lines are typed so that last lines are aligned.

### AMERICAN FOOTBALL LEAGUE STARS: PASSERS

| Year | Player and Team | Passes Attempted | Number of Passes Completed |
|------|-----------------|------------------|----------------------------|
| 1970 | Daryle Lamonica, Oakland | 356 | 179 |
| 1969 | Greg Cook, Cincinnati | 197 | 106 |
| 1968 | Len Dawson, Kansas City | 224 | 131 |
| 1967 | Daryle Lamonica, Oakland | 425 | 220 |
| 1966 | Len Dawson, Kansas City | 284 | 159 |
| 1965 | John Hadl, San Diego | 348 | 174 |
| 1964 | Len Dawson, Kansas City | 354 | 199 |
| 1963 | Tobin Rote, San Diego | 286 | 170 |
| 1962 | Len Dawson, Dallas | 310 | 189 |
| 1961 | George Blanda, Houston | 362 | 187 |

## ■ Lesson 64 ● *70-space line*

### 64a ■ Keyboard Review ● Each line three times

*5 minutes*

Alphabetic SS Mickey Peck will attempt to squeeze five or six juicy oranges by hand.

3d and 4th fingers What size quilts does Sade have? We saw six dozen square zinc plates.

*Quick, snappy stroking of all keys*

Figure-Symbol These fractions ($\frac{1}{4}$ & $\frac{1}{2}$) can be related to two percentages: 25% & 50%.

Easy Bob thought that one must always be alert, ready, cautious, and quiet.

| 1 | 2 | 3 | 4 | 5 | 6 | 7 | 8 | 9 | 10 | 11 | 12 | 13 | 14 |

### 64b ■ Skill Comparison ● Type a 1-minute writing on each sentence in 64a, above. Compare the gwam.

*5 minutes*

### 64c ■ Placement of Quotation Marks

*5 minutes*

**Directions –** Type each sentence three times. The first line gives the rule and the remaining lines apply it. Capitalize and punctuate the last sentence correctly.

1   SS Periods or commas are placed inside, not outside, the quotation marks.

2   Huxley stated, "Facts do not cease to exist because they are ignored."

*Think as you type*

3   "The hardest thing about a job," he stated, "is the work it requires."

4   macy said we get at least 50 percent of our knowledge from reading

| 1 | 2 | 3 | 4 | 5 | 6 | 7 | 8 | 9 | 10 | 11 | 12 | 13 | 14 |

## 22b ■ Spacing of Symbols, Figures, and Fractions—Review

*10 minutes*

**Directions** – Each line twice. Read the explanation for a line before you type it.

### EXPLANATIONS

**Line 1** – Do not space between the dollar sign and the following figure.

**Line 2** – Do not space before or after the apostrophe.

**Line 3** – Do not space between the quotation marks and the words they enclose.

**Line 4** – Space before and after the ampersand.

**Line 5** – Do not space between a figure and the percent sign.

**Line 6** – Do not space between a figure and ½ or ¼.

**Line 7** – Space between a whole number and a "made" fraction. Be uniform in typing fractions.

**Line 8** – Before a figure, # stands for number; after it, for pounds. Do not space between the symbol and a figure.

**Line 9** – Do not space between the parentheses and the words they enclose.

### SENTENCES

1  SS   We got his check for $192 for the table.  He still owes $26.

2      It's much better to know nothing than to know what isn't so.

3      Mr. Bond said, "Do not space before or after an apostrophe."

4      Janet ordered two white leather jackets from Muncie & Young.

5      The new bonds pay interest at the rate of 5%.  Ted wants 7%.

6      The bank discount rate on the secured notes is $6\frac{1}{4}$%, not $5\frac{1}{2}$%.

7      Mix 3 1/8 pounds of clover with 5 1/2 pounds of millet seed.

8      My order #450 is dated May 20.  He ordered 36# of detergent.

9      Caution (although very often wasted) is a good risk to take.

*Think as you type*

*Eyes on this copy*

## 22c ■ Typing on Ruled Lines

*5 minutes*

**Directions** – 1. Set the line-space regulator for triple spacing.
2. Using the underline, type three lines about three inches long, beginning at the left margin. Pica type: 30 strokes. Elite type: 36 strokes.
3. Note the position of the line in relation to the top of the alignment scale (No. 33).
4. Remove the paper; then reinsert it.
5. Align the paper, using the variable line spacer (No. 3) to type on the first line.
6. Type the lines shown at the right.

• *ZIP Code numbers are typed a minimum of 2 spaces following the state name.*

Miss Fran Bloom _____

182 South Formosa Avenue _____

Los Angeles, California  90036 _____

## 22d ■ Paragraph Guided Writings ● Paragraphs appear on the next page.

*15 minutes*

**Directions** – 1. Type a 1-minute writing on ¶1. Note the *gwam*. Add four words to your *gwam* for a new goal. Type two more writings, trying to reach your new goal.

2. Repeat Step 1 for ¶'s 2 and 3. Your teacher may call the half-minute guides on the 1-minute writings to aid you in checking your rate.

# ■ Lesson 63 • *70-space line*

## 63a ■ Keyboard Review • Each line three times

Alphabetic SS Davey Waxler hopes to make a jet flight to Brazil to acquire the land.

Double letters Miss Spratt, from Crossett, will visit Tennessee and Mississippi soon.

Figure-Symbol Johnson & Montgomery paid a stock dividend of $7\frac{1}{2}\%$, plus $2.30 in cash.

Easy We observe that the person who knows everything has the most to learn.

| 1 | 2 | 3 | 4 | 5 | 6 | 7 | 8 | 9 | 10 | 11 | 12 | 13 | 14 |

Quiet wrists
and arms

## 63b ■ Skill Comparison

5 minutes

Directions – Type a 1-minute writing on each sentence in 63a, above. Compare *gwam*.

## 63c ■ Typing from Dictation and Spelling Checkup

5 minutes

Directions – Type the words in 62b, page 131, from your instructor's dictation.
Check for correct spelling. Retype any words in which you made an error.

## 63d ■ Problem Typing

30 minutes

### Problem 1—Three-Column Table with Columnar Headings

Directions – 1. Type this table on a full sheet of paper. Center it in *reading position*.
2. Double-space the items in each column.
3. Leave 8 blank spaces between the columns. Double-space after typing the main heading; triple-space after typing the secondary heading.

## MOTION PICTURE ACADEMY AWARDS
### 1959 – 1971

| Year | Actress | Actor |
|------|---------|-------|
| 1971 | Jane Fonda | Gene Hackman |
| 1970 | Glenda Jackson | George C. Scott |
| 1969 | Maggie Smith | John Wayne |
| 1968 | Katharine Hepburn Barbra Streisand | Cliff Robertson |
| 1967 | Katharine Hepburn | Rod Steiger |
| 1966 | Elizabeth Taylor | Paul Scofield |
| 1965 | Julie Christie | Lee Marvin |
| 1964 | Julie Andrews | Rex Harrison |
| 1963 | Patricia Neal | Sidney Poitier |
| 1962 | Anne Bancroft | Gregory Peck |
| 1961 | Sophia Loren | Maximilian Schell |
| 1960 | Elizabeth Taylor | Burt Lancaster |
| 1959 | Simone Signoret | Charlton Heston |

¶1
30 words
1.2 si

DS  The key to riding a bicycle is motion. As long as the | 11  4  36

wheels turn, we can remain upright. When they stop, we are | 23  8  40

bound to tumble to the hard ground. | 30  10  42

¶2
32 words
1.2 si

Learning works the same way. We learn only as long as | 41  14  46

we meet new ideas and as long as we keep looking for better | 53  18  50

ways to solve the many problems that face us. | 62  21  53

¶3
34 words
1.1 si

When we close our minds, we quit learning. It is true | 73  24  56

that we should give our brain the same care that we give to | 85  28  60

anything else. We must keep it sharp by good exercise. | 96  32  64

1' | 1 | 2 | 3 | 4 | 5 | 6 | 7 | 8 | 9 | 10 | 11 | 12 |
3' | 1 | 2 | 3 | 4 |

## 22e ■ Tabulator Control • Each sentence three times; single spacing.          *5 minutes*

Directions – 1. Clear the tabulator rack as directed on page vii.
2. Type the first sentence at the left margin.
3. Set a tab stop for the second sentence five spaces from the left margin. Set tab stops for the third and fourth sentences as indicated.

• On manual machines depress the tab bar (right index finger) or tab key (right little finger). Hold down the tab until the carriage stops.

• On electric typewriters flick the tab key lightly with the little finger.

Strokes in line
                                                                          Words
60 ——————————→On manuals, keep the tab depressed until the carriage stops.   12

55 ——————————→On manuals having tab bars, use the right index finger.   11
          5

50 ——————————→Use the little finger on the tab key on electrics.   10
          10

45 ——————————→On electric machines, just flick the tab key.   9
          15

## ■ Lesson 23 • *60-space line*

### 23a ■ Keyboard Review • Each line at least twice          *5 minutes*

Alphabetic   SS  Rex paused to see the wolf, jaguar, and zebras move quickly.

Figures          See pages 2, 51, 83, 406, and 927 for the charts and graphs.

                                                                    Sit erect

un               untie hunt fun sun undo gun under unarm unfit jungle plunder

Easy             Every man shows what he is by what he does with what he has.
          | 1 | 2 | 3 | 4 | 5 | 6 | 7 | 8 | 9 | 10 | 11 | 12 |

### TYPING COLUMNS WITH LEADERS

1. Strike the period and the space bar alternately.

2. Type the first period in the second space after the last letter of the first item. Continue typing the periods to a point 2 or 3 spaces short of the longest item in the next column.

3. To align the periods, note on the front of the cylinder scale whether you are typing odd or even numbers for the first line. Use this pattern to type the periods in the remaining lines.

4. End all rows at the same point.

## 62d ■ Problem Typing                    *30 minutes*

### Problem 1—Table with Columnar Headings and Leaders

**Directions – 1.** Type the following table in *exact vertical center.* Use a half sheet of paper.

2. Leave 24 blank spaces between the two columns.
3. Double-space the entries in each column.

## ESTIMATES OF POPULATION OF LARGEST METROPOLITAN AREAS

Double-space ───────────►

(For the Year 1975)

Triple-space ───────────►

| Area | Population |
|---|---|
| New York . . . . . . . . . . . . . | 11,366,000 |
| Los Angeles-Long Beach . . . . . . . . | 7,877,000 |
| Chicago . . . . . . . . . . . . . | 6,688,000 |
| Philadelphia . . . . . . . . . . . | 4,659,000 |
| Detroit . . . . . . . . . . . . . | 3,987,000 |

Double-space ───────────►

### Problem 2—Four-Column Table with Columnar Headings

**Directions – 1.** Type the table on a half sheet of paper in *exact vertical center.* Single-space entries in each column. 2. The numbers in color in the table show the number of spaces to be left between columns.

• *Note that the lines under the columnar headings extend across the entire width of the columns. Either this practice or the practice that was followed in Problem 1 is acceptable.*

## STATE NAMES AND TWO-LETTER ZIP CODE ABBREVIATIONS

### (Only Selected States Are Shown)

| Name | 6 | Code | 12 | Name | 6 | Code |
|---|---|---|---|---|---|---|
| Alabama | | AL | | New Mexico | | NM |
| Arizona | | AZ | | New York | | NY |
| Arkansas | | AR | | Ohio | | OH |
| California | | CA | | Oklahoma | | OK |
| Florida | | FL | | Pennsylvania | | PA |
| Illinois | | IL | | Tennessee | | TN |
| Indiana | | IN | | Texas | | TX |
| Kentucky | | KY | | Vermont | | VT |
| Maine | | ME | | Washington | | WA |
| Michigan | | MI | | Wisconsin | | WI |

## 23b ■ Special Characters • Each line twice

**Times, by:** Small letter x with a space before and after.
**Minus:** Hyphen with space before and after.
**Plus:** Hyphen typed over the diagonal.
**Division sign:** Hyphen typed over the colon.

**Equals sign:** Two hyphens, one below the other. In typing the second hyphen roll platen forward slightly, type hyphen, then return platen to position.
**Minutes, feet:** Apostrophe.
**Seconds, inches, ditto:** Quotation marks.

• *It will be helpful for you to know how to make the plus and equal signs as described above although some typewriters do have special keys for these signs.*

1    SS    This is the way I arrived at the answer: $70 $\times$ .05 $=$ $3.50.

2    They got the balance in this way: $160 $+$ $80 $-$ $110 $=$ $130.

3    John's test score may be obtained as follows: 320 $\div$ 4 $=$ 80.

4    He ran 50' in 10". I need a rug 14'6" $\times$ 9'8" for this room.

## 23c ■ Typing Outside the Right and Left Margins

**Right Margin** – To type outside the right margin after the carriage is locked, depress the margin-release key (No. 25).

**Left Margin** – To type outside the left margin, depress the margin-release key; then backspace to the desired point.

• *Depress the margin-release key with the ; finger. On some electric typewriters the margin-release key is depressed with the a finger.*

**Directions** – 1. Using a 60-space line, type the first line. When the carriage locks, depress the margin-release key and complete the line. Repeat.

2. Now, depress the margin-release key, move the carriage five spaces into the left margin, and type the second line. Repeat.

The margin release is a useful device. Learn how to use it well.

The margin release is a useful device. Learn how to use it well.

## 23d ■ Listening for the Bell; Right Margin Release

**Directions** – Type the paragraph with a 60-space line, then with a 50-space line. Let the bell guide you in returning the carriage. If the carriage locks before you complete a word, depress the margin-release key and complete the word.

• *Remember to set the right margin five to eight spaces beyond the desired line ending. Doing this will give your copy better horizontal balance.*

|  | Words |
|---|---|
| DS  Keep the right margin as straight as you can. | 9 |
| The bell will tell you when you are near the end | 19 |
| 46 words  of a line. When it rings, finish the word; return | 29 |
| the carriage. Divide long words to keep them from | 40 |
| running into the margin too far. | 46 |

# ■ Lesson 62 • *70-space line*

## 62a ■ Keyboard Review • Each line three times

*5 minutes*

Alphabetic SS The Quincy Park Zoo may receive a lynx, four jaguars, and a brown fox.

Underline Donovan read <u>Doctor Zhivago</u>; he states that it is an interesting book.

Figures Is it true that 45 students are typing in excess of 62 words a minute?

Easy Before you borrow any money from a friend, decide which you need more.

| 1 | 2 | 3 | 4 | 5 | 6 | 7 | 8 | 9 | 10 | 11 | 12 | 13 | 14 |

*Quick stroke, quick release*

## 62b ■ Spelling Aids • Each line three times

*5 minutes*

1  SS  eligible superintendent tangible conscientious sympathy hesitant menus

2  theology speculations versatile voracious vigilance privilege venomous

3  authoritative contrary anniversary anonymous conversation conservation

4  gluttonous retroactive laxity possessor treacherous zealous excellence

*Think as you type*

## 62c ■ Concentration Practice • Type as many times as possible in the time allowed.

*5 minutes*

Words

DS  How the continents were formed and how they came to be in their  13

present locations has been a point of much debate for some years.  The  27

62 words  theory of continental drift, that is, the parting of the land from what  41
1.4 si

was originally just one large mass, was brought forth by Alfred Wegener  55

(1880-1930), a German geologist.  62

| 1 | 2 | 3 | 4 | 5 | 6 | 7 | 8 | 9 | 10 | 11 | 12 | 13 | 14 |

---

### CENTERING COLUMNAR HEADINGS

Follow these steps to center headings over the columns of a table:

1. Move the carriage to the exact space at which the column begins.

2. Space forward 1 space for every 2 spaces occupied by the longest line in that column.

3. From this point, backspace once for every 2 spaces occupied by the columnar heading.

4. Type the heading. It will be centered over the column.

---

## 23e ■ Dividing Words; Left Margin Release

*15 minutes*

**Directions – 1.** Full sheet; 60-space line; single spacing with double spacing between items. Start typing on the 21st line space from the top of the paper.

**2.** After you type the first line, reset the left margin stop so the carriage stops under the Y in *You*. To type the figures 2, 3, 4, etc., move the carriage outside the left margin by depressing the margin-release key and backspacing.

2 spaces

Reset left margin stop

1. You will divide words at the ends of lines to keep the right margin as even as possible. You can divide words only between syllables, as your-self and foot-ball.

Double-space

2. When in doubt, use a dictionary to help solve word-division problems. The following guides tell you when *not* to divide words even though some of them may contain more than one syllable.

3. Naturally, you should not divide words of only one syllable, such as thought, friend, or trained.

4. Do not separate a syllable of one letter at the beginning of a word, such as idea, across, or elect.

5. Do not divide a word of five or fewer letters, such as also, duty, or going.

6. Do not separate a syllable of one or two letters at the end of a word, such as ready, greatly, or greater.

7. Do not separate a syllable that does not contain a vowel from the rest of the word, such as didn't or wouldn't.

8. Avoid, if possible, dividing words at the ends of more than two consecutive lines.

## 23f ■ Timed Writings

*10 minutes*

**Directions –** Type two 3-minute writings on the paragraphs in 22d at the top of page 45. Compute *gwam*. Submit the better writing.

# ■ Lesson 24 • *60-space line*

## 24a ■ Keyboard Review • Each line at least twice

*5 minutes*

| | | |
|---|---|---|
| Alphabetic | ss Kip gave Clement exquisite old jewelry for the bazaar today. | |
| Figures | John Sigmund swam 292 miles for the record on July 20, 1940. | Fingers deeply curved |
| Long reach | debt doubt nymph my brace sunny table crimp plumber electric | |
| Easy | A man who empties his purse into his head will lose neither. | |

| 1 | 2 | 3 | 4 | 5 | 6 | 7 | 8 | 9 | 10 | 11 | 12 |

## 61d ■ Sustained Skill Building

**Directions** – 1. Type a 5-minute writing. Circle your errors and figure your *gwam*.
2. Type two 1-minute writings on each paragraph. Type the first writing for speed, the second for control.

3. Finally, type another 5-minute writing on all paragraphs. Circle your errors and figure your *gwam*.
4. Compare the *gwam* and the number of errors for the two 5-minute timings.

● Contains all letters

|  | | GWAM 1' | 5' |
|---|---|---|---|

¶1
60 words
1.4 si

DS    As one reads the advice of experts on how to get more out of his    13  3  52

reading, he is impressed by the fact that nearly all the experts do    27  5  54

have unique suggestions to make. One says that if you have difficulty    41  8  57

getting started, skip the initial chapter. Get into the book; come    54  11  60

back to the beginning later.    60  12  61

¶2
60 words
1.4 si

A practice highly recommended by some experts is to summarize the    13  15  64

high points of each chapter in your own language. When you record    27  17  66

ideas in your own words, you make them your own. As a rule, you will    41  20  69

remember what you read. Prepare the summary, however, with as much    54  23  72

care as you would a telegram.    60  24  73

¶3
62 words
1.4 si

Another expert urges the use of a pencil in reading. With it,    13  27  76

you can underline key passages, number them in the margin, and index    26  29  78

them by subject on the flyleaf. This index will be your guide to    40  32  81

ideas and facts when you need them. If the book is not yours, jot    53  35  84

the page numbers of key ideas down on paper.    62  36  85

¶4
63 words
1.4 si

Because of recent investigations in rapid reading, many individu-    13  39  88

als hold that the rate at which one reads a book reflects the type of    27  42  91

mind one has. Books, though, should be read according to their value.    41  45  94

With good books, the idea is not to see how many you can get through,    55  47  96

but how many can get through to you.    63  49  98

1' | 1 | 2 | 3 | 4 | 5 | 6 | 7 | 8 | 9 | 10 | 11 | 12 | 13 | 14 |
5' |    |    1    |    |    2    |    |    3    |    |

## 24b ■ Superior and Inferior Symbols; Ratchet-Release Lever • Each line twice     *3 minutes*

**Superior and Inferior Symbols** – Follow these steps in typing superior and inferior symbols: (1) pull the rachet-release lever (No. 6) forward; (2) for superior symbols turn the cylinder knob toward you slightly—for inferior symbols turn the cylinder knob away from you slightly; (3) type the symbol; (4) return the ratchet-release lever to its original position. • *The degree symbol is made with the small letter o.*

• *The ratchet-release lever automatically returns the cylinder to the line of writing. The variable line spacer, which is used in typing on ruled lines, will not automatically return the cylinder to the line of writing. It should not be used in typing degree symbols, exponents, or superior or inferior figures or letters.*

1  SS  In Mexico City (7,000 feet above sea) water boils at $180°$ F.

2  Richardson (London) wrote the longest novel ever published.[1]    Use ratchet release

3  The formula for water is $H_2O$; and for sulphuric acid, $H_2SO_4$.

## 24c ■ Listening for the Bell; Right Margin Release     *10 minutes*

**Directions** – Type the paragraphs with a 50-space line, then with a 60-space line. Let the bell guide you in returning the carriage. If the carriage locks before you complete a word, depress the margin-release key and complete the word. Divide words if necessary, but keep in mind the rules in 23e.

| | | GWAM | |
| --- | --- | --- | --- |
| | | 1' | 3' |

¶1
46 words
1.1 si

DS  *The best way to save a part of our income, the experts*     11  4  35
*tell us, is to spend less than we make. How short—yet how*     23  8  39
*very clear! The best way to cut out errors in typing is to*     35  12  43
*type with good form. This, also, is concise and clear.*     46  15  46

¶2
46 words
1.2 si

*In setting up our budget, it is nice to have both ends*     57  19  50
*meet. It is even better if they overlap now and then. The*     69  23  54
*same holds true in typing. It is nice to type with very few*     81  27  58
*errors; it is much nicer to have none once in a while.*     92  31  62

1' | 1 | 2 | 3 | 4 | 5 | 6 | 7 | 8 | 9 | 10 | 11 | 12 |
3' | 1 | 2 | 3 | 4 |

## 24d ■ Technique Builder—Balanced- and One-Hand Phrases     *5 minutes*

**Directions** – Set margins for a 60-space line. Type each line twice.

**Technique Goal** – Type the balanced-hand words more rapidly than the one-hand words.

1  SS  to my | to do my | and look | to set | to you | and in | to see it

2  for him | the date | the case | for you | if you are | if she was     Use flowing rhythm

3  and the trade | to pull | and if you see | they care | to regard

4  with the fact | by the only | and jump | to the great | see them

# ■ Lesson 61 • *70-space line*

## 61a ■ Keyboard Review • Each line three times

5 *minutes*

Alphabetic SS   The jury of six men picked Viv, Larry, and Win for the big radio quiz.

Figure-Symbol   In 1972 Ethel Shane won second place with sales amounting to $684,503.

4th finger   It is apparent that the people appreciate the apparatus at the bazaar.

Easy   Anything one man can imagine in the world today, another man can make.

| 1 | 2 | 3 | 4 | 5 | 6 | 7 | 8 | 9 | 10 | 11 | 12 | 13 | 14 |

Be alert

## 61b ■ Paragraph Guided Writings

5 *minutes*

**Directions** – Type for one minute to establish your base rate. Type three
additional 1-minute writings. Try to hit the exact letter of your base
rate on each writing. Your teacher will call the half-minute guides.

● Contains all letters

DS   Without question, no person can become great until he tackles a

task or problem larger than himself. Experts can tell us that we all

64 words
1.4 si   have talents that remain hidden until we force ourselves to the test.

Those who are too lazy or timid to handle a new job or a tough problem

never seem to develop their hidden talents.

Type at a
controlled
rate

## 61c ■ Technique Builder—Stroking • Each line three times

10 *minutes*

Right hand SS   Paula, please play the part in my play. The play will open in Pamona.

Double letters   Jeff succeeded in getting the committee's letter to our Willcox staff.

Shift keys   M. R. Nolan wrote to P. S. McNeight in Big Rapids, Michigan, in April.

Weak fingers   Zaza politely applauded the plays. The astronauts waited on the pads.

One hand   Dave gave my car a fast grease and oil job at Steve's service station.

Hyphen   Fred and Jim gave a four-hour talk about their month-long trip by car.

Long reach   He joined in the annual hunting fun with the gun snugly under his arm.

Dash   Your own ideas––much like your own children––are especially wonderful.

| 1 | 2 | 3 | 4 | 5 | 6 | 7 | 8 | 9 | 10 | 11 | 12 | 13 | 14 |

Fingers
deeply
curved

Stroking
action in
fingers

**24e** ■ **Paragraph Guided Writings** • As directed in 22d, page 44    *15 minutes*

|  | 1' | 3' |
|---|---|---|

¶1
32 words
1.2 si

DS  The men who grow pears, apples, or some other fruit for    11  4  38

a living will tell you that the more you prune a tree, the    23  8  42

better the fruit. They know from experience.    32  11  45

¶2
34 words
1.2 si

The longer you think about something, the less you have    43  14  48

to write or say to explain it. Thinking is the basis of all    55  18  52

good writing. Think clearly, and you can write well.    66  22  56

¶3
36 words
1.2 si

Learn all you can about your subject, and you will find    77  26  60

the right words to tell your story forcefully and clearly.    89  30  64

If you have all the facts you need, the words will come eas-    101  34  68

ily.    102  34  68

```
1' | 1 | 2 | 3 | 4 | 5 | 6 | 7 | 8 | 9 | 10 | 11 | 12 |
3' |   1   |   2   |   3   |   4   |
```

**24f** ■ **Timed Writings** • Type two 1-minute writings and one 3-minute writing on 24e. Circle any errors. Compute gwam.    *7 minutes*

■ **Lesson 25** • *60-space line*

**25a** ■ **Keyboard Review** • Each line at least twice    *5 minutes*

Alphabetic  DS  Bud Roper may take this quiz next week if Jack will give it.

Figures     On October 1, 1942, the Bell XP59 made the first jet flight.

pol         police polite policy pole polar politic polish polled pollen

Easy        Tact is the knack of making a point without making an enemy.

Quiet wrists and arms

```
| 1 | 2 | 3 | 4 | 5 | 6 | 7 | 8 ! 9 | 10 | 11 | 12 |
```

**25b** ■ **Alignment of Paper—Horizontal and Vertical**    *5 minutes*

Directions – 1. Type the following sentence.

This job requires high skill.

2. Note the relationship of the top of the aligning scale to the bottom of the letters. Note also how the white lines on the scale line up with the letters "i" and "l" in the typewritten matter.

3. Remove the paper from the machine and reinsert it in position to type over the first typing.
4. Align horizontally first by using the paper-release lever and moving the paper to the left or right until the lines on the scale are brought into alignment with the letters "i" and "l."
5. Align vertically using the variable line spacer.
6. Retype the sentence over the first writing.
7. Repeat the problem.

## Table 1

<u>Pulitzer Prizes for Fiction</u> — *all caps*

1960 - 1970 ← *Double-space*

(No Award Given in Year not Listed)

*← Triple-space*

| 1970 | Collected Stories | Jean Stafford |
|------|-------------------|---------------|
| 1969 | House Made of Dawn | N. Scott Momaday |
| 1968 | The Confessions of Nat Turner | William Styron |
| 1966 | Collected Stories of Katherine Anne Porter *Double-space* | Katherine Anne Porter |
| 1967 | The fixer | Bernard Malamud |
| 1965 | The Keepers of the House | Shirley Ann Grau |
| 1963 | The Reivers | William Faulkner |
| 1962 | The Edge of Sadness | Edwin O'Connor |
| 1960 | Advice and Consent | Allen Drury |
| *1961* | *To Kill a Mockingbird* | *Harper Lee* |

## Table 2

PULITZER PRIZES FOR JOURNALISM

1963 - 1970 — *Double-space*

*Triple-space →*

| 1963 | Chicago Daily News | Illinois |
|------|-------------------|----------|
| 1964 | St. Petersburg Times | Florida |
| 1965 | *The* Hutchinson news | Kansas |
| 1966 | Boston Globe | Massachusetts |
| 1967 | The Louisville Courier-Journal and The milwaukee Journal | Kentucky wisconsin |
| 1968 | The Riverside Press-Enterprise | california |
| 1970 | Newsday | New York |
| 1969 | Los Angeles Times | California |

*she*

## 25c ■ Technique Builder—Finger-Action Stroking

*10 minutes*

**Directions** – Type each line twice.          **Technique Goals** – Observe the goals in the right margin.

| | | | |
|---|---|---|---|
| Third row | SS | I quoted their top reporter at your request; he writes well. | Curved fingers |
| First row | | Ben amazed the men with his calm zeal as he explored a cave. | Curved fingers |
| Home row | | Hadla Hall asked Ada Flag if she had a salad. Ada had hash. | Direct strokes |
| Weak fingers | | Zaza Zola played on an apparatus equipped with a large pole. | Quiet wrists |
| Long reach | | A number of the debatable summaries were received by Nygard. | Finger action |
| One hand | | As John Carver asserted, Fred Greer was greeted at the cafe. | Letter response |
| Balanced hand | | These girls may go to the city to do the audit for the firm. | Word response |
| Direct reach | | Gregg Brown hunted with Bret Young in the jungle near Lagos. | Finger action |

| 1 | 2 | 3 | 4 | 5 | 6 | 7 | 8 | 9 | 10 | 11 | 12 |

## 25d ■ Paragraph Guided Writings ● As directed in 22d, page 44

*15 minutes*

● Contains all letters

| | | GWAM | |
|---|---|---|---|
| | | 1' | 3' |

¶1
38 words
1.2 si

DS   A good listener, as a rule, is a popular fellow. What is       12   4   44
more in his favor is that after a while he knows something.        24   8   48
The trouble with many of us is that we do not know how to use      36   12   52
our ears.                                                          38   13   53

¶2
40 words
1.2 si

We all fall into the lazy habit of opening our ears only          49   16   56
to the thoughts we want to hear. We tune out the speaker with      62   21   61
the same ease that we turn a radio dial. As a result, we miss      75   25   65
more than we get.                                                  78   26   66

¶3
42 words
1.2 si

Learn how to listen. Question the speaker's logic, or             89   30   70
try to put his thoughts into your own words. Formulate your        101  34   74
own examples to fit the points he is making. Try to use these      114  38   78
hints in school and on the job.                                    120  40   80

| 1' | 1 | 2 | 3 | 4 | 5 | 6 | 7 | 8 | 9 | 10 | 11 | 12 |
| 3' | | 1 | | 2 | | 3 | | 4 | | | |

## 25e ■ Timed Writings ● Type two 3-minute writings on 25d. Compute gwam. Submit the better of the two writings.

*10 minutes*

## 59d ■ Problem Typing

30 minutes

### Problem 1—Two-Column Table, Subheading

**Directions** – 1. Type this table in *exact vertical center* on a half sheet of paper. Space the main heading and the subheading as shown in the table.
2. Leave 20 blank spaces between the columns.
3. Double-space the items in each column.

### RIVERS OVER 1,200 MILES LONG

Double-space ⟶

### (In the United States)

Triple-space ⟶

| | |
|---|---|
| Mississippi | 2,348 |
| Missouri | 2,315 |
| Rio Grande | 1,885 |
| Yukon | 1,800 |
| Arkansas | 1,450 |
| Colorado | 1,360 |
| Columbia | 1,214 |

### Problem 2—Three-Column Table, Subheading

**Directions** – 1. Type this table in *reading position* on a full sheet of paper. Space the main heading and the subheading as shown in Problem 1.
2. Leave 12 blank spaces between the columns.
3. Double-space the items in each column.

### HIGHEST MOUNTAIN PEAKS

### (In North America)

| | | |
|---|---|---|
| McKinley | Alaska | 20,320 |
| Logan | Canada | 19,850 |
| Citlaltepec | Mexico | 18,700 |
| St. Elias | Alaska | 18,008 |
| Popocatepetl | Mexico | 17,887 |
| Foraker | Alaska | 17,395 |
| Iztaccihuatl | Mexico | 17,343 |
| Lucania | Canada | 17,150 |
| King | Canada | 17,130 |
| Steele | Canada | 16,644 |
| Bona | Alaska | 16,500 |
| Blackburn | Alaska | 16,390 |

## ■ Lesson 60 · *70-space line*

### 60a ■ Keyboard Review · Each line three times

5 minutes

Alphabetic  SS  The boxer jabs a quick volley into a dazed opponent when fighting him.

Figure-Symbol  Bernard & Hunter will buy 47 dozen @ 38¢, less a cash discount of $6\frac{1}{4}\%$.

Short, quick strokes

Dash  Terry saw that production––an interesting movie––at the Bruin Theater.

Easy  Dreary as practice may be, it usually separates the men from the boys.

| 1 | 2 | 3 | 4 | 5 | 6 | 7 | 8 | 9 | 10 | 11 | 12 | 13 | 14 |

### 60b ■ Timed Writings ·
Type two 1-minute and two 5-minute writings on 56d, page 121.
Compute gwam. Submit the better of the 5-minute writings.

15 minutes

### 60c ■ Problem Typing

25 minutes

### Problem 1—Three-Column Table

**Directions** – 1. Type Table 1, page 128, in *reading position* on a full sheet of paper.
2. Double-space the entries in each column.
3. Leave 4 blank spaces between columns.

### Problem 2—Three-Column Table

**Directions** – 1. Type Table 2, page 128, in *exact vertical center* on a half sheet of paper.
2. Single-space the entries in each column.
3. Leave 6 blank spaces between the columns.

# Part 2 ■

# Basic Personal Applications

You are now ready to use the typewriter to prepare some school and personal papers. Here are some of the kinds of problems you will type in Part 2.

**Memorandums, Short Reports, and Announcements** – You will type three different types of memorandum forms, short reports, themes, and announcements in acceptable form.

**Outlines, Class Notes, Book Reviews, and Minutes of Meetings** – In typing these papers, you will use commonly accepted form guides. In addition, the content of the various papers you type will give you information on the many fine points of style to be observed in your typewritten work.

**Personal Notes, Personal Business Letters, and Post Cards** – Personal written communications of various

types are covered in these problems. Acceptable form, standard practice, and content are emphasized.

**Basic Skill** – There is continued emphasis on basic skill in all the lessons in this part. The ideal is to be able to type so well that you can forget the typewriter and concentrate on the papers you are preparing.

**Erasing Errors** – Erasing instructions are given in Lesson 32. Your instructor will tell you if you are to erase and correct errors on problems in lessons following Lesson 32.

**Extra-Credit Assignments** – Problems are given at the end of each unit for students who finish assignments ahead of schedule.

# Unit 5 ■

## Typing Memorandums and Short Reports
### General Directions ■ Lessons 26-35

**Line length** – For drills and timed writings, use a 70-space line. For problems, set the stops as directed. When you type from unarranged copy, return the carriage with the bell.

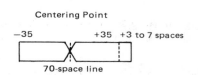

Centering Point

−35    +35   +3 to 7 spaces

70-space line

**Spacing** – Single-space sentences and drill lines. Double-space between repeated groups of lines. Double-space paragraph copy. Space problem copy as directed.

## ■ Lesson 26

### 26a ■ Keyboard Review • Each line at least three times

*5 minutes*

Alphabetic  SS  David and Jack Craig were quite happy for a month in Texas and Brazil.

Fourth finger  Paula quickly quizzed the pupils; prizes were awarded for the puzzles.

Figure  Mount McKinley (20,320 feet) is the highest peak in the United States.

Easy  A sure way to earn the respect of your friends is to respect yourself.

| 1 | 2 | 3 | 4 | 5 | 6 | 7 | 8 | 9 | 10 | 11 | 12 | 13 | 14 |

Sit erect

## Problem 2—Three-Column Table on a Full Sheet

**Directions** – 1. Type the table shown below in *reading position* on a full sheet of paper.
2. Leave 10 blank spaces between the columns.
3. Double-space the items in the columns.

### TELEPHONE AREA CODE NUMBERS OF MAJOR CITIES

| New York | New York | 212 |
|----------|----------|-----|
| Chicago | Illinois | 312 |
| Los Angeles | California | 213 |
| Philadelphia | Pennsylvania | 215 |
| Detroit | Michigan | 313 |
| Houston | Texas | 713 |
| St. Louis | Missouri | 314 |
| Boston | Massachusetts | 617 |
| Baltimore | Maryland | 301 |
| Cleveland | Ohio | 216 |
| Dallas | Texas | 214 |
| Washington | D. C. | 202 |

## ■ Lesson 59 • *70-space line*

### 59a ■ Keyboard Review • Each line three times     *5 minutes*

Alphabetic  SS  Five more bags were packed with a dozen boxes of quail by Randy Jones.

Figures  By the 19th of next month, 368,949 fans will have attended such games.

Shift keys  Milwaukee, Madison, and Green Bay are three large cities in Wisconsin.

Easy  Most people know that there is nothing much busier than an idle rumor.

| 1 | 2 | 3 | 4 | 5 | 6 | 7 | 8 | 9 | 10 | 11 | 12 | 13 | 14 |

*Wrists and elbows still*

### 59b ■ Spelling Checkup • Type the words in 58c, page 125. Check for correct spelling. Retype any words in which you made an error.     *5 minutes*

### 59c ■ Skill Comparison     *5 minutes*

**Directions** – Type a 1-minute writing on each sentence. Compare *gwam*. Try typing all sentences at the rate of the first one.

Easy  SS  Dan earned some money by taking odd jobs after school and on weekends.

Figures  The team's center is 7½ feet tall, and he averages 33 points per game.

Rough draft  When typing, the columns should be typed on straight across--not down!

Script  *His working habits have put him in good stead for timely jumps in pay.*

| 1 | 2 | 3 | 4 | 5 | 6 | 7 | 8 | 9 | 10 | 11 | 12 | 13 | 14 |

*Type without pauses*

## 26b ■ Technique Builder—Flowing Rhythm Practice

5 *minutes*

**Directions** – Type each sentence two times on the response level indicated in the left margin.
**Stroke Response** – Think and type each *letter* as a separate unit.
**Word Response** – Think and type the *words* as units.

**Combination Response** – Think and type the short, balanced-hand words as units. Type the one-hand and difficult words letter by letter. Combine the two response levels into a natural, flowing, rhythmic pattern.

| | | |
|---|---|---|
| Stroke | SS | To cultivate kindness is a valuable part of the real business of life. |
| Word | | The man who knows that a thing should be done can find a way to do it. |
| Word | | This is the type of work she likes to do and the work she can do well. |
| Combination | | From the sublime to the ridiculous there is really but one short step. |
| Combination | | Nothing in the world is more haughty than someone of moderate ability. |

Work for flowing rhythm

| 1 | 2 | 3 | 4 | 5 | 6 | 7 | 8 | 9 | 10 | 11 | 12 | 13 | 14 |

## 26c ■ Paragraph Guided Writings

20 *minutes*

**Directions** – 1. Type a 1-minute writing on the first paragraph. Note your *gwam*. Add 4 words to your *gwam* rate for a new goal.

2. Type a second 1-minute writing on the paragraph. Try to reach your new goal.

3. Type a third writing on the paragraph at your original rate. Try typing with fewer errors.

4. Repeat Steps 1, 2, and 3 for the second and third paragraphs.

5. Type two 3-minute writings on the paragraphs. Figure your *gwam*. Submit the one with the higher rate.

● Contains all letters

GWAM
1'  3'

¶ 1
38 words
1.3 si
DS
The fellow who quits one job after another because they have no
future may be closer to the answer than he realizes. There is no
future in any job. The future lies in the man who holds it.

13  4  45
26  9  50
38  13  54

¶ 2
40 words
1.3 si
It has been said that the feeling of doing a job well is reward
in itself, but knowing that you do a job perfectly can be fatal. It
is vital that one has a desire to improve. Keep this desire alive.

13  17  58
27  22  63
40  26  67

¶ 3
44 words
1.3 si
One of the best habits you can develop is the ability to analyze
your work with a clear eye. You can be proud of your work all right,
but you must not be satisfied with it. If you are, you will never
excel at anything.

13  30  71
27  35  76
40  39  80
44  41  82

1' | 1 | 2 | 3 | 4 | 5 | 6 | 7 | 8 | 9 | 10 | 11 | 12 | 13 | 14 |
3' | 1 | 2 | 3 | 4 | 5 |

## 58b ■ Paragraph Guided Writings

5 minutes

**Directions** – Type for one minute to establish your base rate. Type three additional 1-minute writings. Try to hit the exact letter of your base rate on each writing. Half-minute guides will be called.

DS     You probably believe that luck is simply that good fortune which happens purely by chance. Perhaps you are right, but it is pretty wish- ful thinking to hold that the success others enjoy just happens. The world's biggest optimist is one who waits for his ship to come in when he didn't send it out.

60 words
1.4 si

Type at a controlled rate

## 58c ■ Spelling Aids

5 minutes

**Directions** – Type each line twice. Study the words carefully as you type them.

1   SS  category experience irresistible harebrained nickel paraffin genealogy

2   reconnoiter foreign assistants heroes threshold drier fulfill hypocrisy

3   occasion timeliness likelihood pursuit gaiety ecstasy immaculate route

4   hopeful exhorts substantial protuberant scintillate plebeian paralyzes

Study letter sequences carefully

## 58d ■ Problem Typing

30 minutes

### Problem 1—Three-Column Table on Half Sheet

**Directions** – 1. Center the table vertically on a half sheet of paper. Leave 6 blank spaces between columns.   2. Single-space the entries in each column. Triple-space after the heading.

### STUDENTS GRADUATING WITH HONORS

| Paul Baum | Cum Laude | History |
|---|---|---|
| Thomas Bell | Cum Laude | Chemistry |
| Jay Berger | Magna Cum Laude | English |
| Dorothy Bernd | Cum Laude | Business Education |
| Daniel Blake | Summa Cum Laude | Health Science |
| Keith Evans | Magna Cum Laude | Biology |
| Aaron Fuller | Cum Laude | Speech |
| Susan Ham | Cum Laude | Economics |
| Mary Manos | Magna Cum Laude | Philosophy |
| Steve Marks | Cum Laude | History |
| Patricia Smith | Summa Cum Laude | English |
| Arthur Taitt | Summa Cum Laude | Geography |
| Shirley Teeter | Cum Laude | Geology |
| Albert Wright | Cum Laude | Sociology |

┌─────────────────────────────────────────────────────────────┐

## HORIZONTAL CENTERING STEPS

- *Centering headings and paragraph material so that there will be equal left and right margins is called horizontal centering.*

**Step 1** – Check the placement of the paper guide. Turn to page vi, and read the directions for adjusting the paper guide.

**Step 2** – Move the carriage to the center point.

**Step 3** – Backspace once for each 2 spaces in the line to be centered. If there is one letter left, do not backspace for it. Begin to type at the point where the backspacing is completed.

---

### 26d ■ Practice Problem—Horizontal Centering

8 *minutes*

**Directions** – Using practice paper, center each line horizontally.

ANNUAL CONFERENCE FOR WRITERS

Double-space ——→ Stimulating Lectures and Discussions

Wednesday, October 21, 9:30 a.m.

Ralph Bunche Auditorium, City Convention Center

### 26e ■ Creative Typing

7 *minutes*

**Directions** – Type an answer, in the form of a complete sentence, to each question. For example, the answer to the first question is: Mount McKinley is the highest mountain peak in the United States.

1. What is the highest mountain peak in the United States?

2. Are you typing on a machine with pica or elite type?

3. Name a motion picture in which John Wayne played a leading role.

4. Name the city, state, and country in which you were born.

5. What is your favorite season of the year? Why is it your favorite?

6. Name a service offered by a bank to its depositors.

## ■ Lesson 27 • *70-space line*

### 27a ■ Keyboard Review • Each line at least three times

5 *minutes*

**Alphabetic** SS Jack Mavis will specialize in shipping quantities of goods by express.

**Figure-Symbol** He was insured for $8,400 at the age of 29 years 5 months and 17 days.

Type with purpose

**One hand** We were directed to decrease the maximum number of jumps on this test.

**Easy** Learn that the basic rule of writing good copy is knowing the subject.

| 1 | 2 | 3 | 4 | 5 | 6 | 7 | 8 | 9 | 10 | 11 | 12 | 13 | 14 |

## Problem 2—Two-Column Table on a Full Sheet

**Directions** – Retype the table below; this time type it on a full sheet of paper in *reading position*. Leave 14 blank spaces between the columns; double-space for the items. Use the vertical centering shortcut method.

- **Vertical Centering Shortcut** – *Insert the paper to Line 33, the vertical center. Roll the cylinder back (toward you) once for every two lines in the copy to be typed. This will place the copy in exact vertical center. To type a problem in reading position, roll the cylinder back two additional times.*

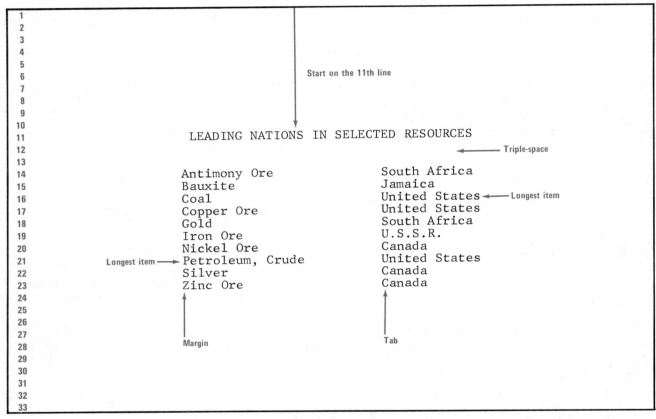

**Simple two-column table**

## ■ Lesson 58 • *70-space line*

### 58a ■ Keyboard Review • Each line three times                                              5 minutes

Alphabetic SS    Zelda did not expect to be in Quincy for my visit with Ginger Jackson.

Word
recognition      It will pay you to do the jobs you must do as well as you can do them.          Quiet
                                                                                                wrists
Figures          The longest river in the world is the Nile; its length is 4,145 miles.          and arms

Easy             All too often a clear conscience is merely the result of a bad memory.
                 |  1  |  2  |  3  |  4  |  5  |  6  |  7  |  8  |  9  |  10  |  11  |  12  |  13  |  14  |

**27b ■ Paragraph Skill Builder** • Type a 1-minute and two 3-minute writings on the paragraphs. Circle errors. Compute gwam.

*10 minutes*

GWAM
1' 3'

¶ 1
30 words
1.2 si

DS    There are but two kinds of clever people in this world. One    12  4 36

group thinks of a witty remark in time to make it, and the other, in    26  9 41

time not to make it.    30 10 42

¶ 2
33 words
1.3 si

Genuine wit is an art all right. It comes from saying the un-    42 14 46

expected at the right time to the right people. Learn how to use it    56 19 51

to bring spice to your conversation.    63 21 53

¶ 3
34 words
1.4 si

The next best thing to being witty yourself is being able to    75 25 57

quote another's wit. Never be clever, though, at the expense of    88 29 61

someone else. This is always in poor taste.    97 32 64

1' | 1 | 2 | 3 | 4 | 5 | 6 | 7 | 8 | 9 | 10 | 11 | 12 | 13 | 14 |
3'       | 1 |       | 2 |       | 3 |       | 4 |       | 5 |

---

## COMMON PROOFREADERS' MARKS

∧ Insert        ⊐ Move right        ∿ Transpose

⌒ Close up        ⊏ Move left        # Space

⧸ Delete        ≡ Capitalize        ¶ Paragraph

---

## 27c ■ Problem Typing

*30 minutes*

### Problem 1—Announcement with Centered Lines

**Directions** – 1. Review the steps for horizontal centering on page 53.
2. Use a half sheet of paper. Set your machine for triple spacing.
3. Start typing on the 10th line space from the top edge of your paper.
4. Center each line horizontally. Refer to the proofreader's marks above as you type your copy.

Foreign Students Association

Triple - space
Welcome new and old students

Informal, Get - Acquainted
at Reception

Sunday
Friday, September 15, 197-

to 5:30 p.m.    Triple - space

House International

415 Gayley Avenue

# STEPS IN ARRANGING TABLES

## Horizontal Placement

1. Center the paper in the machine.

2. Move the left and the right margin stops to the ends of the scale. Clear the tabulator rack.

3. Determine the number of blank spaces to be left between columns. An even number (4, 6, 8, or more) of blank spaces should be left between columns. The directions for problems that follow will tell you how many blank spaces to leave.

4. Move the carriage to the center of the machine.

5. Spot the longest word or entry in each column.

6. Backspace once for every two spaces occupied by the longest word or entry in each column. If the longest word or entry in each column is composed of an uneven number of letters or digits, carry the unused one to the next column.

A letter or digit left over from the last column is dropped.

7. Backspace once for every two blank spaces left *between* the columns.

8. Set the left margin stop at the point at which you stop backspacing. This is the point at which the first column will start.

9. From the left margin, space forward once for each letter, digit, and space in the longest entry in the first column and once for each blank space to be left between Columns 1 and 2. Set a tab stop at this point for the second column. Continue in this manner until stops have been set for all columns.

10. Return the carriage. Operate the tab bar or tab key to determine whether or not all the tab stops have been set.

## Vertical Placement

Vertical placement of material is not new to you. See directions given on page 57.

---

## 57c ■ Problem Typing

*30 minutes*

### Problem 1—Two-Column Table on a Half Sheet

Directions – 1. Type the table on a half sheet of paper as it appears on page 124.

2. Leave 16 spaces between columns.

3. Single-space the items in the columns.

- *The correct placement of the table in* exact vertical center *is shown in the illustration. You will need to plan the vertical placement of the table yourself in subsequent problems.*

- *A half sheet of paper contains 33 lines.*

## Problem 2—Memorandum on Centering

Half sheet
60-space line
Single spacing

**Directions** – Type the following memorandum. Type the date on the 7th line space from the top; then follow the directions given in the illustration. Proofread; circle errors.

```
 1
 2
 3    Type date on 7th line space
 4
 5
 6                                                                    Words
 7    September 16, 197-                                                 4
 8
 9        4th line space from date
10
11    TO:   Typing Students                                             8
12    DS
13    FROM:   Standards Committee                                      13
14    DS
15    SUBJECT:   Horizontal Centering                                  20
16
17    TS
18    Step 1:   To center headings horizontally, check the placement   33
19    of the paper guide; then move the carriage to the center point   46
20    of the paper.                                                    49
21
22    Step 2:   Backspace once for each two letters or letters and     62
23    spaces in the line to be centered.  If one letter remains,       74
24    disregard it.  Begin to type at the point where the backspacing  87
25    ends.                                                            88
26
27
28
29
30
31
32
33
```

**Memorandum centered on half sheet of paper**

## Problem 3—Memorandum on Center Point

Half-sheet
60-space line
Single spacing

**Directions** – For this problem, use the same date and heading lines and the same spacing directions given for Problem 2. Use the body below. Proofread; circle errors.

Standard typing paper is 8½ inches wide and 11 inches long with 66 lines to the page. A half sheet has 33 lines. A line has 102 elite or 85 pica spaces.

The exact horizontal center of the paper is at 51 for elite or 42½ for pica type. Unless otherwise directed, use 50 for the elite center and 42 for the pica center.

## 56e ■ Continuity Practice from Script

5 minutes

**Directions** – After each typing of the paragraph, circle any errors you may have made. Type correctly three times the word in which you made an error, along with the word preceding and the word following the error. See how many times you can type the paragraph without any errors in the time allowed.

DS

64 words
1.3 si

|  | Words |
|---|---|
| Charm in a conversation rests less on using your own wit than in | 13 |
| opening the way for the other fellow to use his. Find his pet subject; | 27 |
| get him to talk about it. You may be surprised to learn how much he | 41 |
| knows about it. Getting the other fellow to talk about his pet topic | 55 |
| is the second rule of the art of conversing. | 64 |

| 1 | 2 | 3 | 4 | 5 | 6 | 7 | 8 | 9 | 10 | 11 | 12 | 13 | 14 |

## ■ Lesson 57 • *70-space line*

### 57a ■ Keyboard Review • Each line three times

5 minutes

Alphabetic  SS  Phil Jackson wanted Terry Gorman to move Zoro to Quebec next February.

Figure-Symbol  IBM is listed at $502\frac{7}{8}$, "3M" at $101\frac{3}{8}$, and American Can at $59\frac{5}{8}$.

Dash  These recommendations––like those of the past––are markedly brilliant.

Easy  We must know that it is better by far to forgive than to gain revenge.

Quick carriage return

| 1 | 2 | 3 | 4 | 5 | 6 | 7 | 8 | 9 | 10 | 11 | 12 | 13 | 14 |

### 57b ■ Speed Ladder Sentences

10 minutes

**Directions** – Type each sentence for one minute as the guides are called. Your teacher will call the return of the carriage every 10, 12, or 15 seconds.

**Technique Goals** – Return the carriage quickly without looking from the copy. Start typing immediately after throwing the carriage.

| | | GWAM 15" | 12" | 10" |
|---|---|---|---|---|
| 1 | SS  I was told to work hard to be a success. | 32 | 40 | 48 |
| 2 | One may work very hard, and yet one may fail. | 36 | 45 | 54 |
| 3 | But, a key to success may not always be hard work. | 40 | 50 | 60 |
| 4 | Success might demand hard work, but it also takes luck. | 44 | 55 | 66 |
| 5 | What may seem to be failure at first may wind up as success. | 48 | 60 | 72 |
| 6 | All famous people have had times of despair and times of failure. | 52 | 65 | 78 |
| 7 | Most people will agree that hard work and a little luck is the answer. | 56 | 70 | 84 |

| 1 | 2 | 3 | 4 | 5 | 6 | 7 | 8 | 9 | 10 | 11 | 12 | 13 | 14 |

## Problem 4—Memorandum from Unarranged Copy

**Directions** – Type the following memorandum on a half sheet of paper. Follow the directions given earlier.

• *Do not type diagonal lines shown in color. They indicate carriage-return points. The symbol ¶ stands for a new paragraph.*

• *The lines in the problem are not set line for line the way you will type them. Set the margin stops properly; return your carriage with the bell.*

November 10, 197– / TO: Chris Chialtas / FROM: Allan Wunsch / SUBJECT: Final Meeting of the Board / The final meeting of the Board of Directors will be held on Thursday, December 10, at 6:30 p.m. at my home. I am letting you know about the meeting at this very early date so that you can make plans to attend. (¶) Please let me know whether or not you will attend the meeting. I shall appreciate an early reply.

## ■ Lesson 28 • *70-space line*

### 28a ■ Keyboard Review • Each line at least three times          *5 minutes*

Alphabetic  SS  May packs two dozen boxes of very good tarts filled with quince jelly.

Double letters  Bill offered to supply the additional glasses to the school next week.

Figure-Symbol  Order #4928 (File 305-C) must be shipped in April to James & Parksons.

Easy  She must never be content to let someone else do her thinking for her.

| 1 | 2 | 3 | 4 | 5 | 6 | 7 | 8 | 9 | 10 | 11 | 12 | 13 | 14 |

*Curve fingers deeply*

### 28b ■ Speed Ladder Sentences          *10 minutes*

**Directions** – Type 1-minute writings on each sentence. Your teacher will call the carriage return every 15 seconds. Figure your *gwam.*

**Technique Goals** – Follow the suggestions to improve your carriage return. Try to increase your rate by 4 words a minute with each succeeding writing.

| | | | Words in Line | GWAM 15" Guide |
|---|---|---|---|---|
| 1 | DS | Learn how to throw the carriage quickly. | 8 | 32 |
| 2 | | To return, use a quick wrist and hand motion. | 9 | 36 |
| 3 | | Return the hand to the correct keys without delay. | 10 | 40 |
| 4 | | The hand should not guide the carriage across the page. | 11 | 44 |
| 5 | | For electric machines, tap the return with the little finger. | 12 | 48 |
| 6 | | Quickly return your finger to typing position and continue typing. | 13 | 52 |
| 7 | | You can raise your rate; merely improve the way you control the return. | 14 | 56 |

| 1 | 2 | 3 | 4 | 5 | 6 | 7 | 8 | 9 | 10 | 11 | 12 | 13 | 14 |

## 56d ■ Sustained Skill Building *25 minutes*

**Directions** – 1. Type one 5-minute writing. Figure your *gwam*.
2. Type two 1-minute writings on each paragraph—the first for speed, and the second, for control.

3. Type another 5-minute writing on all paragraphs. Figure your *gwam*. Compare the *gwam* and the number of errors for the two 5-minute writings. Submit the better writing to your teacher.

● Contains all letters

| | GWAM |
|---|---|
| | 1'   5' |

**¶1**
**60 words**
**1.4 si**

DS    A budding young writer, hoping to become a journalist, asked Ring | 13  3  52
Lardner, a famous American author celebrated for his wit, for his writ- | 27  5  54
ing secret. The amateur writer asked a stock question: "When writing," | 42  8  57
he said, "do you use a formula of some kind? If you do, can you tell | 56  11  60
me just what it is?" | 60  12  61

**¶2**
**60 words**
**1.4 si**

Always known for his candor, Lardner replied as follows: "I cer- | 13  15  64
tainly do use a formula, and I'll be delighted to explain it to you. I | 27  17  66
merely take several sheets of paper and type some widely scattered words | 42  20  69
on them. The rest is very easy. I just go back afterwards and fill in | 56  23  72
the blank spaces." | 60  24  73

**¶3**
**62 words**
**1.4 si**

Lardner's reply, made in jest, drives home an extremely important | 63  27  76
point about writing. Even the experts must work at the art. The facts | 28  30  79
that are to be written on paper for the benefit of one's readers must | 42  32  81
be found, checked for accuracy, and analyzed. There must be strict at- | 56  35  84
tention to the smallest detail. | 62  36  85

**¶4**
**62 words**
**1.4 si**

Writing does take talent, but the magic formula is also made up | 13  39  88
of practice and the submission of one's work to strict self-criticism. | 27  42  91
Some years ago, Cicero admitted the might of talent, but then he went | 41  45  94
on to say that when hard work and practice are combined with talent, | 55  47  96
the result is often quite pleasing. | 62  49  98

```
1' |   1   |   2   |   3   |   4   |   5   |   6   |   7   |   8   |   9   |  10   |  11   |  12   |  13   |  14   |
5' |               1               |               2               |               3               |
```

## VERTICAL CENTERING

Centering material so that it will have uniform top and bottom margins is called vertical centering.

The steps for vertical centering are given in the problem that follows. You will need to know and understand these steps in order to solve many of the problems in typing.

## 28c ■ Problem Typing

### Problem 1—Full-Page Memorandum with Indented Items

**Directions** – 1. Type the memorandum on the next page on a full sheet. Use a 60-space line.
2. Follow the spacing directions given on the problem.
3. Indent the numbered items 5 spaces from the left and right margins.

• *After you type the first line of the indented copy, reset the left margin stop for the short lines of the copy. To type the number for succeeding steps, depress the margin release and backspace to the desired point. This will eliminate resetting the margin stop.*

### Problem 2—Paragraph Centered on Half Sheet

Double spacing
60-space line

**Directions** – 1. Follow the steps in Problem 1 for vertical centering.
2. Center the heading horizontally.

```
1
2
3
4
5
6                                                                          Words
7                            ANTARCTICA                                       2
8
9
10        Antarctica is the highest, driest, coldest, and emptiest           14
11
12    continent on earth.  There is almost no plant life or native           26
13
14    population, except for penguins, seals, and some hardy sea-            38
15
16    birds.  The land area is bigger than that of the United States         50
17
18    and Mexico combined.  Ninety-five percent of this area is             62
19
20    covered with snow and ice that in some places is three miles          74
21
22    thick.  The normal temperature at South Pole Station is minus          86
23
24    55 degrees, and winter temperatures have plunged to more than          99
25
26    113 degrees below zero.                                               103
27
28
29
30
31
32
33
```

**SOLUTION TO PROBLEM**
Lines in half sheet . . . . . . . . . . . . . . . . . . . . . . . 33
Lines and line spaces in copy . . . . . . . . . . . . . . 18
Line spaces in top and bottom margins . . . . . . . . 15
Divide by 2.  Top margin . . . . . . . . . . . . . . . . . . 7*
Bottom margin . . . . . . . . . . . . . . . . . . . . . . . . 7
*Start typing on the 8th line space from the top.

**Paragraph centered on half sheet**

# Typing Tables

## General Directions ■ Lessons 56-65

**Machine Adjustments** – Use a 70-space line length for the lessons in this unit. Single-space lines of words and sentences, but double-space between repeated groups of lines. Double-space paragraph copy. Space problem copy as directed for each problem.

**Correcting Errors** – Your teacher will tell you whether or not you are to erase and correct errors on the problems of this unit. He will also tell you whether or not you may use the suggestions presented for correcting errors by "squeezing" and "spreading" letters.

## ■ Lesson 56

### 56a ■ Keyboard Review • Type each line at least three times for all lessons in Unit 8.   *5 minutes*

| | | |
|---|---|---|
| Alphabetic | SS | We might require about five dozen packing boxes for your July produce. |
| Hyphen | | A door-to-door drive on a city-wide basis results in well-known items. |
| Figure-Symbol | | This bank pays 4½% interest on savings accounts. Joe received $32.96. |
| Easy | | They need less stress on how to stay young and more on how to grow up. |

Quick, sharp stroking

| 1 | 2 | 3 | 4 | 5 | 6 | 7 | 8 | 9 | 10 | 11 | 12 | 13 | 14 |

### 56b ■ Continuity Practice • Each line at least three times   *5 minutes*

1   SS   and do | and do this | and do this for them | and do this for all of them

2   with them | go with them | go with them to | go with them to do this work

3   and they | and if they | and if they go with | and if they go with us now

4   and did | and he did | and he did the work | and he did the work for gold

Rapid, continuous stroking

### 56c ■ Correcting Errors by Squeezing Letters   *5 minutes*

**Directions** – 1. Type the sentences just as they appear below with the errors. Then, make the corrections using the directions that follow.
2. To squeeze an omitted letter within a word, erase the word; then position the carriage to type the first letter of that word.
3. Operate the paper-release lever and move the paper a half space to the right.

4. Retype the word correctly so that the first letter is in half the space following the preceding word, and the final letter is in half the space following the corrected word.
5. To squeeze an omitted letter at the beginning or end of a word, move the carriage a half space before or after the word. Hold the carriage in position with the hand. Type the omitted letter.

| With error | A leter is omitted. | A etter is omitted. | A lette is omitted. |
| Corrected | A letter is omitted. | A letter is omitted. | A letter is omitted. |

**10th line space**

*Today's date*

**4th line space**

TO:   Typing Students                                                                                    7

**Double-space**

FROM:   Committee on Correspondence Policies                              16

**Double-space**

SUBJECT:   Vertical Centering                                                               22

**Triple-space**

Centering copy on a page so that there are uniform top and bot-      34
tom margins is called <u>vertical centering</u>.  To center copy verti-   51
cally, follow these steps:                                                                  56

**Always double-space** ——
**between paragraphs**     Step 1:   Count the lines in the copy to be centered--      67
                                      be sure to count all blank lines in double          76
                                      and triple spacing.                                          80

**Indent 5 spaces** ——▸ Step 2:   Subtract the total lines to be used from the     91
**from both margins**              lines available on the paper you are using.      100
                                      (There are 6 lines to a vertical inch; there-    109
                                      fore, a half sheet has 33 lines, and a full       118
                                      sheet has 66 lines.)                                        123

                            Step 3:   After subtracting, you will know exactly how    134
                                      many blank lines you will have on the paper.   143
                                      Divide these remaining lines by 2.  Disregard  153
                                      any fraction.  The answer is the number of      161
                                      blank lines in the top and bottom margins.     170

                            Step 4:   Insert your paper so that the top edge is ex-   181
                                      actly even with the alignment scale.  Roll      190
                                      the paper up the proper number of lines (the   199
                                      answer from Step 3).  Begin typing on the next  209
                                      line so that you retain the right number of    218
                                      blank lines in the top margin.                       224

                            Step 5:   <u>Reading Position</u>.  If you are directed to      238
                                      center the problem in reading or off-centered  247
                                      position, subtract 2 lines from the normal top  257
                                      margin after Step 3; then do Step 4.              264

**Full-page memorandum with indented items**

## Problem 3—Bibliography for Formal Library Report

**Directions – 1.** Type the bibliography for your formal report on a separate sheet of paper. List the references given below.

**2.** Assemble your report as follows: title page, body of the report, and bibliography. The report should be bound at the left.

● *See page 116 for an illustration of a bibliography.*

Anderson, James W. "How to Save Money with COM." Information and Records Management. Vol. 5 (February, 1971), pp. 27-29.

Carding, A. D. "Microfilm: EDP's Newest Ally." Administrative Management. Vol. 31 (April, 1970), pp. 38-42.

Markowitz, E. N. "Ten Seconds to Answer an Inquiry." Administrative Management. Vol. 31 (March, 1970), pp. 50-51.

Smythe, Terry. "Microfilm and the Computer." Records Management Quarterly. Vol. 5 (April, 1971), pp. 30-33.

## ■ Lesson 55 ● *70-space line*

### 55a ■ Keyboard Review ● Each line at least three times
*5 minutes*

Alphabetic SS  Jack Alexander saw the magnificent painting by Velazquez in the Prado.

Hyphen  We had a two-hour-long debate on the superiority of air-cooled motors.

*Space quickly*

Figure  1 and 2 and 3 and 4 and 5 and 6 and 7 and 8 and 9 and 10 and 11 and 12

Easy  Those who try to get something for nothing may be paying a high price.

| 1 | 2 | 3 | 4 | 5 | 6 | 7 | 8 | 9 | 10 | 11 | 12 | 13 | 14 |

### 55b ■ Timed Writings ● Type two 5-minute writings on 51e, page 111. Compute gwam; circle the errors. Submit the better writing.
*15 minutes*

### 55c ■ Problem Typing
*25 minutes*

**Directions –** Continue typing the manuscript of the formal library report started in Lesson 54. Keep the margins and the spacing uniform throughout the manuscript.

### 55d ■ Extra-Credit Typing

#### Problem 1

**Directions –** Prepare a report of approximately two pages on the topic, "The Value of a Good Education." Include a title page and a bibliography. Follow the directions for typing bound manuscripts given on page 104.

#### Problem 2

**Directions –** Expand the material in 51e, page 111, into a paper of 1½ to 2 pages. Add information from other books. Use footnotes to identify the sources of your material. Provide a title, title page, and a bibliography.

#### Problem 3

**Directions –** Retype the first and second pages of the manuscript on pages 106 and 109. Paraphrase the two direct quotations, but use footnote references to indicate the sources of the material that you have paraphrased.

### 29a ■ Keyboard Review • Each line at least three times

*5 minutes*

| | |
|---|---|
| Alphabetic SS | With a fixed goal in mind, Jim quickly sized up the job before moving. |
| Adjacent keys | The western office ordered the local people to rotate these May plans. |
| Figure-Symbol | Leeds & Ivy gave 6% off on "hand-tailored suits" that sold for $74.95. |
| Easy | One should have the gift to think for himself as he thinks for others. |

*Wrists low and steady*

| 1 | 2 | 3 | 4 | 5 | 6 | 7 | 8 | 9 | 10 | 11 | 12 | 13 | 14 |

### 29b ■ Technique Builder—Flowing Rhythm

*5 minutes*

**Directions** – Type each line three times. Try to feel the difference in typing the balanced-hand and the one-hand words.

**Technique Goal** – Develop a smooth rhythmic stroking pattern.

1    SS    they are | for him | their address | with the case | and the date | for you

2          he was saved | and the tact | if it were | they fear | for the only | as it

3          and see | if they look | and the union | to the state | the facts | for him

4          they grade | and imply | if they saw | and may trade | they were | the case

*Work for flowing rhythm*

### 29c ■ Creative Typing • Type answers to as many of these questions as time permits. Use complete sentences.

*5 minutes*

1. How many horizontal spaces are there in paper 8½ inches wide, either pica or elite?
2. How many lines are there in a vertical inch?
3. How many line spaces are there in a full sheet of paper?
4. How many line spaces are in a half sheet?
5. How many line spaces are subtracted from the top margin if copy is to be in reading position?
6. If copy is to be triple-spaced, how many blank lines appear between lines?

### 29d ■ Paragraph Guided Writing

*5 minutes*

**Directions** – 1. Type a 1-minute writing on the following paragraph. Note your *gwam*. Add 4 words to your *gwam* for a new goal.
2. Type a second and third writing, trying to reach your new goal on each.

3. Type a fourth writing at your first rate. Try typing without errors.

• *Your instructor may call the half-minute guides to aid you in checking your rate.*

|  |  | Words | |
|---|---|---|---|
| DS | When you get a job, why not become an idea man? This is easier | 13 | 67 |
| | than you may think. Look for ways to improve your work. Examine each | 27 | 81 |
| 54 words 1.2 si | task. The old ways of doing it may not be efficient. Write down as | 41 | 95 |
| | many solutions as you can; test them to see which one works best. | 54 | 108 |

| 1 | 2 | 3 | 4 | 5 | 6 | 7 | 8 | 9 | 10 | 11 | 12 | 13 | 14 |

techniques. Many companies have begun successful use of this approach for retrieving data. E. N. Markowitz, Vice President and Controller of Korvette's department store in New York City, reported that his company changed from a manual filing system to a microfilm system. In the original system, even under the best conditions, retrieving vendor data took at least five minutes. With the new microfilm system the same data could be retrieved in seconds.[3]

Another distinct advantage of microfilm is the protection of vital records. For instance, irreplaceable records can be protected against loss by disasters such as fire or flood by filming them and storing the microfilm in a location other than where the original is kept. Many historical records subject to deterioration by frequent use or passage of time can be filmed and kept permanently.

Computer Output Microfilm. A very new concept of microphotography involves the combination of the computer and microfilm. Such a concept is known as computer output microfilm or COM. This is a technique whereby the computer data are printed directly on microfilm and the hard-copy computer printout is eliminated. Smythe, who was quoted earlier, is a strong advocate of COM. He believes the computer paper printout slows down the dissemination of information and makes it very difficult to utilize.[4]

In a COM system the equipment transfers digital data from magnetic tape directly to microfilm at speeds up to 150,000 characters per second. This speed is an important advantage of the COM system. Anderson states, "While a typist can produce but six pages of data in an hour, a high speed computer produces at about the rate of a thousand pages per hour. COM produces 30,000 pages in the same hour."[5]

Summary. To achieve full effectiveness, microphotography must be part of a planned records program––part of an entire system. When properly used, microfilm represents a very important technique in records management. The application has shifted from the restricted area of records storage to the more sophisticated usage of information retrieval. Many leading authorities in records management believe that the future uses of microfilm offer the greatest challenges.

---

[1] A. D. Carding, "Microfilm: EDP's Newest Ally," Administrative Management, Vol. 31 (April, 1970), p. 39.

[2] Terry Smythe, "Microfilm and the Computer," Records Management Quarterly, Vol. 5 (April, 1971), p. 30.

[3] E. N. Markowitz, "Ten Seconds to Answer an Inquiry," Administrative Management, Vol. 31 (March, 1970), p. 51.

[4] Smythe, op. cit., p. 33.

[5] James W. Anderson, "How to Save Money with COM," Information and Records Management, Vol. 5 (February, 1971), p. 27.

### Problem 2—Title Page for Formal Library Report

Directions – 1. Type a title page using the data given at the right. This title page is for the two-page report that you typed in Problem 1.

2. Follow the directions that are given on the illustration of a title page shown on page 114.

- *Remember that there are six vertical line spaces to an inch.*

MICROPHOTOGRAPHY

By

*Your name*

Personal and Professional Typing

*Today's date*

## 29e ■ Problem Typing

*25 minutes*

### Problem 1—Announcement Centered on Half Sheet

Half sheet
Double spacing

**Directions** – Type the announcement shown below in *exact vertical position.* Center each line horizontally.

ART COUNCIL BOARD OF GOVERNORS MEETING

Friday, February 16, 7:30 p.m.

Board Room

County Art Museum

Pittsburgh

Report on Recent Acquisitions

Robert Bacon, Chairman

### Problem 2—Announcement Centered on Full Sheet

Full sheet
Triple spacing

**Directions** – Type the announcement in Problem 1 in *reading position* (see page 58 for directions). Center each line horizontally.

### Problem 3—Poem Centered on Half Sheet

Half sheet
Double spacing

**Directions** – Type the following poem in exact *vertical position.* Center the poem horizontally according to the longest line. Begin typing the poet's name at the horizontal center.

COASTAL BORN

Triple-space →

The sea is in the marrow of my bones

The love of sea, inherent in my blood--

The sibling cry of gull in fog, intones

A tidal symphony of ebb and flood.

The mountaineer may cherish vale and crest,

The inlander may cleave to prairie-less,

But the ocean claims her own; there is no rest,

Away from surfing tides and stormy seas.

← Double-space

--Clara Tonk

## 54c ■ Concentration Practice

5 minutes

**Directions** – Type the paragraph three times without timing.   **Technique Goal** – Try typing without errors.

MATISSE ON MODERN ART

Words
4

DS

*"There are two kinds of artists," Henri Matisse (1869-1954) once* — 17

**69 words**
**1.3 si**

*said in defense of the "claws" of Delacroix: "those who paint each time* — 32

*the portrait of a hand, a different hand every time, Corot, for instance;* — 47

*and those who make the sign of the hand, like Delacroix. With signs one* — 61

*can compose freely and ornamentally."* — 69

| 1 | 2 | 3 | 4 | 5 | 6 | 7 | 8 | 9 | 10 | 11 | 12 | 13 | 14 |

## 54d ■ Problem Typing

30 minutes

• *You will not be able to type the entire report in this lesson. Type as far as you can. You will be given time to complete the manuscript in Lesson 55.*

### Problem 1—Formal Library Report

**Directions** – 1. Prepare a manuscript of the following report. Follow the directions for typing bound manuscripts given on page 104. 2. In the problem that follows, the footnotes are placed at the end of the report. Type them at the bottoms of the pages on which reference is made to them. In numbering the footnotes, start with "1" on each page or number them consecutively throughout the report.

#### MICROPHOTOGRAPHY

Even in today's automated society, more paper work is being generated than ever before. Because of this vast amount of paper, many business organizations are beginning to rely on the medium of microphotography. Microphotography is a photographic process whereby information recorded on paper is filmed in a miniaturized form. Magnification is normally required for reading the data that are on film. All sorts of documents, from auto parts catalogs to police files, from stock market records to rare first editions, are being microfilmed. Microphotography has now begun to take its place as an efficient and vital business aid by offering users the advantages of space savings, security, permanence, and rapid retrieval of data.[1]

**Advantages of Microfilm.** A microfilmed file may require up to 98 percent less space than its original paper counterpart. This saving of space may be a definite advantage to a user of microfilm in certain instances. Costwise, however, the preference might be for storing the original document rather than for microfilming it. Unfortunately, many companies consider microfilming their records only to save space. Terry Smythe, a leader in this field, says "Of all the motives for acquiring microfilm, I believe this to be the least rational and the most difficult to justify."[2]

The use of microfilm for the rapid retrieval of information is creating the prime demand for microphotography today. Large amounts of data can be stored on microfilm and any given item can be found rapidly by automated sorting

• *Report is continued on next page.*

# ■ Lesson 30 • *70-space line*

## 30a ■ Keyboard Review • Each line at least three times

Alphabetic  SS   If Judge Rize acquires the papers, he may solve the robbery next week.

Third finger   On a solo flight to Oslo, Walt saw six owls on the loose from the zoo.

*Be alert*

Hyphen   Here is an up-to-date book for those interested in nation-wide issues.

Easy   The crucial game is being played by two of the best teams in the city.

| 1 | 2 | 3 | 4 | 5 | 6 | 7 | 8 | 9 | 10 | 11 | 12 | 13 | 14 |

## 30b ■ Timed Writings

*10 minutes*

**Directions** – Type a 1-minute writing; then type two 3-minute writings. Circle errors. Compute your *gwam* and submit the better of the two longer writings.

|  | | GWAM | |
| --- | --- | --- | --- |
|  | | 1′ | 3′ |

¶ 1
53 words
1.3 si

DS   The best way to save part of our income, the financial experts   13  4  57

tell us, is to spend less than we make. How short––yet how very clear   27  9  62

and sensible!  The best way to cut out errors in typing is to type   40  13  66

with good form.  This, also, is concise, clear, and sensible.   53  18  71

¶ 2
52 words
1.3 si

In setting up our financial budget, it is nice to have both ends   66  22  75

meet.  It is even nicer if they overlap now and then.  The same idea   79  26  79

holds true in typing.  It is nice to type with very few errors, but   93  31  84

it is much nicer to have no errors at all once in a while.   105  35  88

¶ 3
54 words
1.3 si

Turning out a budget takes careful study and time.  All needed   117  39  92

expense items must be met by income.  Leftover cash can then be saved   131  44  97

for the extras that we hope some day to get.  Cutting down on typing   145  48  101

errors takes careful study, too.  They do not go away by themselves.   159  53  106

| 1′ | 1 | 2 | 3 | 4 | 5 | 6 | 7 | 8 | 9 | 10 | 11 | 12 | 13 | 14 |
| 3′ | | 1 | | 2 | | 3 | | 4 | | 5 | |

## 30c ■ Problem Typing

*30 minutes*

### Problem 1—Short, Informal Report

**Directions** – 1. Type the report on page 62. Use a 60-space line. Indent paragraphs five spaces.

2. Double-space the body. Use a standard margin of 2 inches (12 line spaces at the top).

## Problem 3—Bibliography

**Directions** – Type the bibliography shown below. Use the same margins used in the body of a report; assume that the report is to be bound at the left. Leave a 2-inch top margin.

BIBLIOGRAPHY

5-space indention ←——— Triple-space

Author of article

Brown, Leland. *Communicating Facts and Ideas in Business.* Englewood Cliffs, New Jersey: Prentice-Hall, Inc., 1970.

Double-space ——→

Two authors

Dye, Thomas R., and L. Harmon Zeigler. *The Irony of Democracy.* Belmont, California: Wadsworth Publishing Company, Inc., 1970.

Several authors

Hailstones, Thomas J., et al. *Contemporary Economic Problems and Issues.* Cincinnati: South-Western Publishing Co., 1970.

Anonymous author

"How Dictating Equipment Serves Modern Business," *The Office.* LXXIV (July, 1971), pp. 52-64.

**Bibliography**

# ■ Lesson 54 • *70-space line*

## 54a ■ Keyboard Review • Each line at least three times

*5 minutes*

Alphabetic SS  Mary Tracy's box was packed with five dozen jugs of the liquid veneer.

Long reach  About once each night, Bruce checks the barometer on the bottom level.

Begin slowly; increase speed gradually

Figure-Symbol  The premium of $47.20 on Policy #83195 is due the tenth of this month.

Easy  The world has now achieved a goal of putting peace on a wartime basis.

| 1 | 2 | 3 | 4 | 5 | 6 | 7 | 8 | 9 | 10 | 11 | 12 | 13 | 14 |

## 54b ■ Technique Builder—Stroking

*5 minutes*

**Directions** – Type each line three times.　　　　**Technique Goal** – Keep your wrists and elbows quiet.

Home row SS  Jack Ladd had a full glass of milk at the kiosk; he had a salad, also.

Third row  Peter wrote quite a true report of the weary trip through the prairie.

Hold wrists steady

First row  Ben Vance minimized his chance of failing the exam by cramming for it.

Hyphen  The well-known Pan American author has up-to-date information at home.

| 1 | 2 | 3 | 4 | 5 | 6 | 7 | 8 | 9 | 10 | 11 | 12 | 13 | 14 |

TYPING A SHORT REPORT OR THEME

Triple-space

Short reports or themes of one page or less may be typed
with a 60-space line.  If the number of lines can be counted
easily, center the copy vertically; if not, use a standard
margin of 2 inches (12 line spaces) at the top.

Double spacing is usually used in themes and reports.
Class notes, book reviews, and minutes are usually single-
spaced to provide better groupings of information.

Every report should have a title which is typed in all
capital letters.  It is always separated from the body by a
triple space.

Longer reports or papers--especially those of more than
one page--are usually typed with side margins of 1 inch.  When
the paper is to be bound at the left, however, an extra one-
half inch must be provided in the left margin for binding.

The heading is typed 2 inches from the top of the first
page.  All pages after the first have a top margin of 1 inch.
The bottom margin should not be less than 1 inch.  The copy
usually looks better if this margin runs an extra one-half
inch.

18
30
42
51
62
74
84
95
107
110
122
134
146
158
169
182
194
206
207

◄——— 60-space line ———►

**One-page theme**

**Directions** – Type a 1-minute writing on each sentence.

1  SS  *A man is considered wise if he knows when to speak and when to listen.*
2     *Speed and accuracy in typewriting are achieved only through hard work.*
3     *The hardest tasks may often be the most rewarding and self-satisfying.*
4     *Learning can be aided by making the correct answers immediately known.*

Type without pauses

| 1 | 2 | 3 | 4 | 5 | 6 | 7 | 8 | 9 | 10 | 11 | 12 | 13 | 14 |

## 53d ■ Problem Typing                    *30 minutes*

### Problem 1—Bibliographical Card

● *Bibliographical cards contain information about references to be used in the preparation of a formal report.*

**Directions** – 1. Prepare a bibliography card on 5- by 3-inch card stock from the illustration at the right.

2. Type the first entry on the card about three spaces from the top and three spaces from the left edge. To keep the card from slipping, adjust the card holders to hold the card firmly against the cylinder.

Author — Smythe, Terry

Title — "Microfilm and the Computer"

Publication information — Records Management Quarterly, Vol. 5, April, 1971

Short description —
In this article Smythe tries to discredit the widely held belief that microfilm can only be used to save space occupied by inactive records.  He believes that microphotography's greatest value is in rapid retrieval of data.

Library call number — HF5549 R42

**Bibliographical card**

### Problem 2—Note Card

● *Note cards contain ideas, facts, and quotations to be
used in preparing the body of a formal report or speech.*

**Directions** – 1. Prepare a note card on 5- by 3-inch card stock from the illustration at the right.

2. Type the heading about three spaces from the top and three spaces from the left edge.

Heading — Microfilm as a medium for information handling

Notes —
Broadly speaking, the purpose of microfilm is to store and miniaturize information; the purpose of the computer is to store and manipulate information.  These two technologies, therfore, have a common denominator of "information handling."

Reference and page number —
Smythe, "Microfilm and the Computer," p. 31, Records Management Quarterly, Vol. 5, April, 1971.

**Note card**

## Problem 2—Short Report with Indented Items

**Directions** – 1. Set the margin stops for a 60-space line. Use double spacing and a 2-inch top margin. Type the heading as directed in Problem 1.

2. Indent the numbered paragraphs 5 spaces from each margin. Single-space the indented paragraphs; double-space between them.

### BEING A GOOD CONVERSATIONALIST

Ease in speaking is a quality that should be developed by everyone. Aim to contribute substance to a conversation; if you have nothing worthwhile to add, however, listen to what others are saying—you'll be surprised at what you can learn.

Don't manipulate yourself into a position of having to stay in the background, though; have a reservoir of handy facts and ideas that will make you a welcome addition to any conversation. Accomplish this by resorting to the following sources:

1. Daily Experiences—Be alert to the incidents that occur every day. New acquaintances, travel, and one's own interpretations add interesting highlights to a conversation.

2. Periodicals and Newspapers—Keep yourself informed as to what is happening in international and domestic politics, sports, local affairs, and the stock market through magazines and newspapers.

3. Books—A storehouse of interesting facts and ideas is found in the libraries and bookstores. Read those books you find fascinating, but choose the books which also enrich your vocabulary.

4. Cultural Events—Attend the local drama festivals, concerts, and art exhibits.

These sources comprise only the starting point. Become aware of what's going on around you, and you'll never have the excuse of "just" listening. Here's your clue to making yourself an interesting and interested person.

## ■ Lesson 31 • *70-space line*

### 31a ■ Keyboard Review • Each line at least three times

*5 minutes*

Alphabetic SS   With a fixed goal in mind, Jim quickly sized up the job before moving.

Shift key   J. C. Byrd flew to Washington, D. C., to confer with Gen. R. A. Smart.

Figure   In 1980, the United States will have a population of over 272,600,000.

Easy   Plan to do extra things today since you wasted so much time yesterday.

| 1 | 2 | 3 | 4 | 5 | 6 | 7 | 8 | 9 | 10 | 11 | 12 | 13 | 14 |

*Sit erect*

### 31b ■ Judgment Placement of Headings

*5 minutes*

**Directions** – 1. Set your machine for triple-spacing. Type the headings at the right in what you believe to be the horizontal center of the paper.

2. Roll the paper back to one line below the first heading. Center that heading by the backspacing method. Compare your judgment placement with the exact placement.

3. Center the remaining headings under the first typing of each.

LIFE ON PARADISE ISLAND

CAN TRAINING CURE INFLATION?

TECHNOLOGY WORKSHOP

## Problem 2—Title Page

**Directions – 1.** Type the title page in the illustration on the right. The title page is for the two-page report you just completed in Problem 1.

**2.** Follow the directions given on the illustration. The data on the title page are given below. Type from this copy.

COMMUNICATING EFFECTIVELY

By

*Your name*

Personal and Professional Typing

*Today's date*

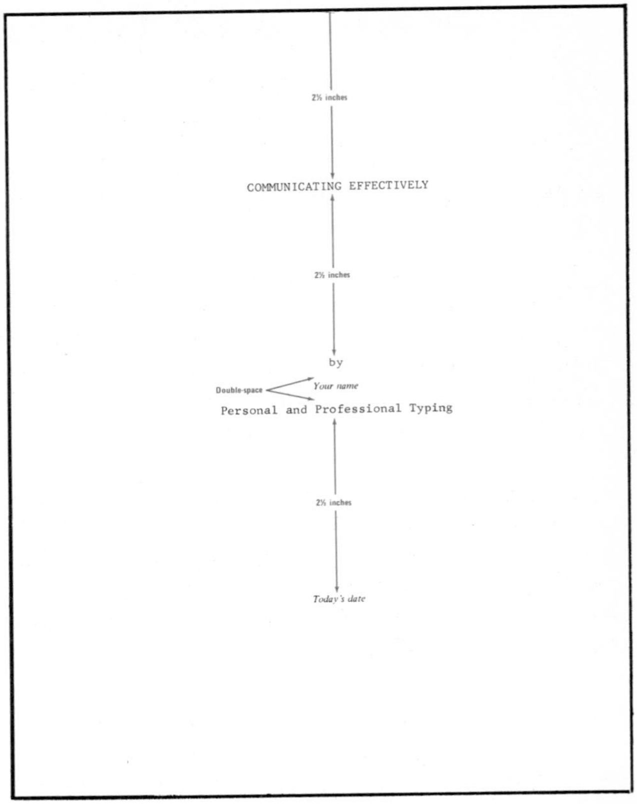

COMMUNICATING EFFECTIVELY

2½ inches

2½ inches

by

Double-space  *Your name*
Personal and Professional Typing

2½ inches

*Today's date*

**Title page**

## ■ Lesson 53 • *70-space line*

### 53a ■ Keyboard Review • Each line at least three times        *5 minutes*

Alphabetic SS  Wilbur Jackson explained the quick-freezing process to every salesman.

pol            Political polls were the policy of polished politicians and policemen.      Eyes and mind on copy as

Figure-Symbol  In the 1820's, good Texas farmland was selling for only 12½ ¢ per acre.     you type

Easy           It is the way someone works, not the way he talks, that really counts.
               |  1  |  2  |  3  |  4  |  5  |  6  |  7  |  8  |  9  |  10  |  11  |  12  |  13  |  14  |

### 53b ■ Skill Comparison        *5 minutes*

**Directions – 1.** Type a 1-minute writing on each of the paragraphs listed at the right.

**2.** Compare your *gwam*.

**3.** Type an additional writing on the one on which you had the lowest rate.

48c   Concentration Practice, page 102

50c   Technique Builder, page 107

52b   Continuity Practice, page 112

### 31c ■ Technique Builder—Stroking • Each line three times

5 minutes

Double letters   SS   The bookkeeper listed the assets in a letter he sent to the committee.

Weak fingers    We were puzzled by the manager's lack of aptitude for the appointment.

One hand    Face the facts; you can get an award only if you exceed Molly's grade.

Flowing rhythm    The main reason that we fail to learn is that we stop before we start.

| 1 | 2 | 3 | 4 | 5 | 6 | 7 | 8 | 9 | 10 | 11 | 12 | 13 | 14 |

Center
stroking
in fingers

### 31d ■ Spelling and Proofreading Aid • Each line at least three times

5 minutes

• *Spelling is basic to accurate typing and proofreading. Study the spelling of each word as you type it.*

1   SS   concede grieve harass professor recipe foresee agreeable definite lose

2    career prefer calendar difference basis column forty weather guarantee

3    excel gauge strength yield tension possess governor ascertain judgment

Think as
you type

### 31e ■ Paragraph Guided Writings • As directed in 26c, page 52

15 minutes

• Contains all letters

GWAM
1'   3'

¶1
40 words
1.3 si

DS    A poet once wrote that life without freedom is like a body    12   4   48
without a spirit and that if one did not exercise his mind, the    25   8   52
spirit would die. Thus, to keep a free spirit alive, you must    37   12   56
use your mind.    40   13   57

¶2
44 words
1.3 si

This is true in all you do. Do not allow your mind to stagnate;    13   18   62
be creative in all things. When you join a willingness to discover    27   22   66
new and different things with a true zest for life, you'll keep your    40   27   71
free spirit alive.    44   28   72

¶3
48 words
1.3 si

In the business world, each person isn't free to do as he chooses.    14   33   77
Accept this fact and adapt to the system. Be excited about your work,    28   37   81
do a little extra, and you will find that the reins which quenched    41   42   86
your freedom will begin to loosen.    48   44   88

| 1' | 1 | 2 | 3 | 4 | 5 | 6 | 7 | 8 | 9 | 10 | 11 | 12 | 13 | 14 |
| 3' | | 1 | | 2 | | 3 | | 4 | | 5 | |

# COMMUNICATING EFFECTIVELY

Far too frequently one hears the complaint that people fail to understand each other—that people cannot communicate with one another. How can this perplexing problem be remedied? William Keefe lists four points that are essential in any type of communication: [1]

1. It must be heard or received.

2. It must be understood.

3. It must be accepted.

4. It must be acted upon.

To convey a message accurately to another individual requires more than just an understanding of the meaning of words. Eric Moonman states that, "No two men will respond to a message in the same way." [2] If a person will realize this fact and will attempt to understand individual differences in people, one can improve the effectiveness of his communications.

A message may seem very clear to everyone but the very person for whom the message was intended. Each person should keep in mind at all times during the communication process that misunderstandings are very easy. The sender of a message must be willing to accept his share of the blame if the receiver does not comprehend it.

Each individual has his own perceptions that only add to the potential confusions that may arise when one communicates. Moonman says:

Communication between one individual and another is a constant and continuous process. It is a means of interaction. To understand requires a consideration of the main forces that have shaped or molded the individual: his background, experience, and education. [3]

There is little wonder that so much of what is said is not understood, or worse yet, is altered to the wrong meaning. Keefe emphasizes the reception of communication and believes that listening is a vital instrument in organizational interaction. [4]

Virtually everyone has the need to express himself and to follow the directions of others in his daily life. Leland Brown gives some excellent suggestions for communicating more effectively:

To adapt language for ease of comprehension and motivation, we need to remember that words in our language not only represent logical relationships, but also provide emotional responses. We use them not only to express what we want to say but also to impress our audience, to move them to action. [5]

---

[1] William Keefe, Listen, Management! (New York: McGraw-Hill Book Company, 1971), p. 44.

[2] Eric Moonman, Communicating in an Expanding Organization (London: Tavistock Publications, 1970), pp. 4-5.

[3] Ibid.

[4] Keefe, op. cit., p. 31.

[5] Leland Brown, Communicating Facts and Ideas in Business (Englewood Cliffs, N. J.: Prentice-Hall, Inc., 1970), p. 86.

## 31f ■ Listening for the Bell—Right Margin Release

5 minutes

**Directions –** 1. Use a 50-space line. Let the bell guide you in returning the carriage. If the carriage locks before you complete a word, depress the margin-release key and complete the word.

2. Retype the paragraph with a 60-space line.
• *Remember to set the right margin 5-8 spaces beyond the desired line ending. Doing this will give your copy better horizontal balance.*

DS ¶ get ready totake a timed writing and before you start typing it: clear the desk; be sure have enought clear paper inthe machine; set place hte margins forthe correct length of line; indent the paragraph; put the the copy as it is easyto read.

48 words
1.3 si

Eyes on this copy

## 31g ■ Skill Comparison

5 minutes

**Directions –** Type a 1-minute writing on each sentence. Try to type all sentences at the rate set on the first one.

Easy DS It is a fact that those who type their papers often get higher grades.

Figure-Symbol Brumel is holder of the world's record high jump (at 7 feet 5 inches).

Rough draft even through a turtle took but onestep at one time, he won hte race.

Script A man must learn to control himself before he tries to control others.

| 1 | 2 | 3 | 4 | 5 | 6 | 7 | 8 | 9 | 10 | 11 | 12 | 13 | 14 |

Type without pauses

## ■ Lesson 32 • *70-space line*

## 32a ■ Keyboard Review • Each line at least three times

5 minutes

Alphabetic SS Fred M. Quigg spoke subjectively and expressed his opinions with zeal.

One hand Johnny and Freda grew limp with fear as they saw the savage lion jump.

Figure-Symbol Mr. Brown's note (due on April 7) for $850 was discounted at 6% today.

Easy This is the way to make the work fit into the pattern of typing power.

| 1 | 2 | 3 | 4 | 5 | 6 | 7 | 8 | 9 | 10 | 11 | 12 | 13 | 14 |

Use sure, quick strokes

## 32b ■ Typing from Dictation and Spelling Checkup

5 minutes

**Directions –** Your teacher will dictate the words in 31d, page 64. Type the words from dictation. Check for correct spelling. Retype any words in which you made an error.

## 52a ■ Keyboard Review • Each line at least three times

Alphabetic SS   Dexter Jaquez may give the prize for the best novel to Dwayne Jackson.

br   Breaking abruptly from the brush, Brad's brash brother was breathless.

*Wrists low and still*

Figure-Symbol   Invoice #5483 lists this charge: 716 gallons of oil @ 29¢ per gallon.

Easy   A mistake is a sign that someone spent time and tried to do something.

| 1 | 2 | 3 | 4 | 5 | 6 | 7 | 8 | 9 | 10 | 11 | 12 | 13 | 14 |

## 52b ■ Continuity Practice from Rough Draft

*5 minutes*

**Directions** – Type the paragraph as many times as you can
without timing. Type for control.

Words

DS  ¶ A man spends the the first half of his life listing to the advice, the   13

second have giveing it. this maybe the reason why there is so much a drug on   27

62 words
1.3 si   the market; the sup ply always exceeds the demand. Advice, just as caster oil, like   41

oil, is easy go give, but awful dreadful to take. it is never, never seldom welcome.   54

Those who seem to need it much most, like it the last.   62

## 52c ■ Correcting Errors by Spreading Letters

*5 minutes*

**Directions** – 1. Type the sentence below just as it appears.
2. Erase *exttra*; then position the carriage to type the *e* in *extra*.
3. Operate the paper-release lever; move the paper a half space to the left.
4. Retype the word correctly so that the first letter is 1½ spaces to the
right of the last letter of the preceding word.
5. Repeat the problem.

• *On typewriters which
have a half-space mech-
anism, it is not neces-
sary to move the paper
in the machine.*

With error   An exttra letter appears in one of the words.

Corrected   An extra letter appears in one of the words.

## 52d ■ Problem Typing

*30 minutes*

### Problem 1—Two-Page Report with Footnotes

**Directions** – 1. Type the report on the next page. Use
the directions on page 104 for typing bound manuscripts. 2. Number both pages. 3. Type each footnote
on the page on which the reference appears even
though all footnotes are given at the end of the report
in the problem. Number the footnotes consecutively
throughout the report. Refer to the directions on
page 107 for typing footnotes. Study the illustrations.

## 32c ■ Paragraph Guided Writings

5 minutes

**Directions** – Type the paragraph for four 1-minute writings. Try typing exactly 40 words a minute. Your teacher will call the quarter-minute marks to guide your typing.

|  |  | Words |
|---|---|---|
| DS | Trade among tribes and clans existed before men knew how to write. | 14 |
| 40 words 1.3 si | The trader's need to keep track of his dealings and the state's need | 27 |
|  | to settle disputes led to the invention of writing and counting. | 40 |

| 1 | 2 | 3 | 4 | 5 | 6 | 7 | 8 | 9 | 10 | 11 | 12 | 13 | 14 |

---

### ERASING

The errors that you make in themes, personal notes, and other papers you wish to use should be corrected. You must, therefore, learn how to erase typing errors. These instructions are given in Problem 1, below. Read them carefully.

- *Your teacher will tell you whether you are to erase and correct errors made in typing the problems that follow.*

---

## 32d ■ Problem Typing

30 minutes

### Problem 1—Simple Paragraph Outline

Full sheet
60-space line
Reading position

**Directions** – Single-space the lines in the paragraphs. Be sure to align the Roman numerals at the right. Use the margin-release key and backspace to the desired point.

Words

### ERASING PROCEDURES

| | Words |
|---|---|
| ERASING PROCEDURES | 4 |

Triple-space ⟶

I. Move the carriage to the extreme right or left so that the eraser particles will not fall into the typewriter. — 16, 27

Double-space ⟶

II. If the error occurs on the upper portion of your paper, roll the paper up two or three spaces to give yourself working room. If the erasure is to be made on the lower third of the paper, turn the cylinder backward to keep the paper from slipping. — 40, 52, 63, 76, 77

III. When you erase, be sure that your hands and the eraser are clean to prevent smudges on the copy. An eraser shield is sometimes used to protect the writing that is not to be erased. — 90, 102, 113, 115

IV. Hold the paper firmly against the cylinder with your fingertips. Erase the error carefully so as not to make a hole in the paper. Brush or blow the eraser particles away from the typewriter. — 128, 139, 151, 155

V. Return the paper to typing position. Make the correction by striking the keys lightly. Restrike the letters, if necessary, to make the stroking even. — 167, 178, 186

## 51e ■ Skill Building

**Directions** – 1. Type a 5-minute writing. Circle errors; note your *gwam*.

     2. Type a 1-minute writing on each paragraph. Try to add 10 words to your 5-minute *gwam* on each one.

     3. Type another 5-minute writing. Circle errors; note your *gwam*. Compare it with that of the first writing.

● Contains all letters

| | | | GWAM |
|---|---|---|---|
| | | 3' | 5' |

**¶1 40 words 1.3 si**    DS    The first step in writing a report is the choice of a subject. Best    5   3   51

practice favors the choice of a topic in which you have an interest and    9   6   54

about which you wish to give your reader some new insights.    13   8   56

**¶2 44 words 1.3 si**    After you choose the topic of your paper, start gathering data.    18   11   59

In most cases, your data will come from books and magazines. Read and    23   14   62

take careful notes. Be sure to record the names of sources from which    27   16   64

you get help.    28   17   65

**¶3 48 words 1.3 si**    Record only one note on a card; label each card with a heading.    32   19   67

You will find these headings to be a real aid in working out the out-    37   22   70

line of your paper. After classifying the note cards, you will find    42   25   73

that the topics of your theme emerge.    44   26   74

**¶4 52 words 1.3 si**    With the outline of your paper and your note cards before you,    48   29   77

start writing the first draft. By now, you should be well acquainted    53   32   80

with your topic, and the ideas should come with ease. Do not worry    58   35   83

about errors. Think only of the ideas you wish to express.    61   37   85

**¶5 56 words 1.3 si**    When you revise the rough draft into final form, be sure that the    66   40   88

copy is grammatical, and that transitional words join the main points.    71   42   90

Type the theme in report form; give thought to margins, footnotes, spac-    75   45   93

ing, and other fine points that add to the proper format of your work.    80   48   96

3'   1    2    3    4    5
5'   1    2    3

Full sheet
60-space line
Double spacing

**Directions** – Type the report in *reading position*. Make the corrections as you type.

• *When rough draft copy must be centered, you can count the lines in the draft and add or deduct lines from the total, depending upon the corrections made; or you can type a corrected copy on practice paper first. The lines can then be counted, and the second typing can be centered as directed. Your teacher will tell you which practice you are to follow for this problem.*

Words

*CONQUERING NEW WORLDS*    4

*Triple-space* →

One of the *most* beguiling fantasies of man *is* his ~~doged~~ dogged    16

belief that his *own* generation (only not) represents the apex of a    28

civilization but also is *constantly* thinking new thoughts, solving new    43

problems, and creating many new worlds. consider the case of    55

Ralph Powers and Blakeslee Barnes, whom in 1917 drove *a* car    67

from Florida to Conneticut--a distance of *some* 1,400 miles--in    79

in 16 days. They ~~packed~~ *loaded* their car with food, tents, axes, a    91

rifle, rope, ~~some~~ chains, and spare parts. The roads were    102

unsurfaced, unmarked, *and* poorly maped; yet they ~~made~~ *completed* the ~~tip~~ *trip*.    116

they had reason to believe that they created a *new* world.    128

Today, *the* ~~our~~ motorist needs *little* more then his credit card    140

to ~~take~~ *make* the *same* trip easily in under three days. the day ~~will be~~ *may come*    153

when even a credit card may not be needed.    162

**Directions** – Type the following announcement in the *exact vertical center*. Center each line horizontally.

Half sheet
Double spacing

Claremont Hills School
SUMMER REUNION—CLASS OF '72
The Star on the Roof
at the
Statler-Piedmont Hotel
8:30 p.m., August 10, 197–
Dinner and Dancing, $16 per Couple
RSVP by July 30 to Sally Byrd, 825-2621

LIBRARY
WAYNE STATE COLLEGE
WAYNE, NEBRASKA

## 51b ■ Concentration Practice

**5 minutes**

**Directions** – Type the paragraph three times without timing.  **Technique Goal** – Work for control.

Words

### NATURALIZATION

3

Triple-space———→

DS    An applicant for naturalization must be at least 18 years old.  16

64 words
1.3 si

He must have been a lawful resident of the United States continuously  30

for 5 years. For husbands and wives of United States citizens, the  43

period is 3 years in most instances. Special provisions apply to  57

certain veterans of the Armed Forces.  64

| 1 | 2 | 3 | 4 | 5 | 6 | 7 | 8 | 9 | 10 | 11 | 12 | 13 | 14 |

## 51c ■ Technique Builder—Flowing Rhythm Practice ● Each line three times

**5 minutes**

Letter    SS  In fact, the manager agreed to include this statement in the contract.

Word    A man can think himself into a new life and make his dreams come true.

Type with
your fingers

Combination    People have no experience of their own until it is too late to use it.

Combination    A plan will help you do the things you should when you should do them.

| 1 | 2 | 3 | 4 | 5 | 6 | 7 | 8 | 9 | 10 | 11 | 12 | 13 | 14 |

## 51d ■ Speed Ladder Sentences

**10 minutes**

**Directions** – Type each sentence for one minute. Try to return the carriage as the guides are called at 15-, 12-, or 10-second intervals.

**Technique Goals** – Return the carriage quickly without looking from the copy. Start typing immediately after the throw.

| | | | Words a Minute 15″ 12″ 10″ |
|---|---|---|---|
| 1 | SS | We need three levels of typing response. | 32 40 48 |
| 2 | | A beginning typist types on the letter level. | 36 45 54 |
| 3 | | He thinks each letter to himself when he types it. | 40 50 60 |
| 4 | | This is necessary when key locations are being learned. | 44 55 66 |
| 5 | | On the letter level each letter is typed as a separate unit. | 48 60 72 |
| 6 | | When a typist types on the word level, he reads words as a whole. | 52 65 78 |
| 7 | | Good typists can combine word and letter levels into a smooth pattern. | 56 70 84 |

| 1 | 2 | 3 | 4 | 5 | 6 | 7 | 8 | 9 | 10 | 11 | 12 | 13 | 14 |

# ■ Lesson 33 • *70-space line*

### 33a ■ Keyboard Review • Each line at least three times
*5 minutes*

| | | |
|---|---|---|
| Alphabetic | SS | John and Wayne quickly replaced the five large itemized express boxes. |
| mu | | Maximum and minimum fees must be paid at the Municipal Hall in Muncie. |
| Figure-Symbol | | The Burns & Son check for the full amount ($92.74) was dated 10/13/71. |
| Easy | | When you type, blend rapid and slow typing into easy, flowing strokes. |

Eyes on copy

| 1 | 2 | 3 | 4 | 5 | 6 | 7 | 8 | 9 | 10 | 11 | 12 | 13 | 14 |

### 33b ■ Speed Ladder Paragraphs
*10 minutes*

**Directions** – Type as many 1-minute writings as time permits. When you can type the first paragraph at the rate specified, type the next one. Climb the speed ladder. See if you can reach the top.

• Contains all letters

|  | | GWAM 1' | 3' |
|---|---|---|---|

¶1
32 words
1.3 si
DS

A topic sentence pinpoints the idea of a paragraph. Once you ... 12 | 4 70
set the train of thought, stick to your guns; add only remarks which ... 26 | 9 75
relate to your central theme. ... 32 | 11 77

¶2
36 words
1.3 si

Before you sit down to write the body of the paper, you should ... 13 | 15 81
have an outline of the ideas you wish to express. In this way, you ... 26 | 19 85
will be able to follow a logical thought pattern. ... 36 | 23 89

¶3
40 words
1.3 si

The topic sentences may be the main points in a short report ... 12 | 27 93
or the items of a key heading in a complex paper. Keep the tran- ... 25 | 31 97
sition between your ideas smooth and join them to form your central ... 39 | 36 102
theme. ... 40 | 36 102

¶4
44 words
1.4 si

To unfold the main thought of your report requires practice. ... 12 | 40 106
Make use of strong facts, precise reasons, or diverse examples to ... 26 | 44 110
result in a well-planned group of sentences. At times, you may com- ... 39 | 49 115
pare and contrast facts. ... 44 | 51 117

¶5
48 words
1.3 si

Link chief ideas. Guide the reader from thought to thought by ... 13 | 55 121
stressing important words and by using pronouns that refer to sub- ... 26 | 59 125
jects. Use clear phrases to connect words; do not throw in fuzzy ... 39 | 63 129
terms that cloud meanings you wish to stress. ... 48 | 66 132

1' | 1 | 2 | 3 | 4 | 5 | 6 | 7 | 8 | 9 | 10 | 11 | 12 | 13 | 14 |
3' | 1 | | 2 | | 3 | | 4 | | 5 |

1 inch

1 inch

Words

If the quotation is quite long and there are omissions 11

1½ inches ⟶ of a paragraph or more, Lesikar says that the omission may 23

be indicated by typing a full line of periods usually with 35

intervening spaces.[1] 39

In using these various documenting techniques, the 49

writer should be very careful to see that the quoted matter 61

is reproduced exactly as it appeared in the original source. 74

Robinson suggests: 78

Quotation single-spaced
and indented ⟶
> Our advice about maintaining the integrity of 87
> the quotations extends even to the preservation of 97
> grammatical errors. Fortunately, there is a method 107
> available to the writer by which he can absolve 117
> himself of guilt for the presence of a misspelled 127
> word or grammatical error. The method involves the 137
> use of the Latin expression sic in brackets follow- 148
> ing the error.[2] 152

Although footnotes normally appear at the bottom of a 162

page on which the quotation appears, some writers advocate 174

putting all of them at the end of the manuscript. Wells 186

believes, however, that the footnotes should be placed at 197

the bottom of the page where they will provide easier ref- 209

erence for the reader.[3] 214

218

Footnotes at bottom
of partially filled page
[1]Raymond V. Lesikar, Report Writing for Business (3d 234
ed.; Homewood, Illinois: Richard D. Irwin, Inc., 1969), 245
p. 283. 247

[2]Robinson, op. cit., pp. 316-317. 255

[3]Walter Wells, Communications in Business (Belmont, 271
California: Wadsworth Publishing Company, Inc., 1968), 282
p. 358. 284

1 inch

**Third page of a manuscript**

## Problem 1—Sentence Outline on Taking Notes

Full sheet
60-space line
Reading position

**Directions** – 1. Type the main points at the left margin. Use tab stops for subpoints. Align Roman numerals at the period.

2. Indent, space, capitalize, and punctuate exactly as shown in the problem. Two spaces follow the period after all numbered or lettered divisions in an outline.

3. Do not type copy line for line, but listen for the bell in returning the carriage.

## SUGGESTIONS FOR TAKING NOTES

Triple-space ⟶

I.   TAKE NOTES ON WHAT YOU HEAR.

Double-space ⟶
4-space indentation ⟶

A.   Record only important facts and ideas.
   1.   Disregard items which are not vital.

8-space indentation ⟶

   2.   If the speaker literally indicates that a detail is important, write it down.
   3.   If the speaker spends much time lecturing about a specific item, write down the major points.
B.   Show the relationship between ideas. Transition words are clues to the organization of the subject.
C.   Correlate what you hear with what you know.

II.   TAKE NOTES ON WHAT YOU READ.

A.   Get an overall view of what the book or article is about by noting major headings and subpoints.
B.   Summarize. Don't try to write down everything that you read.
C.   If you wish to quote a statement, be accurate. Include a complete record of the source of the quotation.
D.   Leave space if you miss a point. Get help in adding the point later.

III.   PREPARE NOTES IN FINAL FORM.

A.   Revise and type notes as soon as possible after you take them while the ideas are still fresh in your mind.
B.   Always indicate the date on which the notes were taken.
C.   Type your notes so that they will be easy to read.
   1.   Use complete sentences.
   2.   Clarify and expand ideas.
   3.   Identify main topics with appropriate headings.
   4.   Itemize points under the headings.
D.   Review your notes frequently.

## 50d ■ Problem Typing

### Problem 1—Footnotes

**Directions – 1.** Assume that the sentence below is the last line that you can type on a page of a bound report before you type the footnotes.

**2.** After typing the last line in correct position (see preceding page for directions), type a divider line followed by the footnotes.

Many ideas were expressed concerning economic changes.

[1] Robert A. Johnson, "Computer Communication," The Journal of Business Communication, Vol. 8 (Spring, 1971), p. 39.

[2] Ibid.

[3] Thomas J. Hailstones et al., Contemporary Economic Problems and Issues (Cincinnati: South-Western Publishing Co., 1970), p. 137.

[4] Thomas R. Dye and L. Harmon Zeigler, The Irony of Democracy (Belmont, California: Wadsworth Publishing Company, Inc., 1970), p. 39.

[5] Hailstones et al., op. cit., p. 251.

[6] John F. Mee, "The Explosion of Knowledge," Business Education Forum, Vol. 25 (April, 1971), p. 44.

[7] Ibid., p. 46.

[8] Johnson, loc. cit.

### Problem 2—Succeeding Pages of a Manuscript

**Directions – 1.** Type the third page of a manuscript illustrated on page 109. The first page of this manuscript is shown on page 106.

**2.** Save at least three lines for each footnote in addition to the normal bottom margin. *Notice in the illustration of page 3 of the manuscript that the footnotes on a page only partially full appear at the bottom of the page.*

## ■ Lesson 51 • *70-space line*

### 51a ■ Keyboard Review • Each line three times

| | |
|---|---|
| Alphabetic SS | Joy King's quixotic views of the traffic problem amazed us completely. |
| my, ym | I myself, as well as my army, was mystified by the mysterious symbols. |
| Symbol | Did the class read "How to Be a Failure" in the Saturday Evening Post? |
| Easy | When you read, you must focus on the most important words in the line. |

*Quick, crisp, short, strokes*

| 1 | 2 | 3 | 4 | 5 | 6 | 7 | 8 | 9 | 10 | 11 | 12 | 13 | 14 |

## Problem 2—Typing Notes in Final Form

**Directions – 1.** Assume that the following notes were written in one of your classes. Prepare a type-written copy of them.

**2.** Use regular theme style. Type the date 1 inch from the top of the page and the heading 2 inches from the top. Space the copy so it is easy to read.

**3.** Do not copy the notes line for line, but listen for the bell in returning the carriage.

**4.** Assume that you will place these notes in a notebook. Set the margin stops for a 1½-inch left margin and a 1-inch right margin.

● *As is illustrated on page vi, there are 10 spaces per inch on a pica typewriter and 12 spaces per inch on an elite typewriter.*

*For pica typewriters, the left margin should contain 15 horizontal spaces; the right margin, 10 horizontal spaces. For elite typewriters, the left margin should contain 18 horizontal spaces; the right margin, 12 horizontal spaces.*

*Because of the wider left margin, the center point will be 3 spaces to the right of the point normally used; this puts the heading in off-centered position.*

*Today's date*

## WRITING INTERESTING, FORCEFUL LETTERS

Put warmth into your writing.

1. Remember that you are writing to real people. Your letters should sound like you, not like a cold recording of last year's news.

2. Your letters reflect your character. Let them smile and radiate sincerity. They should show you as a friendly, unaffected person.

Speak when you write.

1. Say what you mean. Don't beat around the bush.
   a. All letters should be fresh and readable. Avoid stilted, cloudy words and phrases.
   b. Use punctuation to indicate pauses and inflections in your speech. Use periods freely. One thought per sentence is a good rule to adopt.
   c. Write clearly. Use simple, forceful words that say what you mean.
   d. Be concise. Repeating yourself or the letter you are answering is a bad habit which bores your reader.
   e. Avoid long paragraphs, especially at the beginning of your letter.

2. Don't ramble on. Say what you need to say in a clear, friendly way. Then stop.

3. The average sentence in popular magazines contains 17 words, 150 syllables per 100 words, and 6 personal references per 100 words. How about your letters?

**Directions** – Type four 1-minute writings. Try to raise your rate on each writing by 2 to 4 words by cutting out the pauses in your typing.

|  | | Words |
|---|---|---|
| DS | You can type this drill with ease. You can type this drill with | 13 |
| | ease if you cut out waste motions. You can type this drill with ease | 27 |
| 62 words<br>1.1 si | if you cut out waste motions and keep your eyes on the copy. You can | 41 |
| | type this drill with ease if you cut out waste motions, keep your eyes | 55 |
| | on the copy, and set a speed goal. | 62 |

---

## DIRECTIONS FOR TYPING FOOTNOTES

- *All important statements of fact or opinion and all direct quotations that are taken from books or articles for use in a theme must be acknowledged with a footnote. Footnotes give complete information about the references from which materials were taken.*

1. Footnotes are placed at the bottom of the page. Corresponding figures are included in the body of the report. These figures are placed one-half space above the line and at the end of a quotation or after the author's name or a statement of fact for which the source is given.

2. Although footnotes vary in length, in general, the following system works well for determining the placement of the footnotes: (a) roll the carriage down so that a 1-inch margin remains at the bottom of the page; (b) from this point, roll the carriage up 3 line spaces for each footnote on the page; (c) roll up one more space for a divider line—an underline which will be used to separate the last line of the report from the footnotes; (d) make a pencil mark at the point where the divider line will be typed.

3. After typing the last line of a full page of copy, space once; then use the underline key to type a 1½-inch divider line.

4. After typing the divider line, double-space; type the footnote reference.

5. Single-space the footnotes and place a double space between them.

6. In numbering footnotes, you may start with "1" on each page or number them consecutively throughout the report.

7. The following Latin terms are frequently used in footnote references:

   *Ibid.*, the abbreviation for *ibidem* (meaning in the same place), may be found in footnotes when the work referenced is the same as that in the immediately preceding footnote or is the same except for a different page number.

   *Op. cit.*, the abbreviation for *opere citato* (meaning in the work cited), may be used when there are intervening footnotes with the name of the author or authors and a new page number in a work previously cited.

   *Loc. cit.*, the abbreviation for *loco citato* (meaning in the same place), should be used in place of *op. cit.* when the repeated reference is to the exact page or passage of a work previously cited and there have been intervening footnotes. No page number follows *loc. cit.*

   *Et al.*, the abbreviation for *et alii* (meaning and others), is used to replace all but the first author's name when a book or article is written by three or more authors.

- *On a page only partially full, the footnotes appear at the bottom of the page.*

# Lesson 34 • *70-space line*

## 34a ■ Keyboard Review • Each line at least three times

5 minutes

Alphabetic SS Jeff Robac took quite extensive trips through Switzerland and Germany.

Difficult A few minutes ago, my aunts invited many hungry young pupils to lunch.

*Fingers curved; wrists low*

Figure-Symbol After October 29, Flight #834 will arrive in Los Angeles at 12:50 p.m.

Easy A good thing about the future is that it comes just one day at a time.

| 1 | 2 | 3 | 4 | 5 | 6 | 7 | 8 | 9 | 10 | 11 | 12 | 13 | 14 |

## 34b ■ Typing Titles of Books

5 minutes

Directions – Type each sentence twice. The first line gives the rule; the remaining lines apply it. Capitalize and punctuate the last sentence correctly.

1 SS The title of a book may be underlined or typed in all capital letters.

2 Jasper read the book, INNOVATIONS IN SPACE, before he wrote his paper.

*Type book titles correctly*

3 Treasure Island, David Copperfield, and The Road are on this new list.

4 mr case assigned the first chapter in the book the call of the wild

## 34c ■ Technique Builder—Flowing Rhythm Practice • Each line three times

5 minutes

Stroke SS Selected mnemonics can be used, but pseudo-operations are not allowed.

Word The thing that counts is not so much where I am, but where I am going.

*Strike and release keys quickly*

Word Work for the gift of using words that give some life to your thoughts.

Combination The mind gets rusty with disuse; you can keep it sharp with new ideas.

| 1 | 2 | 3 | 4 | 5 | 6 | 7 | 8 | 9 | 10 | 11 | 12 | 13 | 14 |

## 34d ■ Problem Typing

30 minutes

### Problem 1—Topic Outline of Directions for Writing a Book Review

Full sheet
60-space line
Reading position

Directions – 1. Type the main points at the left margin. Use tab stops for subpoints. Align Roman numerals at the period.
2. Indent, space, capitalize, and punctuate exactly as shown in the problem. Two spaces follow the period after all numbered or lettered divisions in an outline.
3. Do not type copy line for line, but listen for the bell in returning the carriage.

2 inches

DOCUMENTING SOURCES OF DATA

Triple-space ⟶

1 inch

Footnoting is a tool by which a writer acknowledges the          17

1½ inches ⟶ sources and gives complete information about the references          29

from which data were taken.  Giving credit where credit is          41

due is a common courtesy that is required at every level of          53

writing.  Conscientious writers always extend this courtesy          65

in their work.  Another reason for footnoting, according to          77

Robinson, is a desire to avoid possible legal problems con-          88

cerning copyright infringement.[1]          95

Generally, a direct quotation of four or more type-          105

written lines should be set off from the text of the report.          118

Lengthy quotations need not always be used in their entirety,          130

however.  If words or phrases are omitted, ellipses should          142

be used.  One explanation of ellipses states:          151

> Ellipses, frequently termed "omission marks,"          161
> are printed devices signifying the deletion of          170
> letters or words in quoted material.  Three marks          180

Quotation single-spaced
and indented ⟶
> or dots with intervening spaces (. . .) are used          190
> to signify an omission at the beginning of quoted          200
> discourse or at any other point where the omitted          210
> portion or section does not end on a period.  Four          220
> marks or dots (. . . .) are used when the omitted          230
> portion does end with a period.[2]          237

Single-space (for full page) ⟶
Double-space ⟶          241

[1]David M. Robinson, Writing Reports for Management De-          258
cisions (Columbus, Ohio:  Charles E. Merrill Publishing Co.,          272
1969), p. 313.          275

Double-space ⟶
[2]Robert Aurner and Morris P. Wolf, Effective Communi-          289
cation in Business (5th ed.; Cincinnati:  South-Western          304
Publishing Co., 1967), pp. 556-7.          310

1 inch

**First page of a manuscript**

# DIRECTIONS FOR WRITING A BOOK REVIEW

## I. ITEMS TO INCLUDE IN A BOOK REVIEW

A. Title and name of the author
B. Central theme of the book
C. Some of the important characters in the book
D. Setting for the story
E. Brief summary of some of the interesting incidents
F. Reviewer's comments and opinion of the book

## II. GUIDELINES TO FOLLOW IN WRITING A SYNOPSIS

A. Should interest the reader
B. Should give examples to support comments
C. Should be well written

## III. FORM REQUIREMENTS OF A BOOK REVIEW

A. Typed in regular theme style
B. Typed with copy single spaced throughout and double spaced between parts
C. Allowance for extra spaces in left margin for binding
D. Heading typed in off-centered position

### Problem 2—Typing a Book Review

**Directions** – Type the book review on the next page using regular theme style; type the heading 2 inches from the top. Single-space the copy, but double-space before and after capitalized headings and between paragraphs. As this book review is to be placed in a notebook, use 1½-inch left and 1-inch right margins.

- *For pica typewriters, the left margin should contain 15 horizontal spaces; the right margin, 10 horizontal spaces. For elite typewriters, the left margin should contain 18 horizontal spaces; the right margin, 12 horizontal spaces.*

*Because of the wider left margin, the center point will be 3 spaces to the right of the point normally used; this puts the heading in off-centered position.*

## ■ Lesson 35 • *70-space line*

### 35a ■ Keyboard Review • Each line at least three times

5 minutes

| Alphabetic SS | Clifford and Jan had a vexing quarrel about who should keep my zither. | |
| br | The bride's brother breathlessly briefed the bridegroom at the church. | Quick, sharp strokes |
| Figure-Symbol | The invoice of March 7 read: 300 pairs @ 21¢, 5% discount in 10 days. | |
| Easy | No one can buy tact at a price; you can get it only by working for it. | |

| 1 | 2 | 3 | 4 | 5 | 6 | 7 | 8 | 9 | 10 | 11 | 12 | 13 | 14 |

## 49d ■ Problem Typing

### Problem 1—Topic Outline

**Directions** – Set the margin stops for a 60-space line. Use a standard 2-inch top margin. The copy is set in problem form. Space and arrange the outline correctly.

## TYPING BOUND MANUSCRIPTS

### I. MARGINS

A. Left margin of 1½ inches
B. Right margin of 1 inch
C. Top margin of first page, 2 inches
D. Top margin of subsequent pages, 1 inch
   1. At least 2 lines of paragraph at bottom of page
   2. At least 2 lines of paragraph carried forward to new page

### II. SPACING

A. Double spacing of contents
B. Single spacing of quoted materials of 4 typewritten lines or more, footnotes, and bibliographical items
C. Triple spacing after the title

### III. PAGE NUMBERS

A. Centered ½ inch from bottom of first page
B. Aligned with right margin ½ inch (4th line space) from top for pages following the first

### IV. BIBLIOGRAPHY

A. References listed alphabetically
B. First line of each entry started at left margin; all succeeding lines indented 5 spaces

### V. FOOTNOTES

A. Underline of 1½ inches separates last line of report from footnote
B. Single spacing before division line, double spacing after
C. Placed at bottom of page when page is only partially full

### Problem 2—First Page of a Manuscript

**Directions** – The first page of a manuscript is illustrated on page 106. Type a copy of it.

• *The illustration was typed in pica type. Students using elite type machines should space 8 times between the last line of the report and the divider line.*

## ■ Lesson 50 • *70-space line*

### 50a ■ Keyboard Review • Each line at least three times

Alphabetic SS  Cedric Ripley kindly gave them the exquisite old jewelry for a bazaar.

Balanced and one hand  and we, and we saw, and we saw him, they saw, and they saw, she saw us

Figure  In 1903 this country was crossed for the first time by car in 65 days.

Easy  If you like to do a thing, you do it as well as it is in you to do it.

| 1 | 2 | 3 | 4 | 5 | 6 | 7 | 8 | 9 | 10 | 11 | 12 | 13 | 14 |

*Check your position at the typewriter*

### 50b ■ Timed Writings • Type a 5-minute writing on 46e, page 99. Circle errors. Take a 1-minute writing on any paragraph in which you had an error.

2 inches

BOOK REVIEW:   THE AGONY AND THE ECSTASY

Triple-space

## THE AUTHOR

Double-space

10

The author, Irving Stone, has written many books, including THEY ALSO RAN, LUST FOR LIFE, and LOVE IS ETERNAL.

Double-space

22

33

## THE STORY AND ITS SETTING

38

The story traces Michelangelo Buonarroti's career during the Sixteenth Century through all the years of his genius beginning with his boyhood apprenticeship in Florence through his assignment to design St. Peter's Basilica in Rome.

49
61
73
85

## INTERESTING INCIDENTS

89

After being denied admittance into the palace of Pope Julius II, Michelangelo left Rome and returned to his home in Florence.  Not until Pope Julius ventured north during one of the military bouts with the French did the artist agree to see the Pontiff.  Following an apology for the way he was treated, Buonarroti received the commission to paint the ceiling of the Sistine Chapel.  Michelangelo considered himself a sculptor and did not like to paint, but he said, "I'm going to paint those figures as though they could move right off that ceiling and come down to earth."

100
112
125
137
150
163
175
187
199
204

Michelangelo also displayed his boundless creativity in architecture.  After he was appointed architect of St. Peter's Basilica, he designed and redesigned the chapel to produce a magnificent edifice.  Before he died, he built a model of the dome which was to be the perfect blending of sculpture and architecture.  The creation had absolute balance and faultless lines, curves, and elegance.  His young helpers asked from where he had gotten the idea for the dome.  He replied that ". . . ideas are a natural function of the mind, as breathing is of the lungs.  Perhaps they come from God."

216
228
240
253
265
276
288
300
312
323

## COMMENTS

325

The reader can quickly recognize the great amount of work that went into the writing of this biographical novel.  More important to a sensitive reader, however, is the feeling of experiencing with Michelangelo the many disappointments and heartbreaks that entered the artist's life.

337
349
361
373
381

**Book review**

1   SS   if it is | if it is to go | if it is to go to us | and if it is go to the

2        if they | if they can | and if they can go | and if they can go with them          Type
                                                                                             rapidly
3        to go | to go with them | to go with them to the | and to go with them to          and
                                                                                             continuously
4        to do the | to do the work | to do the work for | to do the work for them

1   SS   This is a job they can do, and they can do it now if it is to be done.

2        They can go to the city to do this work if it is to be done there now.          Type with-
                                                                                         out pauses
3        As scarce as truth is, we seem to have more of it than we care to use.

4        The man who loses his head is probably the type who would not miss it.
         | 1 | 2 | 3 | 4 | 5 | 6 | 7 | 8 | 9 | 10 | 11 | 12 | 13 | 14 |

---

## DIRECTIONS FOR TYPING BOUND MANUSCRIPTS

● *The directions given here apply to typing theses, formal reports, and other manuscripts that are bound at the left. Use these directions in typing the reports and compositions that follow.*

1. Set margin stops for a 1½-inch left margin (pica, 15 spaces; elite, 18 spaces) and a 1-inch right margin (pica, 10 spaces; elite, 12 spaces).

   ● *As is illustrated on page vi, there are 10 spaces per inch on a pica typewriter and 12 spaces per inch on an elite type-writer. In setting the right margin, 5 to 8 spaces are added for the bell.*

   ● *Because of the wider left margin, the center point will be 3 spaces to the right of the point normally used.*

2. On all but the first page, leave a 1-inch top and bottom margin.

3. Type the title in all capital letters 2 inches from the top of the first page. Triple-space after the title.

4. The body of the report should be double-spaced. Paragraphs should be indented 5, 7, or 10 spaces uniformly throughout the report.

5. A long quotation (4 lines or more) should be single-spaced and indented 5 spaces from each margin; it should be preceded and followed by a double space. Footnotes and bibliographical items included in the report should also be single-spaced. Double spacing should be used between each footnote or bibliographical item.

6. Short quotations (fewer than four lines) should be typed within the text material and enclosed within quotation marks.

7. If the first page is numbered (the number on the first page may be omitted if the writer wishes), center the number ½-inch from the bottom. Subsequent pages are numbered ½-inch (4th line space) from the top of the page and aligned with the right margin. Triple-space after typing the page number to type the body of the report.

8. When typing a manuscript that consists of several pages, at least 2 lines of a paragraph must appear at the bottom of a page and at least 2 lines should be carried forward to a new page.

## 35b ■ Timed Writings

*10 minutes*

**Directions** – Type one 1-minute writing on 31e, page 64. Type two 3-minute writings; compute your *gwam*, and submit the better of the two longer writings.

## 35c ■ Problem Typing

*30 minutes*

### Problem 1—Minutes of a Meeting

**Directions** – Type a copy of the minutes that follow on a full sheet in the form illustrated at the right below. A 1½-inch left margin and a 1-inch right margin are used since minutes are usually placed in a binder.

• *Keep in mind that the center point will be 3 spaces to the right of the point usually used.*

• *The minutes of a meeting are an exact record of what happened at a meeting. There is no set form which is used by all clubs and organizations for recording minutes. The form recommended in this lesson is acceptable and widely used.*

MILL VALLEY BOOK CLUB

Minutes of Meeting

Date:       September 18, 197–
Time:       3:15 p.m.
Place:      Room 210, Mill Valley School
Present:    About 25 students were present in addition to the adviser, Mr. Jerry Dutra

1. Mary Ann Whyte, President, presided. She introduced the officers and our adviser.

2. The president outlined the goals of the club, and the requirements for membership.

3. Mr. Dutra stated that the Book Club raised enough money last year through operation of the copier in the library to buy 12 new books. He suggested that the club consider operating the copier again.

4. A motion to operate the copier to buy books for the library was passed unanimously.

5. The president asked members to list their free periods when they would be available to run the copier.

6. Renee Lindsay reported on The White Dawn by James Houston.

7. Frank Ruiz and Fran Garvey were asked to prepare reports for the next meeting.

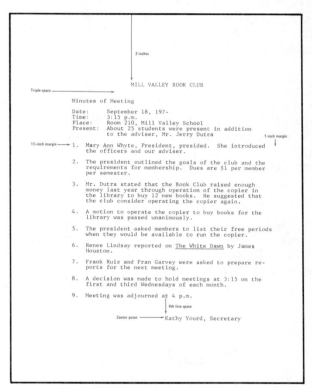

**Minutes of meeting**

8. A decision was made to hold meetings at 3:15 on the first and third Wednesdays of each month.

9. Meeting was adjourned at 4 p.m.

Kathy Yourd, Secretary

## THE BASIC PRINCIPLES OF EFFECTIVE DICTATION

Mr. Chairman, Members of the Conference:

Thank you for inviting me to share some thoughts with you on dictating letters. When one reads some of the letters going through the mails today, he's forced to conclude that we seem to be concerned only with making them as bad as possible. If that is our aim, we're succeeding.

I got a letter two or three days ago, for example, that begged me to "hasten the delay." An earlier letter from the manager of an ice cream store stated flatly that "his prices were the lowest in town and were in keeping with the quality of the ice cream he was selling." What an admission; I'm wondering if he's still in business!

The time has come for all dictators of letters to call a halt to the nonsense that goes into their letters and to do something about improving them. Can this be done? A lot of people working in this field believe that the job is possible. Let's take a look at some of their recommendations. Those I shall give you here have come from many sources.

One source that I've found useful is a booklet with the catchy name of CREATIVE COMMUNICATIONS, published by the Soundscriber Corporation. The authors of this booklet say that the purpose of letters is to inform accurately, persuade convincingly, or decline tactfully. The authors add that to gain these ends, one must be able to think logically and clearly about a subject. He must be able to transmit his thoughts to paper by a careful choice of words and phrases.

The job sounds simple enough. Why is it then that so many of us handle the job so poorly? Perhaps we need to be reminded from time to time that we're getting careless about the letters we dictate and that there are guides that, if followed, can help us do a better job. Let me spend the time that remains discussing with you four of these guides. They are as follows:

1. Be pleasant and natural; talk with your reader.

2. Be prompt in replying.

3. Plan the sequence of events in your letter.

4. Give your stenographer needed help.

### Be Pleasant and Natural; Talk with Your Reader

Don't preach when you dictate. Talk with your reader as if he were in the room with you. Try to anticipate his questions. Answer them in a friendly, natural style. Let your personality shine through. Make your expressions lively, vivid, vigorous, and sincere. Be a wholesome nonconformist instead of a stereotype.

---

## ■ Lesson 49 • *70-space line*

### 49a ■ Keyboard Review • Each line at least three times

*5 minutes*

Alphabetic DS  Felix Z. Marques had jewelry, perfume, book covers, and a leather bag.

One hand  Are you aware of the few errors in my contract that must be corrected?

Figure-Symbol  The Stegosaurus (weight up to 6½ tons) had a brain weighing 2½ ounces.

Easy  We believe that he who falls in love with himself will have no rivals.

| 1 | 2 | 3 | 4 | 5 | 6 | 7 | 8 | 9 | 10 | 11 | 12 | 13 | 14 |

Cut out waste movements

## Problem 2—Typing Notice and Agenda of Meeting

Full sheet
50-space line
2-inch top margin

**Directions – 1.** Type the notice and agenda of a meeting from the copy below. Follow the form used in the illustration.

**2.** Items in the third line are to be typed at the left and right margins of the 50-space line.

MILL VALLEY BOOK CLUB

Notice of the First Meeting

September 18, 197–                    3:15 p.m.

Room 210, Mill Valley School

AGENDA

1. Introduction of officers and adviser

2. Discussion of goals for the forthcoming year

3. Discussion of plan to raise money for the purchase of new books

4. Book report by Renee Lindsay

5. Assignment of reports for the next meeting

6. Decision of dates and time of meetings

7. Adjournment

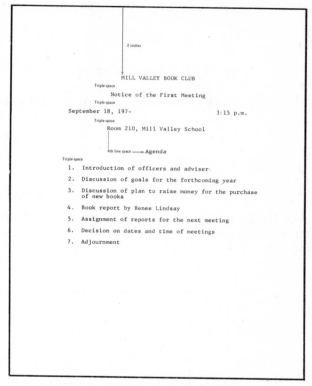

**Notice and agenda of meeting**

## 35d ■ Extra-Credit Typing

**Problem 1** – Type the paragraphs in 31e, page 64, as a one-page report. Follow the guides for typing reports stressed in this unit. Supply an **appropriate** title for the paper.

**Problem 2** – Prepare the manuscript of a short article from a current magazine. Type your paper in report form, following the guides stressed in this unit.

**Problem 3** – Type the review of a book you have read recently. Use the form suggested and used on pages 72 and 73.

**Problem 4** – Type the easy sentences in the keyboard reviews of this unit five times each.

**Problem 5** – Take notes on a lecture or discussion held in one of your classes. Follow the directions given in the outline on page 69 for recording your notes. Type the notes in notebook form as illustrated on page 70.

**Problem 6** – Prepare and type a sentence outline on the notes on writing interesting, forceful letters on page 70. Type the outline on a full sheet; 60-space line; 2-inch top margin.

**Problem 7** – Compose and type in regular report form a short report on writing interesting, forceful letters. Get ideas from page 70, but use your own words.

## 48c ■ Concentration Practice

**Directions** – Type three times for control; think as you type.　　　**Technique Goal** – Work for accuracy.

Words

DS　　　A Hall of Fame for Great Americans was set up at New York Univer-　　13

sity in 1900 to praise famous folks of the United States. Nominations　　27

**70 words**
**1.4 si**　　are to be made by the public. Elections are to be held once every five　　42

years. Each nominee must have a majority of the votes from a college　　56

of electors––a group of eminent people that come from all of the states.　　70

| 1 | 2 | 3 | 4 | 5 | 6 | 7 | 8 | 9 | 10 | 11 | 12 | 13 | 14 |

## 48d ■ Problem Typing

### Problem 1—Speech Notes

**Directions** – 1. Type the heading on the card about three spaces from the top and three spaces from the left edge. Use the spacing shown in the illustration.

2. Notes to be used in giving a speech are usually typed on 6- by 4-inch card stock. If cards are not available, use paper cut to this size.

| | |
|---|---|
| Subject | The Basic Principles of Effective Dictation |
| Purpose | The purpose of letters is to inform accurately, persuade convincingly, or decline tactfully. |
| Major points | Four guides to improved dictation: |
| Subtopics | 1. Be pleasant and natural; talk with your reader. |
| | 2. Be prompt in replying. |
| | 3. Plan the sequence of events in your letter. |
| | 4. Give your stenographer needed help. |
| Conclusions | Dictating combines a number of skills. Improvement comes from attention to these skills in day-to-day practice. |

**Card containing speech notes**

### Problem 2—Manuscript of Speech (First Two or Three Pages)

**Directions** – Type the speech on page 103 in unbound report form, but triple-space the body of the talk. Unbound manuscript form is described on page 62.

● *Directions for typing subsequent pages of a manuscript are given on page 104 under "Directions for Typing Bound Manuscripts."*

# Unit 6 ■

## Typing Personal Notes and Letters

### General Directions ■ Lessons 36-45

Except as otherwise directed, use a 70-space line. Single-space lines of words and sentences, but double-space between repeated groups of lines. Double-space paragraph copy.

• *Your teacher will tell you whether or not to erase and correct errors on problem typing.*

## ■ Lesson 36 • *70-space line*

### 36a ■ Keyboard Review • Each line at least three times                    *5 minutes*

Alphabetic SS  Our amazed executive, Fay Quinn, kept our good will by the adjustment.

One hand  Fred Reader agreed that the wages we pay are in excess of the average.

Figure  1 and 2 and 3 and 4 and 5 and 6 and 7 and 8 and 9 and 10 and 11 and 12

Feet on floor

Easy  Thus, he will not get very far until he learns how to make time count.

| 1 | 2 | 3 | 4 | 5 | 6 | 7 | 8 | 9 | 10 | 11 | 12 | 13 | 14 |

### 36b ■ Technique Builder—Carriage Return and Tabulator Control          *10 minutes*

**Directions – 1.** Clear the tabulator rack as directed on page vii.
**2.** Check to see that the margin stops are set for a 70-space line.
**3.** Type the first column at the left margin.

**4.** Set the first tab stop for the second column 30 spaces from the left margin. Set the second tab stop 30 spaces from the first one.
**5.** Type the list of words once. Type across the page. Repeat if time permits.

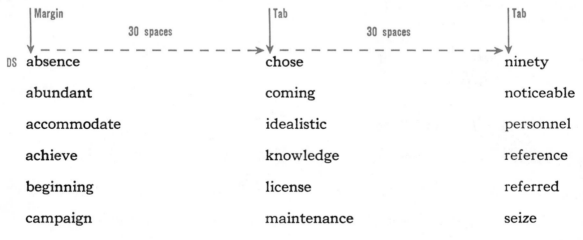

| Margin | Tab | Tab |
| --- | --- | --- |
| 30 spaces | 30 spaces | |
| absence | chose | ninety |
| abundant | coming | noticeable |
| accommodate | idealistic | personnel |
| achieve | knowledge | reference |
| beginning | license | referred |
| campaign | maintenance | seize |

### 36c ■ Aligning Practice                                                   *5 minutes*

**Directions – 1.** Using the underscore, type a 4-inch line. Remove the paper; reinsert it. Type today's date on the line. **2.** Space up; type your name. Remove the paper; reinsert it. Retype your name over the first typing.

## Problem 2—Postal Card Announcement

**Directions – 1.** Center the first, third, and last lines horizontally. Type the items in the second and fourth lines at the margins. **2.** Address the card to yourself.

- *To type items on the second and fourth lines at the right margin, backspace once from the margin for every letter and space in the items, except the last one.*

48-space line
Double-space
Center vertically

### IMPORTANT NOTICE TO COMPUTER CLUB

Computers in Space          Extraordinary Program

Film and Talk by Noted Authority

3:30 p.m.                    March 7

Conference Room, Royce Hall

## Problem 3—Poem Typed on 5½- by 8½-inch Paper

**Directions – 1.** Type the poem on 5½- by 8½-inch paper with the long edge inserted at the left.

**2.** Spread the heading. Triple-space following the heading and double-space the lines of the poem.

**3.** Center the poem vertically on the page in *reading position*. Center the poem horizontally according to the longest line.

- *In typing spread headings, space once between letters and three times between words.*

- *To center a spread heading, backspace once for each letter, except the last one in the line, and once for each space between words.*

### NOT IN VAIN

If I can stop one heart from breaking,

I shall not live in vain;

If I can ease one life the aching,

Or cool one pain,

Or help one fainting robin

Unto his nest again,

I shall not live in vain.

—Emily Dickinson

## ■ Lesson 48 • *70-space line*

### 48a ■ Keyboard Review • Each line three times

*5 minutes*

Alphabetic SS  Viewed by many as lazy speech, excessive jargon shows lack of quality.

One hand  Afterward, we were aware that a few pupils exaggerated test averages.

Figure-Symbol  Founded in 1939, baseball's "Little League" was for boys from 9 to 12.

Easy  In life, everyone should learn how to do as well as how to do without.

Instant release

| 1 | 2 | 3 | 4 | 5 | 6 | 7 | 8 | 9 | 10 | 11 | 12 | 13 | 14 |

### 48b ■ Skill Comparison • Type a 1-minute writing on each sentence in 48a above. Compare the gwam.

*5 minutes*

## 36d ■ Spelling and Proofreading Aids • Each line twice

5 minutes

1  SS  athlete appearance argument apologize altogether huge dormitory across

2  eighth wholly truly unparalleled roommate optimist conscience received

3  similar suing seize safety transferable usage weird forcible miniature

4  irrelevant loneliness laboratory noticeable noticing tragedy surprised

Learn to spell as you type

## 36e ■ Paragraph Guided Writings • As directed in 26c, page 52

20 minutes

• Contains all letters

|  |  | GWAM |
|--|--|--|
|  |  | 1'  3' |

¶1
44 words
1.3 si
DS    Some men are more able than others. This difference forms the — 13  4 52
basis for some of the most puzzling questions facing our country. Here — 27  9 57
is one of them. Should a good worker or a poor one set the standard? — 41 14 62
Think it over. — 44 15 63

¶2
48 words
1.3 si
In golf, should Ben Hogan or passable Joe Doakes set par for the — 13 19 67
course? In medicine, should an able physician or a bad one lead the — 27 24 72
way? In the office, should an incompetent typist or one that can turn — 41 28 76
out a readable letter set the pace? — 48 31 79

¶3
52 words
1.3 si
There is but one right answer to these questions. For the good of — 13 35 83
golf, medicine, business, or anything else you can name, our standards — 28 40 88
should be set by the Hogans, the Salks, the Fords, and the others who — 42 45 93
excel. Only then can some worthwhile gains be made. — 52 48 96

1' | 1 | 2 | 3 | 4 | 5 | 6 | 7 | 8 | 9 | 10 | 11 | 12 | 13 | 14 |
3' | 1 | 2 | 3 | 4 | 5 |

# ■ Lesson 37 • 70-space line

## 37a ■ Keyboard Review • Each line at least three times

5 minutes

Alphabetic SS  The lazy fox was very quick to get away before the dogs jumped on him.

Hyphen  He read a 15-page brochure on the use of large-scale computer systems.

Figures  Last Friday, June 28, I arrived in New York on Flight 317 at 4:50 p.m.

Easy  The quickest way to gain goals you seek is to help others gain theirs.

| 1 | 2 | 3 | 4 | 5 | 6 | 7 | 8 | 9 | 10 | 11 | 12 | 13 | 14 |

Sit erect

## ▪ Lesson 47 ▪ *70-space line*

### 47a ▪ Keyboard Review • Each line at least three times for all lessons in this unit.

5 minutes

Alphabetic SS James Zier expected to fly to Quebec for a short visit with Ken Grace.

Shift key The American inventor, Thomas A. Edison, was the Wizard of Menlo Park.

Figure-Symbol The film grossed a total of $134,508 this week in only three theaters.

Easy The report says that a good leader can put himself in another's place.

| 1 | 2 | 3 | 4 | 5 | 6 | 7 | 8 | 9 | 10 | 11 | 12 | 13 | 14 |

*Reach with your fingers*

### 47b ▪ Creative Typing

10 minutes

**Directions – 1.** Type the following quotation; then expand it into a short report. In your report explain what you think this quotation means and how it could be applied to the development of typewriting skills.

2. Compose, revise, and retype. Give your report a title. Prepare your final copy in manuscript form: 60-space line, pica, 70-space line, elite; double spacing; heading on the 13th line space from the top.

A habit cannot be tossed out the window; it must be coaxed down the stairs a step at a time.––Mark Twain

---

#### FINDING THE CENTER POINT OF ODD-SIZE PAPER OR CARDS

• *In order to center headings on paper or cards of different sizes, you must learn how to find the center point of these papers or cards.*

**Step 1** – Insert paper or card into the machine.
**Step 2** – Add the numbers on the cylinder scale at the left and right edges of the paper or card.

**Step 3** – Divide the sum obtained in Step 2 by 2. The resulting figure gives you the horizontal center point of the paper or card.

---

### 47c ▪ Problem Typing

30 minutes

#### Problem 1—Postal Card Announcement

**Directions – 1.** Use a postal card or paper cut to the size of a 5½- by 3¼-inch card. Insert the card, short side at the left.

2. Center the announcement vertically and each line horizontally. Use double spacing.

3. Address the card to Mrs. Marilyn Rabinovitch / 19172 Boswell Court / Chicago, Illinois 60638

• *Postal card addresses are illustrated on page 96.*

• *For horizontal centering of headings, refer to the directions above for finding the center point of odd-size paper or cards. For vertical centering of the announcement, note that there are 20 vertical line spaces on the card. Subtract the lines needed for the announcement from 20; divide by 2 to find the number of line spaces in the top and bottom margins.*

```
 1
 2
 3
 4          The Chicago Chapter
 5
 6                  of
 7
 8   The Administrative Management Society
 9
10              presents
11
12         DR. FREDERICK MCNUTT
13
14    Monday, December 15, 197-, 7 p.m.
15
16  "CHANGING NEEDS IN ADMINISTRATIVE SERVICES"
17
18
19
20
```

**Centered postal card announcement**

## 37b ■ Typing from Dictation and Spelling Checkup

*5 minutes*

**Directions** – Your teacher will dictate the words in 36d, page 77. Type the words from dictation. Check for correct spelling. Retype any words in which you made an error.

## 37c ■ Paragraph Guided Writings ●

Set a goal for a 1-minute writing. Type four 1-minute writings. Try to type your goal word just as time is called. Type no faster or slower than the goal you select.

*5 minutes*

DS    In the business world, you will find that the best possible lever
      ·           4          ·           8          ·          12

**50 words** for getting a better job or salary raise is the ability to speak and
**1.3 si**    ·    16         ·    20          ·    24

Type at a
controlled
rate

write with clarity and force. It should be comforting to you to learn
  ·    28         ·    32          ·    36          ·    40

that you can acquire these skills in school.
  ·    44         ·    48

## 37d ■ Problem Typing

*30 minutes*

### Problem 1—Personal Note

Half sheet
50-space line
Open punctuation

**Directions** – Type a copy of the personal note that follows. Use the spacing directions given on the note. The date is typed on the 7th line space in half-page personal notes.

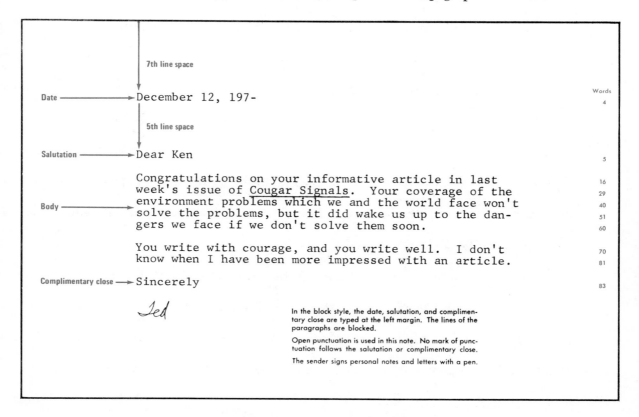

|  |  | Words |
| --- | --- | --- |
| **7th line space** | | |
| Date → December 12, 197- | | 4 |
| **5th line space** | | |
| Salutation → Dear Ken | | 5 |
| Body → Congratulations on your informative article in last | | 16 |
| week's issue of Cougar Signals. Your coverage of the | | 29 |
| environment problems which we and the world face won't | | 40 |
| solve the problems, but it did wake us up to the dan- | | 51 |
| gers we face if we don't solve them soon. | | 60 |
| You write with courage, and you write well. I don't | | 70 |
| know when I have been more impressed with an article. | | 81 |
| Complimentary close → Sincerely | | 83 |
| *Ted* | | |

In the block style, the date, salutation, and complimentary close are typed at the left margin. The lines of the paragraphs are blocked.

Open punctuation is used in this note. No mark of punctuation follows the salutation or complimentary close.

The sender signs personal notes and letters with a pen.

**Personal note in block style**

## 46e ■ Skill Building

**Directions – 1.** Type a 5-minute writing. Circle the errors; note your *gwam*.

**2.** Type a 1-minute writing on each paragraph. Try to add 10 words to your 5-minute *gwam* on each one.

**3.** Type another 5-minute writing. Circle the errors and figure your *gwam*.

**4.** Compare your *gwam* and your number of errors on the two 5-minute writings.

● Contains all letters

**GWAM**
3'  5'

¶1
60 words
1.3 si

Many types of credit exist to help you buy goods you otherwise could not buy; the cheapest way to buy a costly item, however, is to pay for it with your own cash. If you borrow money or if you buy on credit, the cost of the product to you will include the interest on the loan or the credit service.

4  3  51
8  5  53
13  8  56
18  11  59
20  12  60

¶2
60 words
1.3 si

Before you can use your funds in the best way possible, you must be aware of all facts. Receive full value for the dollar you spend when you choose your goods by thinking of the maxim which states: Yesterday is a canceled check, tomorrow is a promissory note, but today is cash, so spend it wisely.

24  15  63
29  17  65
33  20  68
38  23  71
40  24  72

¶3
60 words
1.3 si

The average American has more and better goods and services than a man in any other nation. At times, though, the former sets his sights on raising his standard of living and forgets the people who live near him. Keep in mind that when a man is wrapped up in himself, he makes quite a small parcel.

44  27  75
49  29  77
53  32  80
58  35  83
60  36  84

¶4
60 words
1.3 si

Scientists point out that some of the goods that will be used in the years to come are yet to be produced. Today, as well as tomorrow, you should try to utilize one of your most precious resources––your generous spirit. Do not let the advances of the era blind you to the joy of doing a kindly act.

64  39  87
69  41  89
74  44  92
78  47  95
80  48  96

3' | 1 | 2 | 3 | 4 | 5 |
5' | 1 | 2 | 3 |

## Problem 2—Personal Note in Block Style

Half sheet
60-space line
Open punctuation
Sign your name

**Directions** – Type the personal note below. Type today's date in the proper place. Type the salutation on the 3d line space from the date.

- *Three words are counted for today's date, although the date used may have more or fewer than 15 strokes.*

Words

*Today's date* — 3

↓ 3d line space

Dear Michael — 6

A number of the fellows are planning to write letters to our — 18
principal, Mr. Hugh Bail, about keeping the gymnasium open — 30
on Saturdays, 10 a.m. to 12 noon. There are several reasons — 42
for adopting this practice. — 48

Our city provides limited facilities for playing basketball — 60
and other games. Moreover, the enthusiasm and teamwork devel- — 72
oped through sports has a desirable carryover to school work. — 85

Can we count on you to write a letter to Mr. Bail. — 95

Sincerely — 97

## Problem 3—Personal Note in Block Style

Half sheet
50-space line
Open punctuation

**Directions** – Type the personal note below. Use today's date and your signature. Type salutation on the 4th line space from date.

- *The problems are not set line for line the way you will type them. Set margin stops properly. Return carriage with the bell.*

Dear Van / When I saw you last fall you told me about a book you had read on computers. I believe that you said it was written in plain, nontechnical language understandable by the layman.

(¶) Will you please send me the title of this book and the name of its author. I am preparing a short talk on computers, and the book you mentioned strikes me as being ideal for this purpose. / Sincerely

## ■ Lesson 38 • *70-space line*

### 38a ■ Keyboard Review • Each line at least three times

5 *minutes*

Alphabetic SS The ski jumper talked quickly over the breezeway while fixing my pole.

br Breaking abruptly from the brush, Brad's brash brother was breathless.

Figure-Symbol Ned paid $8.72, plus 4% tax, for the books; John paid $6.95, plus tax.

Easy He knows that no problem is so hard to handle that it lacks an answer.

| 1 | 2 | 3 | 4 | 5 | 6 | 7 | 8 | 9 | 10 | 11 | 12 | 13 | 14 |

Eyes on copy

## 46b ■ Paragraph Skill Builder

*5 minutes*

**Directions** – Type four 1-minute writings. Try to raise your rate
on each writing by 2 to 4 words.

DS      To be a good conversationalist, learn to listen with care to what

the other fellow is saying. Most of us think so hard about what we

**62 words**
**1.3 si**      plan to say that we don't hear him. If you pay close attention to

what others say, they will return the favor when you speak. This is

the first rule of the art of conversing.

Type
without
pauses

## 46c ■ Sentence Guided Writings

*5 minutes*

**Directions** – 1. Type each sentence for one minute.
Try typing each one as the guides are called.

2. Your teacher will call the return of the carriage
every 12 or 15 seconds as a guide.

• *The rates at which you will be typing are given in the columns at the right.*

| | | | GWAM 15" | 12" |
|---|---|---|---|---|
| 1 | SS | Your ballot is stronger than the bullet. | 32 | 40 |
| 2 | | Behind every argument is someone's ignorance. | 36 | 45 |
| 3 | | One cannot let yesterday use up too much of today. | 40 | 50 |
| 4 | | By changing the way one thinks, he can change his life. | 44 | 55 |
| 5 | | The less some men think about a problem, the more they talk. | 48 | 60 |
| 6 | | For some, tomorrow is the best labor-saving device ever invented. | 52 | 65 |
| 7 | | Charm is the glow within one that casts a favorable light over others. | 56 | 70 |

| 1 | 2 | 3 | 4 | 5 | 6 | 7 | 8 | 9 | 10 | 11 | 12 | 13 | 14 |

## 46d ■ Typing Titles of Articles

*10 minutes*

**Directions** – Type each sentence three times. The first line gives the rule. The
remaining lines apply it. Capitalize and punctuate the last sentence correctly.

1      SS   As a rule, the titles of articles should be placed in quotation marks.

2           "New Ways to Finance a College Education" is an article you must read.

3           We found "A Pelican Called Peter" an interesting and humorous article.

4           some of the ideas for my report came from the coming crisis in gold.

Quick, sure
reach to the
shift key

| 1 | 2 | 3 | 4 | 5 | 6 | 7 | 8 | 9 | 10 | 11 | 12 | 13 | 14 |

## 38b ■ Sentence Guided Writings

10 minutes

**Directions** – Type each sentence as a 1-minute writing with the throw of the carriage called each 15 or 20 seconds.

**Technique Goals** – Do not hesitate; throw the carriage with the call and begin typing at once. Keep your eyes on the copy.

| | | Words in Line | GWAM 20" Guide | GWAM 15" Guide |
|---|---|---|---|---|
| 1 | DS They must read to stay in the race. | 7 | 21 | 28 |
| 2 | The ideas you do not use, you will lose. | 8 | 24 | 32 |
| 3 | Read and digest something of value every day. | 9 | 27 | 36 |
| 4 | Time was invented in order to give ideas a chance. | 10 | 30 | 40 |
| 5 | By changing the way one thinks, he can change his life. | 11 | 33 | 44 |
| 6 | Change requires one to trade in his old habits for new ones. | 12 | 36 | 48 |
| 7 | For some, tomorrow is the best labor-saving device ever invented. | 13 | 39 | 52 |
| 8 | All smart men make a mistake now and then; dull ones keep making them. | 14 | 42 | 56 |

| 1 | 2 | 3 | 4 | 5 | 6 | 7 | 8 | 9 | 10 | 11 | 12 | 13 | 14 |

## 38c ■ Problem Typing

30 minutes

### Problem 1—Personal Note in Modified Block Style

Half sheet
60-space line
Open punctuation
Blocked paragraphs

**Directions** – Type the personal note that follows. The dateline and complimentary close start at the center point of the paper. Type the salutation on the 4th line space from the date.

November 28, 197–

Dear Chuck

Congratulations on your election to the presidency of the University Club. You have an outstanding reputation as a leader, speaker, and writer. I am sure that the Club will flourish under your inspired direction.

Best wishes to you and the other officers of the Club. I am looking forward to an eventful and worthwhile year. While my job requires me to make frequent trips out of the city, I hope to attend most of our meetings.

Sincerely

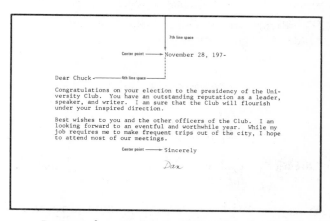

**Personal note in modified block style**

● *In modified block style, the dateline and complimentary close start at the center point of the paper. Paragraphs may be blocked or indented 5 spaces.*

# Part 3 ■

# Applying Typewriting Skills

**Problems** – In Part 3 of this book, you will learn how to organize and type speech notes, manuscripts of articles and reports, a variety of statistical reports and tables, business letters and interoffice memorandums. Studies show that the problems which are included in this cycle are commonly encountered in one's personal and professional typing. Interestingly enough, however, these problems will also give you an opportunity to sample some of the vocational applications of the typewriter.

**Extra-Credit Assignments** – Problems are given at the end of each unit for students who finish assignments ahead of schedule.

**Improving Your Basic Skills** – By this time you have acquired considerable speed and control. Increases in speed do not come as rapidly now as they did early in the course. The drills and timed writings in this cycle will put the finishing touches on your typewriting skill.

# Unit 7 ■

# Typing Manuscripts and Reports

## General Directions ■ Lessons 46-55

**Line Length** – Use a 70-space line for drills and timed writings. Much of the problem copy that you will type will be set in lines either longer or shorter than those for which your margins are set. Therefore, it will be necessary for you to listen for the bell, to use the right margin release, and to divide long words coming at the ends of lines.

**Identifying Papers** – Your teacher will tell you how to identify your papers.

**Spacing** – Single-space sentences and drill lines. Double-space between repeated groups of lines and double-space paragraph copy. Space problem copy as directed for each problem.

**Erasing** – Your teacher will tell you if you are to erase and correct errors made on problem copy.

**Margin Stop Reminder** – Set the right margin stop 5 to 8 spaces beyond the desired right margin.

## ■ Lesson 46

### 46a ■ Keyboard Review

*5 minutes*

**Directions** – Type each line at least three times for all lessons in this unit.

Alphabetic SS  Vincent Jacques expected to make weekly flights to Zambia in December.

awa  I was aware that I must awaken and remain awake to receive that award.  *Fingers deeply curved*

Figure  On December 17, 1903, Orville Wright flew his airplane for 12 seconds.

Easy  You may observe that the less some students think, the more they talk.

| 1 | 2 | 3 | 4 | 5 | 6 | 7 | 8 | 9 | 10 | 11 | 12 | 13 | 14 |

# Problem 2—Personal Note in Modified Block Style

Half sheet
60-space line
Open punctuation
Indented ¶'s

**Directions** – Type the personal note that follows in modified block style.
Type the salutation on the 4th line space from the date.

Words

Center point ⟶ April 5, 197–

3

Dear Don

5

    Funds will be collected from students in all 4th period
classes next Friday, April 15, to support the summer camp for
children from low-income homes.

16
28
35

    The Student Council has asked me to get some students to
help make the collections. We should collect enough money to
send several boys and girls to summer camp. I hope you will
be willing to help. Call me at 418-8983 to let me know if we
can count on you.

46
59
71
83
87

Center point ⟶ Sincerely

89

## Problem 3—Personal Note Typed Lengthwise on 5½- by 8½-inch Paper

**Directions** – 1. Type the note in Problem 2 on 5½- by 8½-inch paper inserted lengthwise. This note is shown at the right.

2. Use a 40-space line. It will give you left and right margins of about one inch on both pica and elite machines.

3. Type the date at the center point of the paper on the 10th line space from the top.

   • *To find the horizontal center of the paper, fold it to bring left and right edges together; crease very lightly at the top.*

4. Type the salutation on the 7th line space from the date.

5. Start the complimentary close at the center point of the paper.

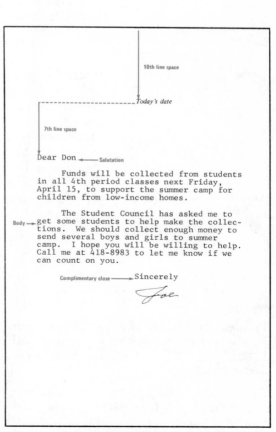

**Note typed lengthwise**

## Problem 2—Addressing a Postal Card

**Directions** – 1. Type the return address and address on the card typed in Problem 1.
2. Type the return address on Line 2 from the top and 3 spaces from the left edge.
3. Type the address about 2 inches from the top and 2 inches from the left edge. Use block style and single spacing for all addresses. The city and state names and ZIP Code must be typed on one line in that order.

- *ZIP Code numbers are typed 2 spaces after the state name.*

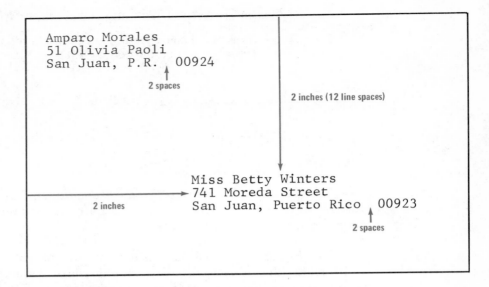

Amparo Morales
51 Olivia Paoli
San Juan, P.R.  00924

2 spaces

2 inches (12 line spaces)

Miss Betty Winters
741 Moreda Street
San Juan, Puerto Rico  00923

2 inches

2 spaces

**Postal card address**

## Problem 3—Postal Card Message

Postal card
48-space line
Open punctuation
Blocked ¶'s

**Directions** – Type as shown in the illustration on page 95. Use single spacing and today's date. Address the card to *your name, street address, city, state, and ZIP Code.* Return address: Alice Sue / 4103 Darlene Way / Honolulu, Hawaii  96821.

Dear (*Your name*)

I am selling unusually nice greeting cards for special occasions. The cards are colorful and appropriate. All profits from the sale of these cards will be sent to the Orphans Relief Fund, Honolulu.

If you are interested in seeing the cards, please call for an appointment:  348-7112.

Alice Sue

## 45d ■ Extra-Credit Typing

**Problem 1** – Prepare and type a topic outline on the points to keep in mind in typing personal business letters, page 83. Use a full sheet, 60-space line, and a 2-inch top margin.

**Problem 2** – Write a letter to the Chamber of Commerce, Santa Fe, New Mexico, requesting information for a paper you are writing on interesting cities in the United States. Type the letter in block style, open punctuation.

**Problem 3** – Type a postal card asking for the same information requested in Problem 2.

**Problem 4** – Assume that you are Albert Ariola. Compose and type a letter in response to the one in Problem 3, page 90. Address the letter to your own name and address. Provide the information requested. Type the letter in modified block style, mixed punctuation, and indented paragraphs. Prepare a carbon copy; address an envelope.

## ■ Lesson 39 • *70-space line*

### 39a ■ Keyboard Review • Each line at least three times

5 minutes

Alphabetic SS Felicitous verbalizing expresses quite kindly just how a man may feel.

Double letters Nell Brooks will sell her zoology books to Hedda Mann of Fayetteville.

Figure-Symbol Omit the decimal point and zeros in the following: $386, $9,205, $47.

Easy He has often said that the brighter we are, the more we have to learn.

| 1 | 2 | 3 | 4 | 5 | 6 | 7 | 8 | 9 | 10 | 11 | 12 | 13 | 14 |

*Think as you type*

### 39b ■ Technique Builder—Stroking • Each line three times

5 minutes

One hand SS refer you | saw him | we saw | look upon | as you were | my grade | dress up

Balanced hand they did | with them | and the | and then | and they did | if she | for them

Combination and look | the case | for only | for him | did look | she saw him | see them

Combination and the joy | she did jump | and did regard | to hop | to see him | for you

*Work for flowing rhythm*

### 39c ■ Paragraph Guided Writings

5 minutes

Directions – Set a goal for a 1-minute writing. Type four 1-minute writings. Try to type your goal word just as time is called. Type no faster or slower than the goal you select.

DS Each letter you write is a character sketch. Test this statement
the next time you read a letter. See if you don't get a mental picture

54 words
1.3 si
of the writer. A clear letter reflects a sharp, clear thinker. A
garbled letter, on the other hand, reflects a fuzzy, unsure mind.

*Control your rate*

### 39d ■ Skill Comparison • Type a 1-minute writing on each sentence. Compare gwam rates on the four writings.

5 minutes

1 SS A leader does his part and a little more to make sure that he is fair.

2 Vatican City (108.7 acres) is the world's smallest political division.

3 We should keep in mind that courtesy may back fire if it is not true.

4 We know, however that a straw vote shows which way the hot air blows.

| 1 | 2 | 3 | 4 | 5 | 6 | 7 | 8 | 9 | 10 | 11 | 12 | 13 | 14 |

*Speed with control*

## ■ Lesson 45 • *70-space line*

### 45a ■ Keyboard Review • Each line at least three times

5 minutes

Alphabetic SS  Jack Gillway expected to visit the old Burt Quill farm in Switzerland.

Long reach  My brother, Myron, brought the extra funds Guy needed to pay the debt.

Figure-Symbol  I raised $15,679 between May 23 and 31—a 48% increase over last year.

Easy  Any man, as a rule, shows what he is by what he does with what he has.

| | 1 | 2 | 3 | 4 | 5 | 6 | 7 | 8 | 9 | 10 | 11 | 12 | 13 | 14 |

*Type with purpose*

### 45b ■ Timed Writings

*15 minutes*

Directions – Type two 5-minute writings on 41b, page 87. Compute *gwam*; circle errors. Submit the better writing.

### 45c ■ Problem Typing

*25 minutes*

• *Personal as well as business messages are often typed on postal cards. The two problems in this lesson will give you experience in typing postal card messages.*

Postal card
48-space line
Open punctuation
Blocked ¶'s

• *Use paper cut to postal card size (5½ by 3¼ inches) if cards are not available.*

• *A postal card address is illustrated on page 96.*

**Problem 1—Postal Card Message**

Directions – 1. Type the postal card that follows, using single spacing and the directions given on the illustration.

2. Address the card to Miss Betty Winters / 741 Moreda Street / San Juan, Puerto Rico   00923

```
1
2                          Triple-space
3   Center point ─────────────► December 3, 197-
4
5                          Triple-space
6   Dear Miss Winters
7                          Double-space
8   The next meeting of the Membership Committee of
9   the San Juan Historical Society will be held on
10  Wednesday, December 10, at 7 p.m., in the San
11  Juan City Library.
12
13  Preparation of the annual report of the Committee
14  will be discussed, and the addition of new items
15  to the museum will be examined.
16
17                          Triple-space
18  Center point ─────────────► Amparo Morales, Secretary
19
20
```

**Postal card in modified block style**

**Card holders**

• *When you insert the card into your typewriter, adjust the card holders, as shown above, and use the paper bail to keep the card from slipping.*

## TYPING PERSONAL BUSINESS LETTERS

* *The most commonly used form for a personal business letter is illustrated on page 84. The typewritten name of the sender below the complimentary close is optional.*

**Step 1** – Set the machine for single spacing for all except very short letters.

**Step 2** – Set the margins. (The margins vary according to the length of the letter.)

**Step 3** – Start typing the return address on the 10th line space. For a modified block style letter, start the return address at the center point of the paper. For a block style letter, position the return address at the left margin.

**Step 4** – Space down for the address. (The number of lines varies with the letter size. The longer the letter, the fewer the number of spaces.)

**Step 5** – Type the salutation a double space below the address.

**Step 6** – Start the body a double space below the salutation.

**Step 7** – Type the complimentary close a double space below the body. For a modified block style letter, start at the center point. For a block style letter, type it at the left margin.

**Step 8** – Type the name of the writer on the 4th line space from the complimentary close.

### 39e ■ Problem Typing

*25 minutes*

#### Problem 1—Personal Business Letter in Modified Block Style

Full sheet
50-space line
Open punctuation

**Directions** – Type the letter on the next page. Follow the directions given for typing personal business letters. Type the address on the 8th line space from the date.

* *ZIP Code numbers are typed two spaces after the state name or abbreviation.*

#### Problem 2—Modified Block Style with Paragraph Indentions

Full sheet
50-space line
Open punctuation

**Directions** – Type the letter in Problem 1 again. Use today's date in the return address. Indent the first line of each paragraph 5 spaces.

## ■ Lesson 40 • *70-space line*

### 40a ■ Keyboard Review • Each line at least three times

*5 minutes*

Alphabetic   SS   Becky Mallard expects to quiz Vince Wolfe about the jade gem he found.

Quiet hands   Lack of poise, without question, can be traced to a lack of knowledge.

Figure-Symbol   On May 30, we sent you our check for $65.94, which was due on June 12.

Easy   You will learn that luck is on the side of men who do not count on it.

| 1 | 2 | 3 | 4 | 5 | 6 | 7 | 8 | 9 | 10 | 11 | 12 | 13 | 14 |

Check your position at the typewriter

### 40b ■ Timed Writings

*10 minutes*

**Directions** – Type two 1-minute and two 3-minute writings on 36e, page 77. Compute *gwam*; circle errors. Submit the better of the 1- and 3-minute writings.

## Problem 2—Personal Letter in Semibusiness Form

● *The semibusiness form is used for letters of congratulation and appreciation and for invitations and acceptances and regrets that could not be classified as purely social. Half-size stationery (5½ by 8½ inches) is frequently used for letters of this type, as will be the case in typing Problems 2 and 3.*

**Directions – 1.** Use 5½- by 8½-inch paper. Type the letter in the form shown at the right.

**2.** Use a 40-space line. Start the return address on the 10th line space from the top, the salutation on the 7th line space from the date.

**3.** Indent paragraphs 10 spaces. Type the address on the 6th line space from the closing.

9472 Trinity Place
Albany, New York    12202
February 19, 197–

Sir

I am grateful to you for inviting me to the informal ceremonies honoring Mr. Joseph Hershey for his many achievements as a foreign correspondent.

Mr. Hershey's talk about his travels and experiences as a reporter was most informative and entertaining. He is a credit to our city, and I am glad that his many contributions are receiving official recognition.

Respectfully yours

Honorable Stephen Nichols
Mayor, City of Albany
Albany, New York    12211

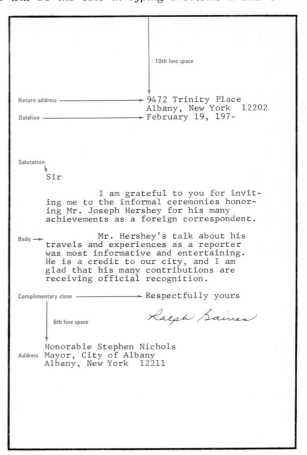

**Personal letter in semibusiness form**

## Problem 3—Personal Letter in Semibusiness Form

**Directions – 1.** Type this letter in semibusiness form, using the directions given in Problem 2. **2.** Use your return address and today's date. Type the salutation on the 7th line space from the date.

Dear Dean Kinzer

On behalf of the guests and members of Delta Pi Epsilon, I want to thank you sincerely for being our guest speaker last Saturday evening. As usual, your words, timing, and delivery kept us on our toes delightfully. (¶) I am sure that Delta Pi Epsilon members would agree that you aroused our interest in education by television. We look forward to hearing from you again on this interesting topic.

Sincerely yours

Dean Frederick Kinzer
419 Thurlow Terrace
*Your city and state*

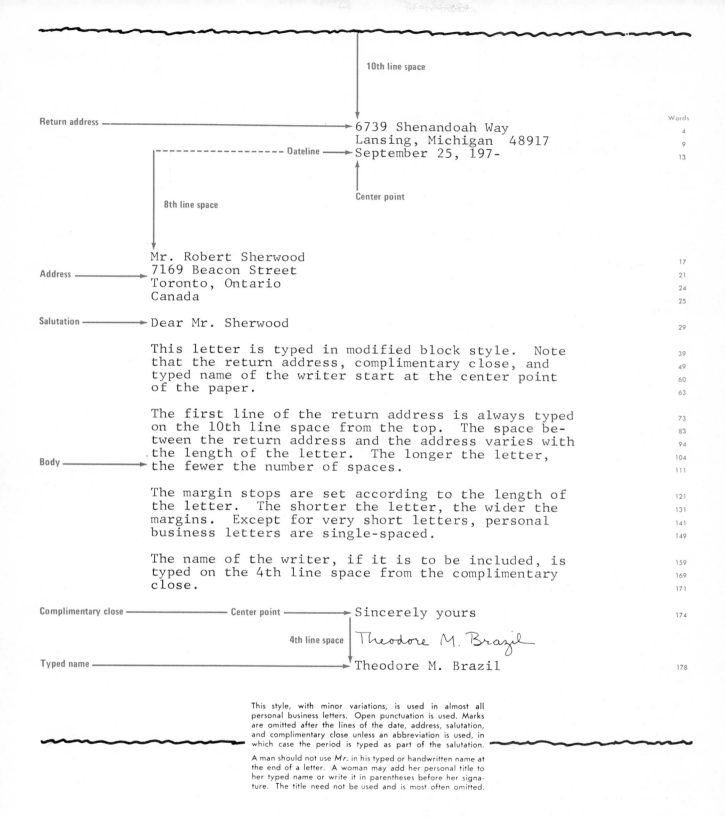

10th line space

Return address ————————→ 6739 Shenandoah Way           Words

                                         Lansing, Michigan  48917      4

— — — — — — — — — — — Dateline ——→ September 25, 197-         9

                                 ↑                      13

Center point

8th line space

                      Mr. Robert Sherwood         17

Address ————————→ 7169 Beacon Street           21

                      Toronto, Ontario           24

                      Canada                    25

Salutation ————————→ Dear Mr. Sherwood          29

                      This letter is typed in modified block style.  Note    39

                      that the return address, complimentary close, and    49

                      typed name of the writer start at the center point    60

                      of the paper.                        63

                      The first line of the return address is always typed    73

                      on the 10th line space from the top.  The space be-    83

                      tween the return address and the address varies with    94

Body ———————————→ the length of the letter.  The longer the letter,    104

                      the fewer the number of spaces.              111

                      The margin stops are set according to the length of    121

                      the letter.  The shorter the letter, the wider the    131

                      margins.  Except for very short letters, personal    141

                      business letters are single-spaced.          149

                      The name of the writer, if it is to be included, is    159

                      typed on the 4th line space from the complimentary    169

                      close.                            171

Complimentary close ———————— Center point ————→ Sincerely yours    174

                                   *Theodore M. Brazil*

                    4th line space

Typed name ————————————————→ Theodore M. Brazil    178

This style, with minor variations, is used in almost all personal business letters. Open punctuation is used. Marks are omitted after the lines of the date, address, salutation, and complimentary close unless an abbreviation is used, in which case the period is typed as part of the salutation.

A man should not use *Mr.* in his typed or handwritten name at the end of a letter. A woman may add her personal title to her typed name or write it in parentheses before her signature. The title need not be used and is most often omitted.

**Personal business letter in modified block style**

• *The following paragraphs describe the steps that should be followed in cleaning your machine. Read them carefully; follow the instructions given.* — *10 minutes*

**Directions** – Type two 1-minute writings on each of the following paragraphs; compare *gwam*. Strive to type Paragraphs 2 and 3 at the same rate at which you can type Paragraph 1.

• Contains all letters

|  | GWAM 1' | 3' |
|---|---|---|

¶1
DS
44 words
1.3 si

The kind of work you prepare on your typewriter will depend to a | 13 | 4 48

great extent upon the care it gets. You cannot expect to do quality | 27 | 9 53

work on a machine that is dirty and that creaks and squeaks from lack | 41 | 14 58

of regular care. | 44 | 15 59

¶2
44 words
1.3 si

First, wipe the dust ~~dirt~~ and erasure clumbs all parts of ~~the~~ type- | 13 | 19 63

writer after each use. do not permit foreign partciles toget loged | 28 | 24 68

~~by~~ in the moveing parts. Use a brush, clear grit the from face of the | 43 | 29 73

type. | 44 | 29 73

¶3
44 words
1.3 si

*Second, to avoid a lazy carriage, clean the grooved bars on which* | 13 | 34 78

*it rides; apply a few drops of oil to them. Two or three drops are* | 27 | 38 82

*usually adequate. For easy typing, clean the bars; then oil them at* | 41 | 43 87

*least once a week.* | 44 | 44 88

1' | 1 | 2 | 3 | 4 | 5 | 6 | 7 | 8 | 9 | 10 | 11 | 12 | 13 | 14 |
3' | 1 | 2 | 3 | 4 | 5 |

## 44c ■ Problem Typing

*30 minutes*

### Problem 1—Personal Business Letter in Modified Block Style

Full sheet
50-space line
Mixed punctuation
Blocked ¶'s

**Directions** – 1. Use today's date and your return address and name. 2. Type the address on the 11th line from the date. 3. Address an envelope; insert letter.

The Nation's News / 88441 Bracewood Road / Waterbury, Connecticut    06706

Gentlemen:

Congratulations on your splendid coverage of the environment problems which we and the world face. As President Nixon told his television audience last week, it is one of the most critical problems we face. We should all be grateful when a magazine with such prestige and wide distribution as yours brings these issues before the public. (¶) I would be delighted to have additional copies or reprints of the article to pass along to some of my friends who are concerned with the environment problem.

Sincerely yours,

## Problem 1—Addressing a Small Envelope

**Directions** – Address a small envelope for the letter on page 84. Fold the letter; insert it. Refer to the illustration below.

- *Use paper cut to envelope size (6½ by 3⅝ inches) if envelopes are not available.*

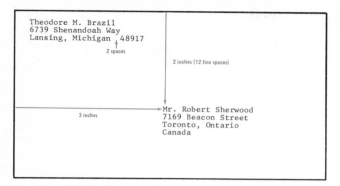

Theodore M. Brazil
6739 Shenandoah Way
Lansing, Michigan 48917
*2 spaces*

*2 inches (12 line spaces)*

*3 inches*

Mr. Robert Sherwood
7169 Beacon Street
Toronto, Ontario
Canada

1. Type the writer's name and his return address in the upper left corner as shown in the illustration. Begin typing on the second line space from the top edge and 3 spaces from the left edge.
2. Type the receiver's name about 2 inches (12 line spaces) from the top of the envelope. Start about 3 inches from the left edge.
3. Use the block style and single spacing for all addresses. City and state names and ZIP Code must be typed on one line in that order.
4. The newer 2-letter state abbreviations may be used, or the state name may be typed in full or in the standard abbreviation.

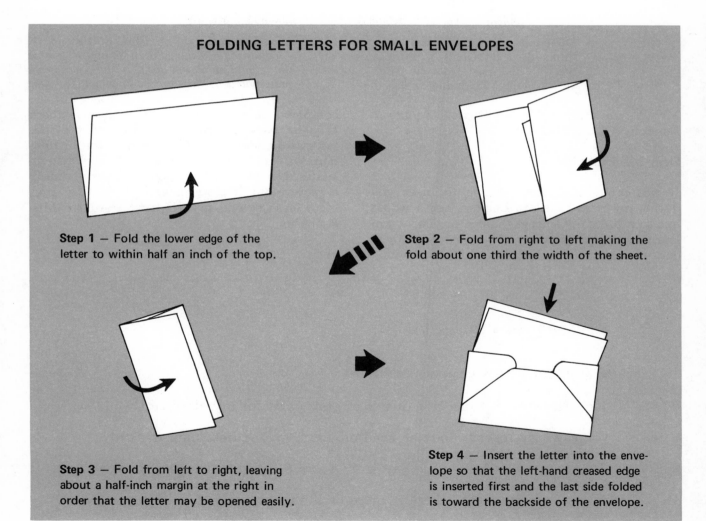

## FOLDING LETTERS FOR SMALL ENVELOPES

**Step 1** – Fold the lower edge of the letter to within half an inch of the top.

**Step 2** – Fold from right to left making the fold about one third the width of the sheet.

**Step 3** – Fold from left to right, leaving about a half-inch margin at the right in order that the letter may be opened easily.

**Step 4** – Insert the letter into the envelope so that the left-hand creased edge is inserted first and the last side folded is toward the backside of the envelope.

## Problem 2—Personal Business Letter in Block Style

full sheet
50-space line
Open punctuation
Blocked ¶'s

**Directions** – Use your return address, today's date, and sign the letter. Decide for yourself how the letter should be spaced.

Mr. Hunter M. Goldman / 12915 Kurtz Avenue / Green Bay, Wisconsin   54301

Dear Mr. Goldman

Mr. Woodrow Byrd, president of the National Flower Growers Association, has asked me to write to a number of our members regarding the annual meeting next summer. Will you please respond to each of the following questions:

1. During which month should the meeting be scheduled?

2. Do you have a preference as to the city in which the meeting should be held?

3. Do you prefer informal discussions by members to formal presentations by outside speakers?

I shall appreciate your answers to these questions. Since we must plan the meeting soon, I look forward to an early reply. Thank you for your assistance.

Sincerely yours

## Problem 3—Personal Business Letter in Modified Block Style

Full sheet
50-space line
Mixed punctuation
Blocked ¶'s

**Directions** – Use today's date and your return address and name. Type the address on the 13th line space from the date. Address an envelope. Fold and insert the letter.

- *Mixed punctuation is used in this letter. A colon follows the salutation, and a comma the complimentary close. Other parts are punctuated as they are in open punctuation.*

Mr. Wayne F. Franklin / Russell Square / London, WC1 / England

Dear Mr. Franklin:

It was a great pleasure to me to meet you during my recent visit to London, and I would like to express my sincere thanks for your warm and generous hospitality. (¶) I greatly enjoyed our evening at the Paladium. The convivial company, delightful music, and entertainment brought back pleasant memories of previous visits to London. (¶) After leaving you in London, we had a very interesting 10-day trip to Wales, Devon, and Cornwall. This is certainly a picturesque, historical, and fascinating area. (¶) Please extend my kindest regards to Mrs. Franklin.

Sincerely,

## ■ Lesson 44 • *70-space line*

### 44a ■ Keyboard Review • Each line at least three times

5 minutes

Alphabetic SS  Jack Hazzard will mix five quarts of gray paint for my old board wall.

One hand  you saw, my regards, look at, read on, exert my, address him, was only

Figures  Type exact ages in figures: Jay is 47 years 6 months and 29 days old.

Easy  Advice is very cheap; there is more of it than most of us care to use.

| 1 | 2 | 3 | 4 | 5 | 6 | 7 | 8 | 9 | 10 | 11 | 12 | 13 | 14 |

*Practice with purpose*

## Problem 2—Personal Business Letter in Modified Block Style

Full sheet
50-space line
Open punctuation
Indented ¶'s

**Directions** – Use your address in the return address. Use today's date. Type the address on the 10th line space from the date. Type your name as the writer.

- *When you supply the information, 11 words are counted for the heading, which includes the return address and date. Three words are counted for your typed name.*

Words

Mr. Lawrence Potter      11
CBS-TV General Offices      15
7800 Beverly Boulevard      20
Los Angeles, California    90036    24
   30

Dear Mr. Potter      34

Mr. John O'Neil of the University of California,    43
Los Angeles, has suggested that I talk to you re-    53
garding a project on which I am working. The pro-    63
ject relates to the validity and reliability of    73
television audience measurement devices.    81

As it will be most helpful to me to know the uses    91
that CBS makes of various measuring devices, may I    101
have an appointment with you at your convenience    111
to discuss them. I can come to your office any    121
day after 3 p.m.    124

I shall appreciate an opportunity to talk with you,    135
as I believe the information you can give me will    145
be very valuable to the completeness of the study.    155

Sincerely yours      158

## Problem 3—Addressing a Small Envelope

**Directions** – Address a small envelope for the letter in Problem 2 of this lesson. Fold the letter; insert it.

# ■ Lesson 41 • *70-space line*

## 41a ■ Keyboard Review • Each line at least three times      *5 minutes*

Alphabetic SS    The quick-mix angel food cake Yvonne just baked won first prize today.

Hyphen    My son-in-law won a hard-earned victory in the coast-to-coast contest.

Correct position

Figures    1 and 2 and 3 and 4 and 5 and 6 and 7 and 8 and 9 and 10 and 11 and 12

Easy    Art, however, washes away from man's soul the dust of everyday living.

| 1 | 2 | 3 | 4 | 5 | 6 | 7 | 8 | 9 | 10 | 11 | 12 | 13 | 14 |

## 43b ■ Typing from Dictation and Spelling Checkup

**Directions** – Type the words in 42b, page 89, as your teacher dictates. Check for correct spelling. Retype any words in which you made an error.

## 43c ■ Paragraph Guided Writings

**Directions** – Set a goal for a 1-minute writing. Type four 1-minute writings. Try to type your goal word just as time is called. Type no faster or slower than the goal you select.

DS

50 words
1.3 si

Great men do not have to spend their time telling others how wonderful they are. One mark of greatness is modesty. When you meet a really great person, he seems so genuine, humble, and modest that you almost have a new faith in your own potential.

Control
your
rate

## 43d ■ Problem Typing

### Problem 1—Personal Business Letter in Block Style

**Directions** – 1. Type the following letter in block style, using a 50-space line and open punctuation, as illustrated at the right.

2. Type the address on the 12th line space from the date. Use your name as the writer.

783 Keen Avenue / Duluth, Minnesota  55808 / November 17, 197–

Miss Kathryn Marts / 1573½ Gloria Drive / Jackson, Mississippi  39208

Dear Miss Marts

This letter is written in block style. It is used by some writers. The modified block style is, however, much more popular. (¶) Please note that the return address and complimentary close are typed at the left margin. In the block style, the paragraphs are always blocked. The vertical spacing between the parts is the same as it is in the modified block style. (¶) The block style is used by letter writers because it saves typing time. / Yours truly

**Personal business letter in block style**

**Directions** – Type 1-minute writings on these paragraphs. When you can type one at the rate specified, type the next; half-minute time guides will be called.

**Alternate Procedure** – Follow the directions at the left, but move from one paragraph to the next only when you can type at the specified rate *without error*.

• Contains all letters

| | | GWAM | |
|---|---|---|---|
| | | 3' | 5' |

**¶1**
**36 words**
**1.4 si**   DS

Amy Vanderbilt, an expert on good manners, says that they reflect 4 3 58
the respect you have for others. She adds that they are like traffic 9 5 60
rules. Without them, life would be chaotic. 12 7 62

**¶2**
**40 words**
**1.3 si**

A knowledge of etiquette makes you feel comfortable when you deal 16 10 65
with other people. Without question, when you know what to do, you do 21 13 68
it with confidence. When you don't, doubt makes a dupe of you. 25 15 70

**¶3**
**44 words**
**1.3 si**

Good manners are vital in writing personal notes. A point often 30 18 73
raised is whether notes can be typewritten. The rules say they can be, 34 21 76
except for a few notes such as those of condolence, which should be 39 23 78
written by pen. 40 24 79

**¶4**
**48 words**
**1.3 si**

In writing to a man, use "Mr." in both the letter and envelope 44 26 81
address. In writing to a woman, use "Miss" or "Mrs.," whichever is 49 29 84
correct. If you do not know, use "Miss"; or if you prefer, you may 53 32 87
use "Ms.," which stands for either title. 56 34 89

**¶5**
**52 words**
**1.3 si**

A man should not use "Mr." in his typed or handwritten name at the 60 36 91
end of a letter. On the other hand, a woman may add her personal title 65 39 94
to her typed name or write it in parentheses before her signature. The 70 42 97
title need not be used and is most often omitted. 73 44 99

**¶6**
**56 words**
**1.3 si**

Good manners also dictate that you use judgment in typing letters. 78 47 102
They should look neat and clean. Fuzzy copy should be avoided by using 83 50 105
a dark ribbon and sharp, firm strokes. The paper used should be free 87 52 107
of blots and smudges. All letters should be well-spaced and centered. 92 55 110

3' | 1 | 2 | 3 | 4 | 5 |
5' | 1 | 2 | 3 |

## Problem 2—Personal Business Letter in Modified Block Style

Full sheet
50-space line
Open punctuation
Blocked ¶'s
Carbon copy

**Directions** – Type the address on the 13th line space from the date. Address an envelope. Fold the letter; insert it into the envelope.

• *When the return address consists of only a city and state name, type both on one line, separating them by a comma.*

Sioux City, Iowa   51101
November 20, 197–

National Park Service
United States Department of the Interior
Washington, D.C.   20240

Gentlemen

Will you please send me a list of the films, filmstrips, and posters that are available on the Grand Teton National Park.

I am preparing a talk on this park for one of my classes and would like to illustrate parts of my presentation. The talk will cover the chief scenic features and hotel and camping accommodations in the park.

I shall appreciate hearing from you soon, as I must give my talk on December 15.

Sincerely yours

Scott Biel

## Problem 3—Personal Business Letter in Modified Block Style with Listed Items

Full sheet
60-space line
Open punctuation
Indented ¶'s
Carbon copy

**Directions** – 1. Use today's date and your return address and name as the writer. 2. Type the address on the 10th line space from the date. 3. Indent the listed items 5 spaces from the side margins. Address an envelope.

Mr. Albert Ariola, Editor
Palmer Publishing Company
1537 Atlanta Avenue, South
Tulsa, Oklahoma   74104

Dear Mr. Ariola

I have recently been awarded a prize for writing a paper on the quality of television programs. The title of my paper is "A High School Student Looks at Television." It may have publication possibilities.

1. May I send the article to you to see if it is suitable for publication in the Palmer Times?

2. If you are not interested in an article on this subject, can you suggest a publisher who might be?

I shall appreciate a reply from you soon. I am hopeful that you will consider my article.

Yours very truly

## ■ Lesson 43 • *70-space line*

### 43a ■ Keyboard Review • Each line at least three times

5 *minutes*

Alphabetic SS  Zita quickly gave them six jars of sweet honey for the birthday party.

Third row  He quoted the reporter of your paper on problems of equipping an army.

Be alert

Figures  Type this line: we 23 or 94 to 59 up 70 or 94 you 697 row 492 owe 923

Easy  Work for the gift of using words that give some life to your thoughts.

| 1 | 2 | 3 | 4 | 5 | 6 | 7 | 8 | 9 | 10 | 11 | 12 | 13 | 14 |

### 41c ■ Technique Builder—Stroking

*5 minutes*

**Directions** – Each sentence three times.    **Technique Goals** – Type on the response level indicated. Work for a flowing rhythm pattern.

| | | |
|---|---|---|
| Letter | ss | As you stated, there are errors that must be corrected in my abstract. |
| Letter | | Edward addressed my letter to the weaver who has an office in Baraboo. |
| Word | | Any man who uses few words does not have to take so many of them back. |
| Combination | | John traded the shelter on the estate for a small house near the lake. |

Flowing rhythm pattern

| 1 | 2 | 3 | 4 | 5 | 6 | 7 | 8 | 9 | 10 | 11 | 12 | 13 | 14 |

### 41d ■ Skill Comparison • Type two 1-minute writings on each sentence. Compare gwam rates on the writings.

*10 minutes*

1  ss  A man is rich according to what he is, never according to what he has.

2  There are only a few men who can run the 100-yard dash in 9.3 seconds.

3  We ~~should~~ *must* keep i/mine that *n* what we do*d*not under stand we/not do/pos*s*ess.

4  *Anyone can judge a person by his looks, by his words, or by his deeds.*

Type without pauses

| 1 | 2 | 3 | 4 | 5 | 6 | 7 | 8 | 9 | 10 | 11 | 12 | 13 | 14 |

### 41e ■ Continuity Practice from Script

*5 minutes*

**Directions** – Type as many copies of this paragraph as you can in the time that remains.    **Technique Goals** – Work for quick, sharp stroking. Type at a steady pace.

DS

**40 words**
**1.3 si**

*Man needs to be creative, but he must have a sense of humor, too. He must have imagination to help him compensate for what he is not. A sense of humor is needed to console him for what he really is.*

| Words |
|---|
| 11 |
| 22 |
| 34 |
| 40 |

| 1 | 2 | 3 | 4 | 5 | 6 | 7 | 8 | 9 | 10 | 11 | 12 | 13 | 14 |

## ■ Lesson 42 • *70-space line*

### 42a ■ Keyboard Review • Each line at least three times

*5 minutes*

| | | |
|---|---|---|
| Alphabetic | ss | Sam Crale quit working for Marv and got a job at a zoo with extra pay. |
| Fourth finger | | Alex Pasqual and Pat Squires are away at a political meeting in Azusa. |
| Figure-Symbol | | Mr. B. J. Jones (Bob) worked a total of 304 days and earned $6,597.21. |
| Easy | | As a rule, those who have nothing to say take the most time saying it. |

Eyes on copy

| 1 | 2 | 3 | 4 | 5 | 6 | 7 | 8 | 9 | 10 | 11 | 12 | 13 | 14 |

## 42b ■ Spelling and Proofreading Aids • Each line twice

1   ss   relevant publicly prairie preferable preceded privilege repel souvenir

2   renown persuaded pamphlet occurrence occasionally nowadays interfered

3   nickel mortgaged intercede infallible inoculate incense fulfill varies

4   hygiene fiery February extension exaggerate embarrass disappoint ninth

## 42c ■ Technique Builder—Stroking • Each line three times

Double letters   ss   Professor Tripp arranged to have the matter referred to the committee.

Weak fingers   This political quiz proved to be popular with large numbers of people.

Long reach   Mr. Hunt's debt has been greatly reduced in amount by annual payments.

One hand   Look in on my nylon mill, Joy Polk. I'll hook pink poplin on my loom.

| 1 | 2 | 3 | 4 | 5 | 6 | 7 | 8 | 9 | 10 | 11 | 12 | 13 | 14 |

---

### CARBON COPIES

To make carbon copies, place the carbon paper (with glossy side down) on a sheet of plain paper. The paper on which you will prepare the original is then laid on the carbon paper, and all the sheets are inserted into the typewriter. The dull surface of the carbon sheet should be toward you when the sheets have been rolled into the typewriter. Erasing on carbon copies is explained on page xii.

- *Carbon copies are called for in this lesson. Your teacher will tell you if you are to prepare carbon copies in any other lessons in this unit.*

---

## 42d ■ Problem Typing

### Problem 1—Personal Business Letter in Modified Block Style

Full sheet
50-space line
Open punctuation
Indented ¶'s

**Directions** – Use your return address, today's date, and your name as the writer. Type the address on the 11th line space from the date. Make one carbon copy. Proofread your finished copy. Address an envelope; fold the letter and insert it.

Sanitation Department
1386 Gabriel Street
Corpus Christi, Texas    78415

Gentlemen

Thank you for the informative letter you sent to me about the correct method of maintaining the chemical balance in our swimming pool.

Please allow me to make one suggestion.

It would be very helpful for the many owners of swimming pools in this area if they could receive the same information that you sent to me. Perhaps you could include the steps outlined in your letter in a small booklet or folder for distribution to persons seeking advice.

Thank you again for the information. It has been most helpful.

Sincerely yours

S0-AFD-753

# Essential
# MONET

This is a Dempsey Parr Book
This edition published in 2000

Dempsey Parr is an imprint of Parragon
PARRAGON
Queen Street House
4 Queen Street
Bath BA1 1HE, UK

Copyright © Parragon 1999

Created and produced for Parragon by
FOUNDRY DESIGN AND PRODUCTION,
a part of The Foundry Creative Media Co. Ltd,
Crabtree Hall, Crabtree Lane
Fulham, London, SW6 6TY

ISBN: 1-84084-705-0

All rights reserved. No part of this publication may be
reproduced, stored in a retrieval system, or transmitted
in any form or by any means, without the prior written
permission of the copyright holder.

A copy of the CIP data for this book is available from
the British Library, upon request.

The right of Vanessa Potts to be identified as the author of this
work has been asserted in accordance with Section 77 of the
Copyright, Designs and Patents Act of 1988.

The right of Dr Claire O'Mahony to be identified as the
author of the introduction to this book has been asserted in
accordance with Section 77 of the Copyright, Designs and
Patents Act of 1988.

Printed and bound in Singapore.

# *Essential*
# MONET

VANESSA POTTS

Introduction by Dr Claire O'Mahony

DEMPSEY PARR

# CONTENTS

# ❋ CONTENTS ❋

# INTRODUCTION

*C*LAUDE OSCAR MONET is in many senses the quintessential Impressionist painter. The spontaneity and vivacity of his painting technique and his devotion to the close observation of nature have been the focus of most discussions of his art. However, the range of his subject matters, the complexities of his exhibiting strategies and his responses to the variety of artistic and socio-historical transformations experienced during his long lifetime are fundamental to understanding his unique contribution to the history of art.

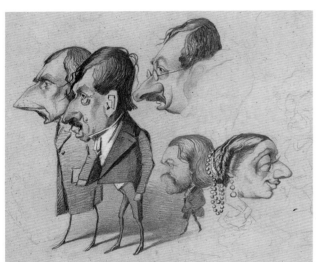

Born in 1840 in Paris, where his father was a wholesale grocer, Monet lived in Le Havre from the age of five; the Normandy region was to be a vital influence on him throughout his life. His earliest artistic reputation was as a caricaturist, but by the mid-1850s Monet, with the encouragement of the atmospheric landscape painter Eugène Boudin (1824–98), had begun to paint from what he saw in the open air.

Monet's artistic career began in earnest with his first trip to Paris in 1859. On his arrival in the capital he was befriended by a number of painters associated with the Realist movement, most notably the Barbizon painter Constant Troyton (1810–65) and the young Camille Pissarro (1830–1903). He also received his first formal training, becoming a pupil for two years in the studio of the academic painter Charles Gleyre (1808–74). It was there that he made a number of artistic friendships that were to have a formative influence on him; he met Pierre Auguste Renoir (1841–1919), Frédéric Bazille (1841–70), and Alfred Sisley (1839–99).

Despite legends stating the contrary, Monet had a degree of success at provincial exhibitions as well as at the annual state-sponsored art exhibition held in Paris each year in May, the Salon. In 1865,

having made painting trips to the forest of Fontainebleau and the
Normandy coast at Honfleur and Le Havre, where he met the Dutch
open-air landscape painter Johan Barthold Jongkind (1819–91), Monet
sent two of his seascapes to the Salon exhibition, and they were
accepted. A portrait of his mistress, Camille Doncieux, and a landscape
were also accepted in 1866, and another seascape in 1868.

Inspired in part by the controversial paintings produced by
Edouard Manet (1832–83) in the last years of the 1860s, Monet began
to wrestle with subjects derived from the modern life of Paris. The
capital had been undergoing a process of extraordinary transformation
on the initiative of Emperor Napoleon III's prefect, Baron Haussmann.
"Haussmannisation" cut a series of huge boulevards, lined with
large-scale, expensive apartment blocks and arcades of shops, through
the city's labyrinthine medieval streets, so beloved of an earlier
generation of Romantic poets and artists. These changes necessitated
the transplantation of the workers of Paris—who had lived in small
upper rooms of the old buildings above the more lavish apartments of
wealthier Parisians—to a new region of suburbs beyond the city walls.
Monet, like many artists of the Impressionist circle, became fascinated
with both the new phenomena of boulevard culture and the suburban
districts, in which many pleasure spots blossomed alongside the
factories on the banks of the river Seine.

Monet's technique and style reflect a wonderful awareness of the
achievements of his teachers and contemporaries while also creating a
unique and constantly transforming personal vision. The young Monet
synthesized the open-air techniques practiced by Boudin and Jongkind
and theorized by the drawing master Lecoq de Boisbaudran with the
controversial subject matter of modern experience. The more abrupt
handling and traditional palette of his earliest works were derived from
the manner of Realist painters such as Gustave Courbet (1819–77) and
followers of the Barbizon School. In the following decades, Monet
moved away from the traditional modeling in black and white, known
as *chiaroscuro*, to a sense of depth and volume created entirely through
color relationships. Rather than using the dark, reddish-brown

underpainting typical of the nineteenth century, Monet began to paint on canvases primed in white or light beige tones to enhance the brilliance of his colors.

Monet experimented with varying degrees of finish throughout his career, although it was not until the 1880s that he would exhibit his most sketchy works publicly. (Sketches such as the famous paintings of La Grenouillère and the beach at Trouville, now in the National Gallery, London, were almost certainly intended as private notations rather than as works for public exhibition.) However, his practice of building up a work was to be fairly consistent throughout his life. He

would first lay in the main elements of the composition in the appropriate colors in a loose underpainting, and he would then work up all these areas in a range of broad contours and small surface brushstrokes, as fitting to the feature being described. Despite his protestations in later life, this process of elaboration was not always performed in front of the subject, but rather over a period of days or often months in the studio, as Monet's letters of the 1880s to the dealer Durand-Ruel testify.

Many of Monet's views of Paris from the 1860s adopt unusual viewpoints and incorporate ambiguous hints of narratives about the relationships of the tiny figures evoked through his summary brushstrokes. The overall effects of these compositional devices had many precedents, not only the unusual perspectives typical of the Japanese prints of which Monet was an avid collector, but also his awareness of the world of the *flâneur* described with such verve in Charles Baudelaire's *The Painter of Modern Life*. This delightful and influential essay, which nominally describes the achievement of

Constantin Guys (1802–92), a draftsman who evocatively captures the
fashions and social types of the Second Empire, articulates the unique
freedom and anonymity available to the young man as he wanders
around absorbing the spectacle of the new Paris. Monet eloquently
captures this mood of exploration
and mystery in his aloof aerial views
of the manicured public gardens,
bridges, and boulevards at the heart
of Paris and the chance encounters
of its suburban fringes.

In 1866, Monet began his
response to Manet's scandalous
painting *Déjeuner sur l'Herbe*, which
had been rejected by the Salon of
1863 on the grounds of indecency,
with a monumental painting of a
picnic enjoyed by elegant Parisian
men and women. Regrettably, it never came to fruition, and only a
sketch and a few fragments survive. Monet did complete a second
large-scale painting of fashionable women at play, *Women in the Garden*,
which he executed entirely in the open air. However, it was rejected by
the Salon of 1867. This was a period of some personal and professional
strain for Monet. His mistress, Camille, was pregnant with their son
Jean and, although Monet's father had been supportive of his son's
artistic career, he would not tolerate this romantic alliance. Suffering
financial difficulties, Monet returned to the family home in Le Havre
and left Camille in Paris. However, they were reunited after Jean's
birth, living first at Etretat and then in Bougival, where Renoir and
Pissarro were frequent visitors and colleagues on sketching trips around
suburban pleasure spots such as the floating restaurant, La Grenouillère.

In 1870, Monet and Camille were married and made a
honeymoon trip to Trouville, a resort on the Normandy coast. With
the outbreak of the Franco-Prussian War in July of 1870, the Monets
took the decision to flee to London. A number of other artistic figures

had also left for London, including, most significantly for Monet, the leading art dealer Paul Durand-Ruel, who soon became a vitally important and lifelong patron for Monet and the Impressionist circle. During the nine months the family spent in London, Monet painted numerous views of the city's parks and of the River Thames. After traveling through Holland in the summer, where he painted at Zaandam near Amsterdam, the Monets returned to France and settled in a suburb to the west of Paris called Argenteuil. Monet remained there until 1878, and many of his friends—Renoir, Sisley, Gustave Caillebotte (1848–94), and Manet—joined him there to paint the life of the River Seine, a site of pleasure boating, swimming, and river cafés, as well as a burgeoning industrial town.

Durand-Ruel had been an avid buyer for these paintings, but in 1873 he suffered financial losses. Monet and his friends had to find a new set of patrons, and they embarked on planning an independent exhibition to draw attention to their work. On the Boulevard des Capucines in the studio of Nadar, a leading photographer of the day, the *Société Anonyme des Peintres, Sculpteurs, et Graveurs* held its first exhibition in April of 1874. A contemporary critic coined the term "Impressionism" in response to Monet's unusually sketchy view in grayish-blue and orange of the industrial harbor at Le Havre

enshrouded in fog entitled *Impression, Sunrise*. This exhibition achieved a certain notoriety, although it did little to raise the prices that the artists could ask for their works, as proved by the 1875 auction of the Jean-Baptiste Fauré collection of works by Berthe Morisot (1841–95), Renoir, and Sisley. Monet also showed paintings at the second, third, fourth, and

seventh of the eight exhibitions mounted by the Impressionist group
between 1876 and 1884.

Monet met Ernest Hoschedé and his wife Alice in 1876, and
they were to play an important role in his later life. Hoschedé
commissioned Monet to paint four paintings to create a decorative
ensemble for the main receiving-room at his home just outside Paris,
the Château de Rottembourg at Montgeron. After Hoschedé's
bankruptcy and the birth of Monet's second son, Michel, in 1878,
the two couples and their eight children decided to form a joint
household in Vètheuil. However, Camille, who seemingly had a
disease of the womb, died in the fall of the next year. Alice Hoschedé
and Monet were to form an open, rather unconventional relationship
that may have contributed to Monet's gradual distancing from his
Parisian painter friends and their exhibitions.

Though intimate, the couple lived largely autonomous lives.
Although Ernest Hoschedé had created a separate life for himself in
the 1880s, Monet and Alice did not marry until after Ernest's death
in 1892. After a brief sojourn in Poissy, the family moved to their
now-famous house in Giverny. They rented this house until Monet
was able to purchase it in 1890, due to a new-found affluence achieved
in a large part by Durand-Ruel's adept and financially rewarding
cultivation of American collectors interested in purchasing Monet's

works. The family were
to spend the rest of their
lives at Giverny.

With Alice caring
for his children, Monet
embarked on a period of
frequent painting trips to
picturesque corners of
France throughout the
1880s. He returned
several times to the
Normandy and Brittany

coasts, as he had always done, but now he chose to paint the more remote sites rather than the tourist-filled resorts. The Parisians at play in Trouville and Ste.-Adresse, celebrated in his canvases of the 1860s, gave way to the lonely, tempest-tossed shores and rock pools of Fécamp and Pourville and the majestic isolation of the hilltop church at Varengeville in 1881 and 1882. He found a favorite motif in the dramatic cliffs and needles of Etretat (a subject made famous a decade before by Courbet). He returned there in 1883, 1885, and 1886, when he also painted many views of Belle-Ile off the southern coast of Brittany. In 1886, Monet also began to explore more distant regions within France and even the tulip fields of Holland. His life-long fascination with the cool light and coastal storms of the north was coupled with new explorations of the warm brilliance of the Mediterranean. He visited the southeastern tip of France, painting Bordighera, Antibes, and Juan-les-Pins in 1884 and 1889. He also traveled to the Creuse Valley in the heart of France in 1889.

The 1880s and '90s saw a shift of focus in Monet's life on many levels, in the kind of subject matter he explored, the venues he selected for exhibiting his works and the huge success and fame that he achieved. Like so many artists and writers at the end of the nineteenth century, he became dissatisfied with the themes of modernity and urban experience. His art became much more focused on a world of personal sensation before the wonders of nature. A monumental, decorative quality creeps in to his late works. Rather than the external spectacle that delighted Manet and Baudelaire, these paintings offer private spaces of contemplation that engulf the viewer in their gentle color harmonies and bold compositions. These paintings achieve a world of escape and private reverie which was analogous to the artistic ambitions championed by the Symbolist painters and poets, and Art Nouveau designers.

These new subjects not only widened Monet's own experience and modes of expression but they also attracted keen buyers and dealer-patrons. After the acceptance to the Salon of a painting of an ice floe in 1880, Monet embarked on a new cycle of one-man and group exhibitions with several of the leading private art dealers of the day. In 1883 Monet held a one-man show at the gallery of his old friend and supporter Durand-Ruel. He participated in the group shows organized by Georges Petit in 1885, 1886, and 1887. This relationship with Petit culminated in a retrospective of Monet's work in 1889 which confirmed the popularity and sales of his work. On his return from the trips to Antibes, Monet also exhibited 10 paintings with the dealers Boussod and Valadon, which their manager, Theo van Gogh, had purchased. Interestingly, Monet ended this hugely successful exhibition by refusing one of the highest accolades from the French state, the *légion d'honneur*. While rejecting honors for himself, he sought a place in the nation's museums for his mentor Manet by orchestrating a campaign of subscriptions to pay for the purchase of the famously scandalous and innovative painting of a Parisian courtesan, *Olympia*, of 1865.

The artistic explorations undertaken on Monet's many painting trips of the 1880s were essentially preliminary work for his great series paintings of the 1890s. In the series, Monet would select a particularly resonant site and subject, such as grainstacks, poplar trees on the River

Epte or the façade of Rouen Cathedral, and paint suites of paintings portraying the motif under various different conditions of light and season. These series lay at the heart of Monet's public exhibiting career in the last decade of the nineteenth century. In a one-man exhibition held in Durand-Ruel's gallery in 1891, Monet included 15 paintings from the grainstack series. He also created single-theme exhibitions for subsequent motifs throughout the following years. He showed the poplars at Durand-Ruel's gallery in 1892, the façade of Rouen Cathedral in 1893, the first water-garden series in 1900, the London views in 1904 and a series of 48 water lily paintings, known as "waterscapes," in 1909. The views of Pourville and of early mornings on the Seine were included in his one-man exhibition at the Georges Petit Gallery in 1898, and the Venice views were shown at the Bernheim-Jeune Gallery in 1912.

Monet's other great artistic project of the 1890s was the creation of his water garden at Giverny. As soon as he had purchased the house, he began to create an elaborate flower garden incorporating every shade of color and variety of bloom—a palette made of flowers. In 1893, he had the opportunity to buy a second plot of land on the opposite side of the road and railway track that run through the property to this day. Monet elaborated on the indigenous pond and stream by gaining planning permission to alter the flow of water entering the stream and by repeatedly enlarging the pond in 1901 and 1910. Perhaps his most dramatic addition was a bridge, of typical arched Japanese design, which he built at one end of the pond. This peaceful idyll of his own devising was to be Monet's final subject, which he painted daily for 20 years.

The water lily series paintings led Monet to his last, great project: the decorations for the Orangerie. Decorative painting had witnessed an extraordinary revival in the last quarter of the nineteenth century in both official and more esoteric artistic circles. In a speech at the awards banquet for the Salon of 1879, Jules Ferry, Minister of Fine Arts and Education, had called for the decoration of all France's public buildings. Town halls, schools, churches, and museums throughout France were decorated with vast mural schemes celebrating the Third

Republic. This revival of decorative art was paralleled among a set of
wealthy patrons who commissioned numerous decorative paintings to
ornament the salons of their villas. Similarly, many leading restaurants,
such as Maxime's and Le Train Bleu, the latter built at the Gare de Lyon
for the World Fair of 1900, sought sympathetic decorative schemes to
enhance the Belle Epoque elegance of their diningrooms. Leading
artists from every aesthetic camp of the day were commissioned to
create these decorations, from the members of the Nabis group, such
as Pierre Bonnard (1867–1947) and Edouard Vuillard (1868–1940), to
leading Salon painters such as Albert Besnard (1849–1934) and Henri
Gervex (1852–1929).

The powerful Republican
politician Georges Clemenceau was a
close friend and a vociferous champion
of Monet's painting. Concerned at his
friend's gloom after the death of both
his beloved wife Alice in 1910 and his
elder son Jean in 1914, Clemenceau
cajoled the old painter to embark on
a colossal decoration inspired by the
water garden. Monet built a special
studio in his garden so that he could
work in comfort on such monumental
proportions. In 1918, he decided to
donate the work to the French state.
Despite suffering from cataracts in both
eyes, Monet worked on the project continuously until his death in
1926. Initially, the ensemble was to be housed in a specially built
pavilion in the grounds of the Hôtel Biron (now the Musée Rodin),
but in 1921 it was announced that the murals would be housed in the
Orangerie in the Tuilleries Gardens near the Louvre. The architect
Camille Lefèvre designed two oval rooms at ground level to house the
paintings, and they were opened to the public on May 16, 1927.

Dr. Claire O'Mahony

## *DANDY AU CIGARE* (c. 1857–58)
## Dandy with a Cigar
*Musée Marmottan. Courtesy of Giraudon*

MONET started his artistic career as a caricaturist in his home town. His caricatures were displayed in the local frame shop, where they attracted much attention because he frequently used well-known and therefore recognizable people from Le Havre as his subjects. Thanks to the success of these caricatures, Monet was able to save enough money to study art in Paris.

The frame shop manager also displayed landscapes by the then more famous artist Eugène Boudin (1824–98). This effected an introduction between the two artists, and Boudin took Monet painting with him on many occasions. Boudin believed that an artist should have a full experience with his art and complete the entire landscape outdoors. This was unheard of before Boudin and became known as *plein-air* technique. Monet embraced this concept wholeheartedly, and it became an important feature of his work throughout his career.

*Dandy au Cigare* is a typical caricature, complete with exaggerated features and the recognizable accessories of a dandy. The oversized cigar distorts the face, rendering the man ridiculous. In the more serious *Portrait de Poly* (1886), Monet retains some sense of the caricature that is especially obvious with the treatment of the sitter's large red nose. Notice this dandy has a similar affliction.

**Portrait de Poly (1886)**
*Portrait of Poly*
*Musée Marmottan. Courtesy of Giraudon. (See p. 148)*

### PETIT PANTHÉON THÉÂTRAL
### (c. 1857–60)
### LITTLE THEATRICAL GROUP
*Courtesy of Giraudon*

*T*HE object of a caricature is to exaggerate the features that make an individual identifiable for humorous purposes. This unfinished picture demonstrates Monet's abilities in this field to great effect.

In particular the nose of each person best illustrates Monet's skill. He does not appear to have a stock of funny noses that he simply applies to the face; each person in the picture has a different nose from the others. These range from a gallic monstrosity on one gentleman to a tiny button of a nose on another. Their eyes, lips, and foreheads are also uniquely individual. The whole effect is to create a face that the viewer can "read" in order to understand the character of the person portrayed. Thus each man could appear intelligent, mean-spirited or kind, depending on how Monet has drawn his characteristic features.

What this picture does show is the quickness of eye that Monet had. He notes the details of the features and then interprets them in a new way. This is the approach he takes with other more serious paintings where the subjects he chooses to paint are not an exact replica of reality but his response to it.

## *TROPHÉE DE CHASSE* (1862)
## SPORTING PRIZES

*Musée d'Orsay. Courtesy of Giraudon*

*T*ROPHÉE *de Chase* is unusual when compared with Monet's later work. However, what cannot be overlooked is his determination to succeed as an artist: this led him in the early years to paint what can be considered conservative paintings. His choice of subject matter was frequently based on what would be acceptable to the art community.

The colors used here are true to life and lack the brilliance that was to emerge later in Monet's life. They are blended together to create a more traditional palette. Still life was never to be a priority in his career, and this is one of the rare examples of it. However, he took two still lifes with him to Paris to show round the art schools.

The elaborate composition and detailed treatment of the birds demonstrate how Monet was growing in confidence about his abilities at that time. The quality of execution shows how determined Monet was to understand the basics behind good art through traditional training. This level of detail would not be of such great concern in his later career, when the general impression became more important.

## *La Rue de la Bavolle, à Honfleur* (c. 1864)
## Bavolle Street, at Honfleur

*Mannheim Stadtische Kunsthalle. Courtesy of Giraudon*

THERE is some confusion over the exact date in which *La Rue de la Bavolle, à Honfleur* was painted. However, it is definitely an early piece and one that is distinctly unusual for Monet.

Honfleur has many buildings dating from the sixteenth century, making the village very picturesque. For this reason it is an unusual subject for Monet to pick, as he normally veered away from the picturesque, particularly when it came to buildings. His preference was for modern subjects, such as St. Lazare Station. The painting *Le Pont de l'Europe, Gare St Lazare* (1877) has all the hallmarks of the sort of city scene that Monet liked. There are modern buildings in the background, a new bridge built in contemporary materials and, most impressive of all, a steam engine. The street scene from Honfleur lacks all of these attributes— its old-fashioned buildings and quiet street are lacking in the bustle and action characteristic of the later painting.

There is no sense of urgency; the scene has the tranquility that Camille Corot (1796–1875), one of Monet's artistic predecessors, would have been proud of. There is no hint at the style that was to become synonymous with Impressionism.

**Le Pont de L'Europe, Gare St-Lazare (1877)**
*Europe Bridge, St Lazare Station*
*Musée Marmottan. Courtesy of Giraudon. (See p. 96)*

## LE DÉJEUNER SUR L'HERBE (1865)
## THE PICNIC ON THE GRASS

*Pushkin Museum, Moscow. Courtesy of Giraudon*

THE subject-matter of this painting is not controversial, but Monet's treatment of it is. Monet started work on this massive canvas with the intention of submitting it to the Salon exhibition of 1866 and causing a sensation. The sheer scale of the work meant it was not ready in time, and Monet abandoned it.

The unfinished canvas reveals a conventional scene of picnickers in the forest. However, Monet is attempting to treat the people as a natural part of the landscape. There is no story to the painting, and this is emphasized by the uncentered composition: the eye is not drawn to any one point, and the people are simply a part of their surroundings. Monet wanted to create a sense of spontaneity with this painting, as if it were the capturing of a moment. This is underlined by the casual actions of the figures. One woman is caught in the act of touching her hair; another is about to put down a plate. This realism was very unusual in art of this period. Manet's influence is felt in the painting, but Monet hoped to avoid the moral judgement that Manet suffered with *Olympia* by not using controversial subject matter such as nude figures.

### CAMILLE OU LA FEMME À LA ROBE VERTE (1866)
### CAMILLE (WOMAN IN THE GREEN DRESS)
*Bremen Kunsthalle. Courtesy of the Visual Arts Library, London*

CAMILLE Doncieux, Monet's mistress and later his wife, was the artist's favorite model and he used her repeatedly in his work. Here she is posed in an attitude that is relatively informal.

The most striking aspect of this painting is the green of the skirt. Monet's love of color and his desire to paint modern subjects probably prompted the choosing of this dress for the painting. The skirt dominates to the point where the woman's personality is secondary. Camille as an individual in her own right is not captured.

The lack of background detail is quite deliberate so that the woman is the only focus of attention. By not providing a setting, her character remains mysterious, with only her clothing hinting at her background. Camille has been painted as if captured mid-action, a spontaneous reaction on the part of the artist to the aesthetic picture her image makes.

Monet submitted this painting to the Salon exhibition and was successful in it being chosen. The Salon was the state-run exhibition, which had a strict and traditional selection process for inclusion in one of its exhibitions. An unknown artist could expect to achieve some notoriety from being selected, and with notoriety often came financial reward.

Claude Monet

## *FEMMES AU JARDIN* (1866)
## WOMEN IN THE GARDEN
*Courtesy of Topham*

CAMILLE Doncieux posed for all four women in this painting, wearing hired dresses: the impoverished Monet could not afford clothes like these. Monet submitted the painting, which was painted at Ville d'Avray, to the 1867 Salon, but it was rejected. Artists such as Daumier and Manet also criticized the picture.

Monet was aiming to make two significant points with *Femmes au Jardin*. This large canvas was traditionally reserved for historical or religious paintings that carried a moral message for the viewer. By painting an unremarkable, modern scene, Monet was declaring that these everyday moments, painted in a realistic manner, were just as important in the art world as esteemed historical or religious subjects.

His second point was concerned with the spontaneity of art and painting exactly what was in front of the artist. Instead of sketching the scene and then completing it in a studio, Monet painted the entire work in the open air. This was the *plein-air* technique that Eugène Boudin had introduced him to. So determined was he to make this painting seem real that he dug a trench in the garden in order to have the canvas at the right level.

### *Jeanne-Marguerite, le Cadre au Jardin* (1866)
### Jeanne-Marguerite, the Image in the Garden
*The Hermitage, St Petersburg. Courtesy of Topham*

A NOTHER work that was inspired by Manet's artistic style, *Jeanne-Marguerite, le Cadre au Jardin* completes the isolation of the individual that Monet had attempted to capture in *Femmes au Jardin* (1866). In the slightly earlier work, although the women form a group, they seem removed from each other. Here Monet finalizes that isolation by leaving a lone female in the garden.

Her isolation is further completed by placing her to the far left edge of the canvas, so that she is removed from the main focus of the picture. This gives an unsettled feel to the composition that is similar to that achieved in the earlier work. In *Femmes au Jardin* three of the women are placed left of center, and the eye struggles to find a main focal point between the women. This is achieved in *Jeanne-Marguerite, le Cadre au Jardin* by patches of color. The viewer is drawn repeatedly from the yellow to the red flowers and then across to the white dress.

The technique of using blocks of colors employed in *Femmes au Jardin* is repeated here with more vigor. The sky is almost a solid patch of blue, the dress a block of white and the grass a strip of green. This gives a flat effect to the picture.

**Femmes au Jardin (1866)**
*Women in the Garden*
*Courtesy of Topham. (See p. 29)*

## *CAMILLE AU PETIT CHIEN* (1866)
## CAMILLE WITH A LITTLE DOG

*Private Collection, Zurich. Courtesy of Giraudon*

*T*HIS intimate portrait is one of the few that shows Camille in a formal pose. Although not shown face on, her features have been recorded in the kind of detail lacking in many of the paintings she posed in for Monet as a model.

The difference in his attitude to the woman between this painting and *La Liseuse* (1872) is interesting. In the main picture his aim is to create a portrait of Camille: there is no vivid background to distract the eye and she is definitely the center of attention. Her profile is emphasized by being painted against a dark color. The quick brushstrokes representing the shaggy dog, contrast with the careful work on Camille's face, and underline that Monet was trying to make Camille the only subject of interest. This is not the case with *La Liseuse*. Here the background, and even Camille's dress, are perhaps more important than who she is. She is painted as part of the scenery, almost an incidental feature of the landscape.

By posing Camille with her face turned down toward her book, her features are not easily distinguishable. In *Camille au Petit Chien*, she looks steadily forward, and some sense of her character can be gleaned from the attitude of the head and the quiet pose.

**La Liseuse (1872)**
***The Lover of Reading***
*Walters Art Gallery, Baltimore. Courtesy of Giraudon.* *(See p. 62)*

### *LA CHARRETTE, ROUTE SOUS LA NEIGE À HONFLEUR* (1865)
### THE CART, ROUTE THROUGH THE SNOW AT HONFLEUR

*Louvre, Paris. Courtesy of Giraudon*

IN 1865, Monet successfully exhibited two paintings, including this one, at the Salon in Paris for the first time. This was an important breakthrough in his career. One of the pictures exhibited was a marine scene painted at Honfleur.

*La Charrette, Route sous la Neige à Honfleur* shows the town as seen from the approach road. It is a winter's day, but the painting is not dark and gloomy as Monet's snowscapes often are. Instead there is a light in the sky that seems to be generated by the sun, which is not yet visible. The white of the snow is not diluted by too much darkness from the buildings or the cart. The overall effect is quite bright.

Although this is an early work, some elements of Monet's later technique are evident within it. There is some short brushwork, using contrasting shades of white, on the snow on the road. Also, Monet is conscious of the parallel lines formed by the cartwheels in the snow and the ditch by the side of the road. This use of lines and shapes in the landscape would become very important in his later work.

## *PORTRAIT D'HOMME* (1865)
## PORTRAIT OF A MAN

*Kunsthaus, Zurich. Courtesy of Giraudon*

*T*HIS is a portrait of Victor Jacquemont, a watercolorist and engraver who worked for several newspapers at the time. However, the picture has been repeatedly cataloged with varying titles and it is difficult to confirm which is the correct one. As a result, it is known simply as *Portrait d'Homme*.

Manet's influence can be seen in the picture, as it can be in other paintings by Monet from this period; the lack of detailed shading on the figure means he has been painted with solid contrasting colors. Working up the body, Monet starts with white only for the shoes. He then switches to gray for the trousers, with only a little shading around the knees and ankles, brown for the jacket and waistcoat, and flesh for the face. The colors are not varied in tone, so that the figure seems very flat on the canvas. The effect of sunlight or the shadow from the umbrella is not painted in.

A similar technique was used in *Camille sur la Plage* (1870–71). However, in the latter, Monet has taken it to its logical conclusion. The brushstrokes have become thicker and the paint is laid on heavily. He concentrates purely on color, so that Camille's face does not have any features. The sky is one solid color, and even the sea has little variety.

**Camille sur la Plage (1870–71)**
***Camille on the Beach***
Courtesy of Giraudon. (See p. 48)

## *La Route de la Ferme,*
## *St.-Simeon en Hiver* (1867)
## The Road to the Farm,
## St.-Simeon in Winter

*Private Collection. Courtesy of Image Select*

S NOW interested the Impressionist painters because of the effects it created with light and because of the way it changed the shape of the landscape. Like other snowscapes that Monet painted, this one contrasts the white of the snow with dark patches. This is a very different treatment of color from that used in *Norvège, les Maisons Rouges à Bjornegaard* (1895), where the white emphasizes the red of the buildings and the blue of the sky.

The contrast between white and dark in the St.-Simeon painting makes the picture seem somber. The figures on the road are alone in their surroundings, their isolation echoed in the birds in the sky. Both form dark patches against a light background, and each seem equally unconnected to their companions. The sky and snow are painted in the same colors, giving the painting a timeless quality. In contrast, the Norwegian buildings are caught with the sun falling on them, giving the painting some specificity of time.

The Norwegian painting is not as stark as the earlier work. The snow reflects pink from the sun, and the blue sky is more welcoming than the gray in the St-Simeon picture. The paint is laid on with quick brushstrokes, whereas the earlier picture has an air of precision to its brushwork.

**Norvège, les Maisons Rouges
à Bjornegaard (1895)**
*Norway, the Red Houses at Bjornegaard*
Courtesy of Giraudon. (See p. 196)

LA ROUTE DE LA FERME, ST.-SIMEON EN HIVER ❊

## GLAÇONS SUR LA SEINE À BOUGIVAL (1867)
## ICE FLOES ON THE SEINE AT BOUGIVAL
*Musée d'Orsay. Courtesy of Image Select*

*T*HE composition of this painting, and its date, suggest that Monet was still interested in the same techniques that he had been using while in Normandy. Three years earlier, he had been engrossed in painting snow scenes, but not in the same style as this.

Monet uses an almost monochromatic color scheme with little variety between the gray and white of the palette. This seems suitable for recording a dull winter's day. It is in contrast to his later treatment of the Seine in winter as depicted below. In *La Seine a Bennicourt, Hiver* (1893) the color scheme is more varied, and the touches of yellow and light blue help to give the picture a warmer tone. In addition, he is preoccupied with laying on small brushstrokes of individual colors to create an all-encompassing atmosphere. In *Glaçons sur la Seine à Bougival*, however, the technique is more concerned with toning brushstrokes in to create a solid block of color.

The trees to the left are painted as vertical lines that form a screen that is reflected in the water. This is reminiscent of contemporary Japanese art. The use of color and the decorative and simplistic interpretation of the landscape are all in keeping with Japanese art, which was very popular at this time.

**La Seine à Bennicourt, Hiver (1893)**
*The Seine at Bennicourt in Winter*
*Courtesy of Christie's Images. (See p. 186)*

### *Terrasse à Ste.-Adresse* (1867)
### Terrace at Ste.-Adresse
*M.O.M.A., New York. Courtesy of Giraudon*

*P*OVERTY forced Monet to return from Normandy to the family home around 1867, and while there he painted this view from one of the upstairs rooms. The man seated is Monet's father. Monet's stepson commented later that the abundance of flowers on the terrace suggests that Monet's love of flowers was inherited from his parents. The painting appears composed and almost artificial when compared with some of the earlier works, which are deliberately given a spontaneous feel.

Monet later referred to this painting as the "Chinese painting with flags." At that time the words "Japanese" and "Chinese" were often interchanged. He owned some Japanese prints, and their influence is seen in this work. The flags that dominate the picture dissect the three horizontal bands of the painting—the terrace, the sea, and the sky—providing a vertical balance.

The composition itself is unconventional, with the faces of the people turned away from the viewer. The boats and ships in the background emphasize the modernity of the scene, as they were vital to trade in the town. Their shapes on the horizon are sharply geometric, contributing to the oriental tone of the painting. While Monet's treatment of the sky is flat, the sea shows signs of his fascination with its every changing color, a fascination that emerges strongly in later works.

## *Portrait de Madame Gaudibert* (1868)
## Portrait of Madame Gaudibert

*Musée d'Orsay. Courtesy of Image Select*

MADAME Gaudibert was the wife of one of Monet's patrons, who commissioned this life-size portrait from him at a time when he was in desperate financial straits.

Monet had painted portraits earlier in his career. In particular, *Camille, ou la Femme à la Robe Verte* (1866) was especially successful. However, this slightly later work, while mimicking the pose of the earlier portrait, has advanced in technique; the composition is more complex. The averted face is intriguing, particularly as this was a commissioned portrait. As can be seen in the later work *Essai de Figure en Plein Air* (1886), this pose was one Monet favored greatly. The head turned to one side turns the woman into an anonymous figure. Monet has painted a fashionable woman of society rather than a detailed individual portrait.

The later painting reveals how Monet takes the anonymity of the figure to new levels. In *Portrait de Madame Gaudibert*, the face of the woman may not be shown fully, but the features that are revealed can be discerned easily. In the secondary image, the face is not averted as far as Madame Gaudibert's, yet the features are blurred and unidentifiable. As the title of the painting suggests, the later work was concerned entirely with aesthetic composition.

**Essai de Figure en Plein Air (Vers la Gauche) (1886)**
*Study of a Figure Outdoors (Facing Left)*
*Courtesy of Giraudon. (See p. 160)*

## *VOLTIGEURS DE LA GARDE FLANANT AU BORD DE L'EAU* (1870)
## SOLDIERS STROLLING BY THE RIVERSIDE

*Courtesy of Christie's Images*

THE steamboat on the water and the guards patrolling the riverbank give *Voltigeurs de la Garde Flanant au Bord de l'Eau* a modern element, preventing the rural setting from being timeless. Similarly *Prairie de Limetz* (1887) relies on the dress of Alice Hoschedé to date the painting to contemporary times.

The figures in both pictures are treated in a similar cursory technique that does not allow for any detailed paintwork. However, they do draw the eye toward them. Alice achieves this by her prominent position in the painting and the pink splash that her dress makes. She is, however, just another aspect of the landscape. The guards in this painting also attract the eye through the bright color they make against a dusty, brown background. The eye then moves from them to the woman seen further along the road. Monet creates a depth in both paintings by using two distinct groups of people with a distance between them. In *Voltigeurs de la Garde Flanant au Bord de l'Eau*, the road running straight ahead into the distance adds to the depth.

**Prairie de Limetz (1887)**
***Limetz Meadow***
*Courtesy of Christie's Images. (See p. 166)*

Monet's treatment of light on the surface of the water is interesting. He shows an incomplete reflection of the steamboat as a result of light reflecting strongly off the water and cutting the boat off from its reflection. Water, light, and reflection become increasingly important elements in his work.

## *CAMILLE SUR LA PLAGE* (1870–71)
## CAMILLE ON THE BEACH

*Courtesy of Giraudon*

THE treatment of the subject in this painting is simplistic. The figure poses on the beach facing toward the viewer and in close proximity, yet she has no features to her face, with the merest hint of an outline for her nose and eyes. She is an anonymous woman without identity.

Monet's formal portrait of Camille (*Camille au Petit Chien* (1866)) is in stark contrast to this work. It depicts Camille in profile but with careful attention paid to her features, so that her face is revealed in detail. Her clothes are treated to the same level of care, and she would be recognizable as the subject in reality. Part of Camille's lack of detail in *Camille sur la Plage* may be due to the unfinished nature of the work— in places the canvas shows through. While this alone does not necessarily indicate that a work is unfinished, the lack of a signature adds weight to the assumption. Monet did not sign all his finished work, but in this case it seems certain he had not finished the painting.

**Camille au Petit Chien (1866)**
*Camille with a Little Dog*
*Private Collection, Zurich.*
*Courtesy of Giraudon. (See p. 32)*

The brushstrokes are laid on thickly and are clearly visible to the viewer. The work has an air of spontaneity that is especially evident when examining the sea, which is painted in with a few brushstrokes using only three colors.

### SUR LA PLAGE À TROUVILLE (1870–71)
### ON THE BEACH AT TROUVILLE

*Musée Marmottan. Courtesy of Giraudon*

P AINTED while on vacation with Boudin, this picture depicts both Camille and Boudin's wife on the beach at the popular French tourist spot of Trouville. Monet's choice of subject again reflects his desire to record modern scenes. He chose to show this familiar resort in an untraditional way.

First the viewer is thrust in very close to the two women. This is the opposite technique to that used in *La Plage à Trouville* (1870). The result is to make the viewer slightly uncomfortable, as if he were invading an intimate scene. This discomfort is furthered by the relationship between the two women. The central space between them is empty; neither woman acknowledges the presence of the other. Their features are not detailed, so there is an air of anonymity about them. Similarly, the people walking in *La Plage à Trouville* are not painted in detail.

In the background other tourists can be seen, also devoid of identifiable features. This, combined with the quick, heavy brushstrokes, adds to the spontaneity of the painting. In both works Monet is advocating the *plein-air* technique of painting.

**La Plage à Trouville (1870)**
*The Beach at Trouville*
Courtesy of Christie's Images. (See p. 52)

### *LA PLAGE À TROUVILLE* (1870)
### THE BEACH AT TROUVILLE
*Courtesy of Christie's Images*

IN both *La Plage à Trouville* and *Barques de Pêche devant la Plage et les Falaises de Pourville* (1882), Monet sought to perpetrate the concept of *plein-air* painting. The cursory depiction of the figures and the quick dashes of paint on the canvas add to the idea that these are works of spontaneity. Each depicts leisure activities being carried out.

However, the Trouville painting shows a number of people walking along the beach. In contrast, the Pourville work depicts a solitary individual, the lack of buildings in the picture adding to his air of isolation. In *La Plage à Trouville* the viewer becomes the isolated person. A strip of sand at the front of the painting is empty of people, and the viewer is facing the approaching tourists, which means the viewer has the sensation of walking against the general flow of people. Despite the fashionable location, the viewer is removed from the main action.

The colors used in this work are brilliant. The flags give the painting a lively air, and the luminosity of the sunshine makes the whole picture warm. In contrast, the colors used in the Pourville painting are more muted. The sky is nearly filled with cloud, and the palette used is less jewel-like.

**Barques de Pêche devant la Plage et les Falaises de Pourville (1882)**
*Fishing Boats in front of the Beach and Cliffs of Pourville*
*Courtesy of Christie's Images. (See p. 124)*

### CHASSE-MARÉE À L'ANCRE, ROUEN (1872)
### FISHING BOAT AT ANCHOR, ROUEN

*Louvre, Paris. Courtesy of Giraudon*

*T*HERE is an overwhelming feeling of
loneliness to this painting. The stillness that
surrounds it adds to that sensation. The lack
of movement in the water and on land, and the
non-specific time of day, give it a timeless quality.

The figure on the ship is isolated in his
environment by the sheer size of the boat and its
masts thrust up into the sky. The straight lines formed
by the masts mimic the lines of the poplars, which
pierce the sky behind the ship on the banks. The
sky itself covers a large part of the canvas, adding to
the timeless nature of the painting. The vastness of
the sky is exaggerated by its becoming almost one
with the water, so that the painting is dominated by
their blueness.

Against this background, the ship stands out.
Her masts dissect the sky, preventing it from
completely overwhelming the picture. The detail of
the ship's rigging is a
complex arrangement of
lines that contrast with
the restful simplicity of
sky and water.

### *BATEAUX DE PLAISANCE* (1872)
### PLEASURE BOATS

*Musée d'Orsay. Courtesy of Giraudon*

BOATING as a hobby and pastime became very popular in France in the nineteenth century. At the time many people worked long days in the city, choosing the weekends to either visit the country or seaside, where many went aboard the pleasure boats.

For Monet, his boating scenes represented the attempts by a typical Frenchman to enter into a dialog with nature. For this reason the paintings are frequently empty of people and seem to be very isolated moments. In this picture there are only a couple of people on the bank, and their features are indiscernable. In *Chasse-Marée à l'Ancre* (1872) there is only one man on board the ship, and his isolation is exaggerated by its size. Both paintings devote a lot of space to the sky, which adds to the insignificance of the individuals.

Prior to his move to Argenteuil, Monet painted only merchant ships and working boats.

**Chasse-Marée à l'Ancre, Rouen (1872)**
*Fishing Boat at Anchor, Rouen*
*Louvre, Paris. Courtesy of Giraudon. (See p. 54)*

*Chasse-Marée à l'Ancre* shows such a ship. Once at Argenteuil, however, Monet rarely produced marine paintings that did not feature pleasure boats, and *Bateaux de Plaisance* is typical of those he painted at the time.

## CARRIÈRES-ST.-DENIS (1872)

*Courtesy of Giraudon*

THIS landscape shows many of the traditional Impressionist trademarks. Some of the techniques within it can be traced to later landscapes, such as *Antibes, Vue de Cap, Vent de Mistral* (1888). Even though they treat contrasting subjects, one being a natural landscape, the other a town, there are some similarities.

*Carrières-St-Denis* has three broad horizontal bands going across the canvas. In the foreground is the water; above it is the town with its patchwork of roofs forming blocks of colors. To the left, some bushes and poplar trees break the horizontal created by the town. The poplars reach into the blue sky that forms the third band. In *Antibes, Vue de Cap, Vent de Mistral*, the banding is made up of four elements of land, sea, mountains, and sky. The presence of water in both was to become a common element in Impressionist work and appears repeatedly in later paintings.

The brushstrokes on the water form strong linear bands in places that disrupt the reflection of the poplars to the point where they disappear in patches. The later painting is concerned with capturing the color of the sea to such an extent that the strength of the blue prevents any reflections from appearing.

**Antibes, Vue de Cap, Vent de Mistral (1888)**
*Antibes, View of the Cape in the Mistral Wind*
*Courtesy of Christie's Images. (See p. 170)*

## NATURE MORTE AU MELON (1872)
## STILL LIFE WITH MELON

*Courtesy of Giraudon*

MONET painted very few still lifes. This study of fruit is treated in a similar manner to his landscape paintings, in the sense that the composition is structured around parallel planes. *Nature Morte au Melon* is not treated with the obvious banding approach evident in some of Monet's landscapes, although this compositional technique is present. The wall in the background forms one strip of color; the tablecloth creates another square of color that is prevented from reaching completely across the canvas by the strip of dark tabletop painted in the middle and side of the picture. These lines of varying color create strong geometric shapes on the canvas. It is easy to see a triangle in the right-hand corner where the wood meets the tablecloth and the frame. Similarly, the wall forms a rectangle.

These geometric shapes are disrupted by the fruit and plates used as the focal points of the composition. It is not by accident that Monet chose round fruits as his subject: the roundness of the melon, grapes, peaches, and the plate contrast with the geometric shapes of their background. The treatment of varying color and light on these draw the eye away from the solid colors with which the backdrops have been painted in. As a result, the whole is harmonized.

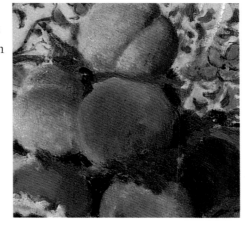

## *LA LISEUSE* (1872)
## THE LOVER OF READING

*Walters Art Gallery, Baltimore. Courtesy of Giraudon*

**D**URING the eighteenth century, women often featured in paintings as allegories or with allegorical subjects. There would be a narrative context to the paintings that could be read by the symbolism included in the painting.

In *La Liseuse*, Monet has taken Camille and painted her in an attitude that is reminiscent of these earlier paintings. However, he has given the treatment a modern rendition and there is no symbolism or allegory to the work. Camille's face is shown in profile and her expression is serene. There is no story to be read into the work; as it is a painting of purely aesthetic purpose. The woman in her pink dress reflects the flowers around her. This association between nature and the female as a flower is evident in *La Barque* (1887), where the color of the women's dresses echo the color of the flowers on the bank.

*La Liseuse* was unusual in its time for posing the woman outdoors. This later became a common practice, but at the time it added to the originality of the painting. Both paintings celebrate the female in harmony with a natural background of flowers.

**La Barque (1887)**
***In the Rowing Boat***
*Courtesy of Topham. (See p. 162)*

## LA CAPELINE ROUGE,
## PORTRAIT DE MADAME MONET (1873)
## THE RED CAPE, PORTRAIT OF MADAME MONET

*Cleveland Museum of Art. Courtesy of Giraudon*

PAINTED at Argenteuil, this work depicts Camille Monet caught as she passes the window. The air of spontaneity about the picture contrasts strikingly with the more formal pose of *Femme Assise sur un Banc* (1874). The intimacy of Madame Monet's portrait is conveyed in the glance she throws over her shoulder at Monet as she passes.

Unlike the composition of *Femme Assise sur un Banc*, in *La Capeline Rouge, Portrait de Madame Monet* the artist uses a very obvious frame around his central subject in the form of the curtains and windowed doors. The frame invades that painting to the point of covering most of the canvas. In the secondary image the subject fills the canvas to the extent that all of her dress cannot be contained in the picture. In this painting the woman is set apart from her natural background. In Madame Monet's portrait, the outside and inside world are connected through the white of the snow and the white of the curtains.

**Femme Assise sur un Banc (1874)**
*Woman Seated on a Bench*
Courtesy of the Tate Gallery. (See p. 84)

The red hood draws the viewer's gaze to Madame Monet; her face turned toward the viewer is intimate. Her central position between the curtains, the bright hood and her inward gaze make her the focus of the painting. In a similar way the seated woman of 1874 is striking against her green background. Her eyes also form a connection between the viewer and the subject of the painting.

### *LA FALAISE DE STE.-ADRESSE* (1873)
### STE.-ADRESSE CLIFFS
*Courtesy of Christie's Images*

$I$N both these paintings Monet has restricted himself to the essentials only, his aim to create an overall impression. For this reason there is no detail on the sea or the shore of *La Falaise de Ste.-Adresse* but merely strokes of color. The difference between these two paintings lies in Monet's tension between land and sea in *Etreat, La Plage et la Falaise d'Aval* (1884) and the calmer landscape of *La Falaise de Ste.-Adresse*.

The horseshoe of land provides a balanced curve in the main painting. The curves and rounded ends to the cliffs give the whole picture a softer feel than in the later work. In this, the jagged point of the cliff end and the uneven beach and sea surface make for a more dramatic painting. *La Falaise de Ste.-Adresse* has a wash of yellow that encompasses the land and the beach, creating a warm glow that is reflected in the sky.

The paintings that Monet produced of the Normandy coast were exhibited in 1898 and proved very popular with the buying public. The combination of familiar scenes and aesthetic presentation meant that these pictures sold easily.

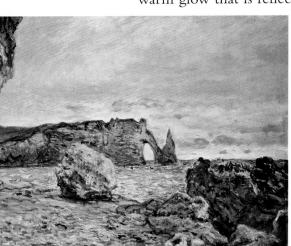

**Etreat, La Plage et la Falaise d'Aval 1884**
*Etreat, the Beach and the Aval Cliff*
Courtesy of Christie's Images. (See p. 140)

## BOULEVARD DES CAPUCINES (1873)
*Courtesy of the Visual Arts Library, London*

DEPICTING a modern scene, Monet shows a Paris that is bustling and full of action. He has caught the fleeting nature of movement precisely by dabbing on paint to represent people, rather than dwelling on their detail. This technique is also used in *La Plage à Trouville* (1870) where the people are equally as lacking in detail. He also picks another modern subject; that of the tourist resort.

As well as creating a spontaneous painting that dwells on the instantaneousness of the moment, Monet is also investigating the effects of winter light in *Boulevard des Capucines*. This is the cause of the off-white glow in the sky which reflects on to the street below. Against this, the people seem like dark marks, and this earned them the description of "black tongue-lickings" from the critic Leroy. The different effects of sunlight would especially be understood by the contemporary viewer as the work was displayed with a companion piece depicting the street in summer.

In *La Plage à Trouville*, Monet paints on a level with his subject, so that everything is seen to scale and the numbers of people are camouflaged. In the main picture, his view is from above, looking down. This increases the impression of the people as a small, scurrying crowd in a city of wide boulevards and tall, modern buildings.

**La Plage à Trouville (1870)**
*The Beach at Trouville*
Courtesy of Christie's Images. (See p. 52)

## *ZAANDAM* (1871)
*Courtesy of Image Select*

MONET visited Holland on his way back from England at the end of the Franco-Prussian War. While there, he painted 24 canvases in just three months. The combination of architecture and water in a flat landscape was what attracted him most. This combination appears again and again in his work.

This painting is reminiscent of some of the marine pictures from Argenteuil, particularly in the technique used on the water. The reflections of the buildings are sharp and the colors clear. *La Zuiderkerk, Amsterdam* (1872) has the same clarity of color but the surface of the water has been treated differently. It is not the mirror that the canal is in the main picture. The strokes used on the water are short flecks of varying colors. In *Zaandam* the water is painted with smooth brushwork. Long white lines are used to indicate where the water reflects light alone. The ripples of the water are also depicted by the wobbly reflection, particularly evident when looking at the reflected masts of the boat.

Both paintings use blocks of colors when it comes to the buildings. In *Zaandam*, a block of red is placed next to a block of blue, representing the house fronts. The architectural nuances are not detailed.

**La Zuiderkerk, Amsterdam (1872)**
***Zuiderkerk at Amsterdam***
*Philadelphia Museum of Art. Courtesy of Image Select. (See p. 72)*

### *LA ZUIDERKERK, AMSTERDAM* (1872)
### ZUIDERKERK AT AMSTERDAM

*Philadelphia Museum of Art. Courtesy of Image Select*

THERE is some confusion about the date of this painting. Monet visited Holland in the summer of 1871, yet this painting is dated 1872. It is now generally agreed that, despite the date, this and another painting, also dated 1872, are part of the 1871 series.

The composition of this painting is centered on the spire, with the canal leading up to it. On the right are the tall buildings of Amsterdam, with people moving along the pavement and over the bridge. These people are painted as flecks. The reflections of the buildings on the water are represented by yellow brushstrokes. This is the same as in *Le Parlement, Couchant de Soleil* (1904), where the buildings' reflection is identified only as a dark patch on the water.

A comparison of these two paintings reveals that by 1904 Monet was less concerned about observing the boundaries between building and water. It is difficult to identify where building ends and reflection begins. In *La Zuiderkerk, Amsterdam* the water is clearly separated from the buildings and there is no danger of building and reflection merging. The painting is in focus and uses strong blocks of color, whereas the London painting has a mist over it that prevents a detailed look at the subject.

**Le Parlement, Couchant de Soleil (1904)**
***Houses of Parliament, Sunset***
*Courtesy of Christie's Images. (See p. 224)*

## *IMPRESSION, SOLEIL LEVANT* (1872)
## IMPRESSION, SUNRISE

*Courtesy of Giraudon*

THIS painting is responsible for the birth of the term "Impressionist." It was included in the first exhibition held by the Society of Painters, Sculptors, and Engravers in 1874. Monet was a founding member of this society, which had originated from the express desire to end the artistic stranglehold of the Salon.

A critic who attended the exhibition, M. Louis Leroy, wrote a now famous article in *Le Charivari* in which he used the term "Impressionist" based on the title of this painting. Despite the fact that Leroy had used the word derisively, the group decided to adopt it and painters such as Renoir and Degas were happy to be called Impressionists. Impressionist art is concerned with capturing on canvas the light and color of a fleeting moment, usually with brilliant colors painted in small strokes, side by side, rather than blended together.

Ironically, *Impression, Soleil Levant* is not typical of Monet's work, although it does carry elements of his usual style. The horizon has disappeared and the water, sky, and reflections have merged. The buildings and ships in the background are only vague shapes and the red sun dominates the painting. As Monet himself commented: "It really can't pass as a view of Le Havre." His aim was not to create an accurate landscape, but to record the impressions formed while looking at that landscape.

## *LES COQUELICOTS, ARGENTEUIL* (1873)
## POPPIES AT ARGENTEUIL

*The Louvre, Paris. Courtesy of Giraudon*

*T*HIS scene from nature contrasts with the recent paintings that Monet had been doing, which were mainly of city subjects. Its soft tranquility reflects some of the warmth of a summer's day: the figures merge with their surroundings, almost melting into them; the body of the boy in the foreground disappears into the grass, and the dress of the woman matches some of the darker shades of grass on the right.

Figures that fade into a rural background are entirely appropriate to Monet's views on nature. He felt that nature was not there to serve man but that man was a part of nature. Hence, the figures in this painting are not the main focus. If it were not for the sloping edge of the poppies drawing the eye of the viewer back from the first group of people to the second on the horizon, the figures could be overlooked. The dominant force of this painting is without doubt the poppies.

Painted in an almost abstract style, the splashes of red draw the observer's eye at once, despite the fact that roughly half the canvas is given over to sky, creating a feeling of an airy summer's day. The blue of the sky contrasts with the red of the poppies and ensures that the landscape, as opposed to the people, leaves the strongest impression on the viewer.

## LE PONT DE CHEMIN DE FER, ARGENTEUIL (1874)
## THE RAILWAY BRIDGE, ARGENTEUIL

*Musée d'Orsay. Courtesy of Giraudon*

MONET was fascinated with painting this railroad bridge during his time at Argenteuil. For him it represented the coming together of modernity and nature. He always painted it with a train rushing across and billowing smoke. This explosion of energy was contrasted with the tranquility of the water. The bridge, which has contact with both, links the two different worlds.

This is in contrast with *Les Déchargeurs de Charbon* (1875), where the bridge appears to be a barrier separating the workers from the passers-by. The solid paint on the bridge in the main painting is contrasted with the colors used on the water. In places the brushwork is applied sketchily. However, when Monet wishes to illustrate the movement of light over the water he uses denser and more detailed strokes. This is especially evident on the water moving under the bridge.

*Les Déchargeurs de Charbon* has dark colors used repeatedly to give the whole painting a gloomy appearance. The main painting does not have one dominant color or tone; instead each section is given a color of its own that complements its neighbor and also separates it: for example, the greenish-yellow of the grass is not related to the gray of the bridge, but the tones manage to complement one another.

**Les Déchargeurs de Charbon (1875)**
**Unloading Coal**
*Courtesy of Giraudon. (See p. 86)*

## *AU PONT D'ARGENTEUIL* (1874)
## THE BRIDGE AT ARGENTEUIL

*Musée d'Orsay. Courtesy of Giraudon*

A NUMBER of paintings from Argenteuil depict boats and this is a classic example. Monet had a very commercial mind and, as boating was a popular pastime for Parisians in the 1890s, his choice of subject matter was guaranteed to appeal to the buying public. The whole is a tranquil scene that has a translucent air to it.

The colors harmonize to help create an aesthetic view. Broken color is used where it is necessary to depict the surface of the water affected by light, and under the arches of the bridge where the light reflects off the water. By using adjacent lines, an almost translucent effect is created. The bridge to the right is another feature that Monet favored in paintings at this time. In this picture the lines and arches provide a geometric balance to the translucence of the water.

*Les Déchargeurs de Charbon* (1875) is a contrasting vision both of the river and of a bridge. In this painting the river is a source of industry, not relaxation. The bridge is used as a dark frame across the top half of the painting and appears threatening. In *Au Pont d'Argenteuil* the river is peaceful and the bridge a complement to it.

**Les Déchargeurs de Charbon (1875)**
*Unloading Coal*
*Courtesy of Giraudon.* *(See p. 86)*

## *LE PONT D'ARGENTEUIL* (1874)
## THE BRIDGE AT ARGENTEUIL
*Courtesy of Image Select*

WHAT makes this landscape dramatic is the railroad bridge in the background. Its presence dominates the painting and forms a solid structure that spans the canvas.

Its solidness contrasts with the bushes and the woman—both of which are curved and rounded shapes—the antithesis of the straight lines of the bridge. Similarly the green of the grass is fresh and natural compared with the gray of the bridge. Monet is painting the meeting of modernity with tradition. The line of the bridge is echoed in the horizon. However, the natural world and modern are not harmonized in the same way as they are in *Waterloo Bridge* (1902). In this painting, bridge, water, and sky fuse. The focal point is the patch of sunlight on the water rather than the bridge. Even the smoking chimney stack in the background seems to be a balanced part of the painting.

It is interesting to note that in *Le Pont d'Argenteuil*, Monet deliberately chose this view of the bridge so that it did not include the factories that lay just to the left of where the canvas ends. He obviously felt that he could not harmonize industry into a natural background as he had learned to do when he painted *Waterloo Bridge*.

**Waterloo Bridge (1902)**
*Courtesy of Christie's Images.* (See p. 220)

## *FEMME ASSISE SUR UN BANC* (1874)
## WOMAN SEATED ON A BENCH
*Courtesy of the Tate Gallery*

THIS woman is a striking presence on the canvas, in a dress of pink and white, against a backdrop of a green bench and green trees. She is deliberately placed out of harmony with her surroundings, and this gives her a commanding presence.

Her parasol, hat, and dress define her as a fashionable woman. Monet uses these to form shapes and solid lines that are geometric in

design. Little effort is made to shade her dress or to make use of any shadowing in the painting. The strong, solid shape of the woman is balanced by regular horizontal lines on the bench and vertical lines representing the foliage behind. This style has often been compared to Manet's.

The bench itself is flat and, were it not for the woman seated on it, would appear as a screen of green rather than with depth to it. Perspective and depth are not of importance in this painting. Monet is primarily concerned with creating an overall impression using strong shapes and lines.

## LES DÉCHARGEURS DE CHARBON (1875)
### UNLOADING COAL
*Courtesy of Giraudon*

*P*AINTED just outside Argenteuil, this picture is unique in Monet's work: it is the only one of his paintings that depicts laborers at work. The result is a dramatic painting that has a schematic composition to it.

A sense of mechanization is achieved by the regular spacing and number of men walking up and down the planks. The men are a part of the machine. The regularity of their movement and the depiction of industrial work going on are countered by the casual passersby on the bridge. This subject is a very marked contrast to the idyllic boating paintings from the same period. The color scheme is dark and gloomy compared with the lighter tones of the boating paintings. However, although the subject matter is different, Monet's ability to create harmony and balance is not compromised and is achieved by his use of the vertical and horizontal. The bridge forms a strong network of grid lines that provides a frame over the picture.

The men moving across the planks are a strong vertical balance to the horizontal lines of the planks. The overall effect is to create an order within the painting that harmonizes the picture and adds to its machine-like qualities.

## *LA JAPONAISE* (1875)
## THE JAPANESE WOMAN

*Boston Museum of Art. Courtesy of Giraudon*

*I*NCLUDED in the second Impressionist Exhibition, this work was an abrupt departure from the style that Monet had been cultivating over the preceding decade. At the time the painting caused a sensation. One critic praised its "solid coloring" and "emphatic impasto."

It harks back to *Camille, ou la Femme à la Robe Verte* (1866), which was painted in a style that the Salon would appreciate. Monet was very poor at this time, and one theory holds that he chose deliberately to paint a conventionally posed painting that would have a high chance of selling, with perhaps the added benefit of attracting a new patron. Monet had a strong commercial instinct that lies behind some of his choices of subject matter and style.

The careful composition and posing of Camille in this painting lacks all the spontaneity that Monet had been looking to capture in other works. Camille is not true to life, as she is wearing a blonde wig. The robe itself is magnificent, and Monet's depiction of the samurai warrior contrasts with the sweetness of Camille's face. Monet's interest in Japanese art, an influence on some of his earlier work, was obviously still strong at this time.

## Un Coin d'Appartement (1875)
## A Corner of the Apartement
*Courtesy of Giraudon*

IN *Un Coin d'Appartement* and *Le Capeline Rouge*, Monet experiments with framing his subject. In *Un Coin d'Appartement*, he repeats the shape of the curtains and plants in the foreground in the curtains in the background. The frame has the dual purpose of drawing the eye into the painting and also focusing the viewer's perception of the subject. By making the frame well lit compared with the subject, Monet emphasizes the darkness of the room.

Monet is clearly experimenting with light and dark. In the earlier painting of 1873, Madame Monet is in contrast with the dark interior because she is well lit and wears a bright color. In the later picture, Jean Monet, who stands at the center, is one of the darkest patches on the canvas; the light reflecting from the floor at his feet emphasizing his darkness.

Jean Monet is isolated in the room and is separated from the woman at the table. He makes a disturbing figure because he is painted so dark and because of the steady gaze he directs at the viewer. Madame Monet has a similar direct gaze, but hers is a more intimate, loving look. Jean Monet is also vulnerable; his size is exaggeratedly small when compared with the height of the plants, which appear to threaten to engulf him.

**La Capeline Rouge, Portrait de Madame Monet (1873)**
***The Red Cape, Portrait of Madame Monet***
*Cleveland Museum of Art. Courtesy of Giraudon. (See p. 65)*

## EN PROMENADE PRÈS D'ARGENTEUIL (1875)
## WALKING NEAR ARGENTEUIL

*Courtesy of Giraudon*

MANY of Monet's paintings of summer days in the countryside around Argenteuil share an intensity about them. Both *Les Coquelicots, Argenteuil* (1873) and *En Promenade près d'Argenteuil* are concerned with capturing the essence of a summer's day. The passion with which Monet wanted to preserve this particular day is evident in the colors used.

Both paintings have a beautiful blue sky with soft, white clouds billowing across it, but the real color comes from the flowers. In the earlier painting, Monet concentrated on capturing the incredible strength of the red poppies. In the later painting, the poppies are again present, but other flowers also shine through so there are blues and whites as well as red in the grass. In both paintings the flowers are represented by a dash of color rather than a detailed presentation.

In *Les Coquelicots, Argenteuil*, the flowers appear to threaten to swamp and overwhelm the people. In *En Promenade près d'Argenteuil*, the figures stand out above the flowers and are seen full length. They are not dominated by their environment but form a family unit that is in harmony with the natural world around them. No buildings appear in this painting, adding to its pastoral tone.

**Les Coquelicots à Argenteuil (1873)**
*Poppies at Argenteuil*
*Louvre, Paris. Courtesy of Giraudon. (See p. 76)*

# LES DINDONS (1876)
## THE TURKEYS
*Courtesy of Giraudon*

IN 1874, Ernest Hoschedé invited Monet to stay on his estate and commissioned four decorative panels from him. This is one of them. While the subject matter itself is very traditional, Monet's treatment of it is not.

One can compare this with *Trophée de Chasse* (1862), which was created early in Monet's career, while he was still careful to follow the traditions of art. It depicts dead game birds in a conventional composition, the whole carefully arranged for the artist's benefit. The formality of this earlier painting is not in evidence in *Les Dindons*. The birds, painted realistically to life size, ramble across the painting at will. This has the result of making the composition seem asymmetrical. The carefully arranged triangular symmetry of the still life is not in evidence here. Monet even has the audacity to cut one bird off at the neck, unheard of in paintings of the establishment, adding to the spontaneity of the painting.

The viewer is placed on a level with the birds, as if he were lying on the grass. In *Trophée de Chasse* the distance is carefully maintained between subject and viewer. The different angle taken in the later painting adds to the informality of the whole picture.

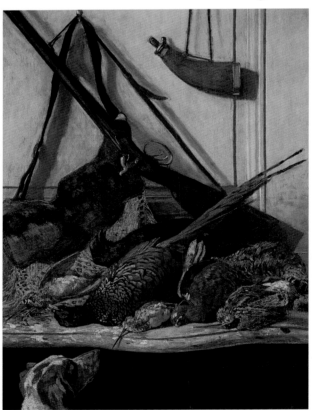

**Trophée de Chasse (1862–63)**
*Sporting Prize*
*Musée d'Orsay. Courtesy of Giraudon. (See p. 20)*

# *Le Pont de l'Europe, Gare St.-Lazare* (1877)
## Europe Bridge, St. Lazare Station
*Musée Marmottan. Courtesy of Giraudon*

ETWEEN January and April 1877, Monet painted 12 pictures of the Gare St. Lazare. Although these are sometimes referred to as Monet's first attempt at a series of paintings, they differ from each other too widely to justify such a title, although they do show his growing interest in using the same subject again and again. Monet's choice of a station as a subject reflects his desire to paint modern scenes. The author Emile Zola described them as "paintings of today."

Monet uses the smoke from the engines in a similar way to the fog in *Charing Cross Bridge, La Tamise* (1903): as a tool to distort light and color patterns. However, whereas this is made into a localized effect in *Le Pont de l'Europe, Gare St.-Lazare*, the later painting is dominated by fog, creating a haze over the setting. The architecture is not recreated in detail, as in the earlier work, but becomes shadowy as a result of the fog. Monet's aim with *Le Pont de l'Europe, Gare St.-Lazare* is to paint a modern subject. The buildings, the bridge, and the train are all synonymous with modern Paris. There is an air of bustle in this scene that is missing altogether from the serene Charing Cross Bridge painting.

**Charing Cross Bridge, La Tamise (1903)**
*Charing Cross Bridge, The Thames*
Courtesy of Christie's Images. (See p. 222)

## *LA ROUTE À VÉTHEUIL* (1878)
## THE ROAD TO VÉTHEUIL

*Phillips Collection. Courtesy of Image Select*

*L*A ROUTE *à Vétheuil* is very similar in composition to *La Route de la Ferme, St.-Simeon en Hiver* (1867). Both show the broad sweep of a road approaching buildings in the distance; however, the two works are set in contrasting seasons and the effect of these different seasons is that the snow muffles the winter scene.

*La Route à Vétheuil* is dominated by geometric shapes and lines. The road in both paintings draws the eye in and forms two meeting diagonals on the canvas. However, although the snow markings in the St. Simeon painting underline this linear aspect, the concentration of white effectively dampens the overall impact. The road in the later painting is not only free of snow but has been painted using obvious vertical brushstrokes. The bank forms a triangle on the canvas, and the hills in the background also form a geometric shape.

Monet uses light to emphasize the geometry of the painting so that the dark hills in the background of *St.-Simeon en Hiver* contrast with the well-lit bank in the foreground. Similarly, the shadows of trees not visible in the painting fall across the road, creating parallel horizontal bands of darkness that contrast with the vertical band of the road.

**La Route de la Ferme, St.-Simeon en Hiver (1867)**
*The Road to the Farm, St. Simeon in Winter*
*Private Collection. Courtesy of Image Select. (See p. 38)*

## *CHRYSANTHÈMES* (1878)
### CHRYSANTHEMUMS

*Courtesy of Christie's Images*

*T*HE strange, almost three-dimensional effect of the flowers on the wallpaper is reminiscent of the Japanese fans in *La Japonaise* (1875). The flowers float in an uncomfortable way behind the basket of flowers. This effectively causes two different points of interest in the painting, so that the eye struggles between the wallpaper and the flowers to find a central focal point.

This is in contrast to *Les Roses* of 1925–26, where Monet's treatment of the flowers is based purely around the pattern they create. The flowers are painted without the detail afforded to the chrysanthemums. In *Les Roses,* Monet's aim is entirely decorative. Here the flowers do not float across the canvas but are given a strong background and are placed in an obvious domestic setting. Although not a conventional still life, this picture does depict flowers in a more traditional way.

The quick brushstrokes that cross each other create a blurring around the center of the flowers. Out of the mass of pink and white, the individual petals emerge to spiky effect. The roses are painted as dashes of color that have little definition. By this time Monet is more concerned with the impression of the flower than with the detail.

**Les Roses (1925–26)**
*The Roses*
*Courtesy of Giraudon. (See p. 254)*

## L'ESCALIER (1878)
### THE STAIRS
*Courtesy of Christie's Images*

*T*HIS painting is one that was sold to an American buyer, although later it was bought back by the collector Durand-Ruel. America proved to be a profitable market for the Impressionists, thanks to Durand-Ruel, who opened it up to them through exhibitions.

The appeal of *L'Escalier* lies in its subject matter and composition. The stairs leading up are inviting, while the archway provides a provocative glimpse into the courtyard. This is in contrast to *Vétheuil* (1901), where the town is seen from a distance and the viewer is set apart by an expanse of water. *L'Escalier* is an intimate and inviting view of a building at close hand, with the viewer now at the heart of the town. *L'Escalier* is unusual for its choice of an everyday rural building as its subject. Most of Monet's paintings of buildings depict either modern or Gothic architecture or groups of buildings seen from a distance, as in *Vétheuil*.

The warm pinks and golden colors used in this painting combine with the deep blue of the sky to create the effect of a balmy, lazy summer's day. Even the shadow falling across the bottom left corner does not detract from the warmth.

**Vétheuil (1901)**
*Pushkin Museum, Moscow. Courtesy of Topham.* *(See p. 216)*

### *POMMIERS PRÈS DE VÉTHEUIL* (1878)
### APPLE TREES NEAR VÉTHEUIL
*Courtesy of Christie's Images*

THIS painting depicts the view down into the valley of Vienne-en-Artheis. It is typical of the rural scenes that Monet produced once he moved to Vétheuil. There is no evidence of industrialization in this painting, which instead focuses on the apple trees in the foreground.

Monet uses small brushstrokes of different colors on the trees to create the effect of sunlight falling across the blossoms. These smaller strokes gradually become longer as he moves down into the valley. These longer strokes have the effect of merging colors together and creating a blurring of lines so that the trees in the foreground appear to be strongly in focus compared with the valley in the background.

The critic, Philippe Birty, saw this painting exhibited at Durand-Ruel's gallery, along with others by Monet. His response was as follows: "It is from afar that these paintings must be judged, and the near-sighted and insensitive will only perceive a confused mixed-up, tough or shaggy surface resembling the underside of a Gobelin tapestry with an excessive use of chromium-yellows and orange-yellows"

## *LA RUE MONTORGEUIL FÊTE DU JUIN 30, 1878* (1878)
## MONTORGEUIL STREET FAIR, JUNE 30, 1878
*Musée d'Orsay. Courtesy of Giraudon*

*T*HIS painting is easily confused with *Rue St.-Denise Celebrations, Juin 30, 1878* (1878) as they depict virtually identical scenes. It is a testimony to Monet's enthusiasm for the subject that he devoted two canvases to the cause of reproducing the excitement in the streets on one day.

The occasion was a celebration of the World Fair that Paris had been hosting. As can be seen from the painting, the streets were decked with flags and banners. A sense of national pride is present in this work, as well as an incredible air of spontaneity. Monet's pride in his country is evident in the overpowering national colors of red white, and blue. The quick brushstrokes and pulsing colors are all testimony to Monet's desire to capture quickly the atmosphere of the scene. His rendition of a street below had been painted in a similar manner earlier in *Boulevard des Capucines* (1873). The view Monet paints in both pictures is from an upper story, providing a similar perspective.

**Boulevard des Capucines (1873)**
*Courtesy of the Visual Arts Library, London.*
*(See p. 68)*

In addition, Monet chooses to depict the crowds in both paintings by using quick, dark brushstrokes that emphasize the individuals being caught in mid-movement. In both these works, the people are anonymous, but in the later work this has developed to the extent that even the men and women cannot be differentiated.

## *LE GIVRE* (1879)
## THE FROST

*The Louvre, Paris. Courtesy of Giraudon*

*T*HIS period was a desolate one for Monet. Financially, the household was stricken, and he was heavily in debt. The winters of 1878 and 1879 were severe, forcing prices up. In September 1879 Camille died.

Many critics have attempted to draw parallels between Monet's mood at this time and his paintings. It is true that the gloom of *L'Eglise à Vétheuil, Neige* (1879) could reflect his emotions, but a look at *Le Givre* undermines this. Although the subject matter itself could represent Monet's personal desolation, his treatment of it suggests that this is not the case. *Le Givre* shows ice and frost sparkling in the sunlight, the white frost warmed up with pink and blue. Although a barren scene, the colors used give it a warmth lacking in the buildings of *L'Eglise à Vétheuil, Neige*. The whole scene is harmonized through the use of strong horizontal strokes on the ice and small vertical strokes on the bushes. The vertical of the poplars balances the horizontal of the river bank. This use of horizontal and vertical balance can be found in *L'Eglise à Vétheuil, Neige* as well.

Although it is difficult to try to read the artist's personal life into his work, these paintings do reveal that Monet's changing moods meant that he was being attracted to very different styles.

**L'Eglise à Vétheuil, Neige (1879)**
*The Church at Vétheuil, Snow*
*Louvre, Paris. Courtesy of Giraudon.*
*(See p. 110)*

### *L'EGLISE À VÉTHEUIL, NEIGE* (1879)
### THE CHURCH AT VÉTHEUIL, IN SNOW
*The Louvre, Paris. Courtesy of Giraudon*

*P*AINTED from the opposite bank of the river, this somber work is very different from some of Monet's summer paintings in Vétheuil. The palette of colors used is extremely restricted, offering very little relief from the white and dark colors. *Le Jardin de Vétheuil* (1881) provides a useful contrast to demonstrate how tightly controlled this palette was.

Matching this rigid color scheme, Monet adheres as doggedly to the rules of symmetry. The bank forms a solid, horizontal line that is repeated in the hedgerow growing above, counterbalanced by the vertical of the church tower and the poplar trees. The buildings all form solid shapes on the canvas, making a pattern of oblongs, squares, and triangles. In *Le Jardin de Vétheuil*, the house, veranda, and steps form similar shapes on the canvas and attempt to replicate the balance of horizontals and verticals. However, this is disrupted by the garden with the strong, twisting shape of the tree dominating the rigid shape of the house.

Some relief from the rigidity of the painting is given by the short, broken brushstrokes used to create the water surface; these help to soften the impact of the flatter bank above.

**Le Jardin de Vétheuil (1881)**
*The Garden at Vétheuil*
*Courtesy of Christie's Images.*
*(See p. 120)*

## PORTRAIT DE MICHEL MONET BÉBÉ (1878–79)
## PORTRAIT OF MICHEL MONET AS A BABY
*Courtesy of Giraudon*

THIS painting was produced not long after Michel was born. He still has the full cheeks of a very young baby, although he does have a lot of hair. Despite the quick brushwork, Monet succeeds in creating an impression of Michel that is immediately recognizable as the same child in later portraits.

This style of creating an impression of the person rather than producing a detailed portrait was a change from his earlier work; Monet treats his portraits from this period in the same style as his landscapes. There are a number of portraits of his sons from around this period. His family had, until now, often featured as the human presence in many of his landscapes. However, from around 1880 onward Monet included people less and less in his landscapes, which might explain his desire to record them in portraits.

The portrait of Michel is intimate and does not attempt to exaggerate any features or caricature the child. This is a very different style from that used in *Portrait de Poly* (1886), where the man posing is painted in a manner suggestive of his personality. When looking at Michel's portrait, there is no indication as yet of his character.

**Portrait de Poly (1886)**
***Portrait of Poly***
*Musée Marmottan. Courtesy of Giraudon. (See p. 148)*

## *PORTRAIT DE JEUNESSE DE BLANCHE HOSCHEDÉ* (1880)
## PORTRAIT OF THE YOUNG BLANCHE HOSCHEDÉ
*Musée des Arts, Rouen. Courtesy of Giraudon*

*B*LANCHE Hoschedé, daughter of Monet's friend and patron Ernest whom he met in 1876, was 14 when this portrait was painted. It is the essence of a young girl, her rosy cheeks, bright eyes, and red lips making her the epitome of youth.

This portrait is very different from that of Camille made 14 years earlier. The style is more typical of Monet's Impressionism. The brushwork is more obvious across the portrait, whereas *Camille au Petit Chien* (1866) has this type of brushwork only on the dog. The colors fuse across the painting, so that there is a blurred effect especially noticeable on Blanche's dress. Although her features are clear, they are not painted in the same sharp style as Camille's. Blanche is painted with a strongly patterned wallpaper behind her that prevents her figure from dominating in this painting in the same way that Camille does.

The colors used are mostly pastels, but the red of the hat attracts the eye. This color helps to emphasize Blanche's red lips, but it also draws the viewer's gaze away from the face. Blanche is painted as part of an overall design, Camille as a separate entity.

**Camille au Petit Chien (1866)**
***Camille with a Little Dog***
*Private Collection, Zurich. Courtesy of Giraudon. (See p. 32)*

## PORTRAIT DE MICHEL EN BONNET À POMPON (1880)
## PORTRAIT OF MICHEL IN A POMPOM HAT
*Courtesy of Giraudon*

MICHEL Monet was Monet's second son by Camille. At the time of this portrait he was two years old. Monet had initially felt uncertain about fatherhood, but this doubt had gone by the time Michel was born. Both this portrait and *Portrait de Jean Monet* (1880) are a testimony to the love that he felt for his children.

In Michel's portrait, the two-year-old sat apparently docile while his father painted him. The quick brushstrokes, used on the red coat and the red of his cheeks in particular, suggest that Monet at least wanted to create the impression of the portrait having been dashed off. This is especially noticeable when compared to the shorter strokes used on Jean's portrait. Although Michel's features are identifiable, the nose, lips, and eyes are not painted in as much detail as the features are in Jean's portrait.

Both paintings share an anonymity of background. A blanket color has been applied so that each boy is the focus of the painting. In some of Monet's portraits of fashionable women, the background and clothing are given as much detail as the face and body of the woman. This makes a statement about how the women are perceived. With both of these portraits the individual child is the center of attention.

**Portrait de Jean Monet (1880)**
*Portrait of Jean Monet*
Courtesy of Giraudon. (See p. 118)

## PORTRAIT DE JEAN MONET (1880)
## PORTRAIT OF JEAN MONET
*Courtesy of Giraudon*

JEAN Monet would have been about 13 when this portrait was painted. Monet had used Jean frequently in landscape paintings before this portrait, sometimes with Camille and sometimes on his own. However, in all of these, he can be identified only as a small child rather than as an individual in his own right.

This portrait is entirely concerned with Jean as Jean. Care is taken to record his features, and he is painted as a full-face portrait. When compared with *Portrait de Madame Gaudibert* (1868), where the woman's face is averted to the point that her features are almost hidden, the intimacy of *Portrait de Jean Monet* is understood. Monet is recording Jean in a very personal style. The lack of detail to the background compared with *Portrait de Madame Gaudibert*, where even her clothes are carefully recorded, indicates clearly that Monet is interested in illustrating the individual that is Jean. Madame Gaudibert is recorded as yet another society woman whose identity is found in her clothes and her home rather than in her face.

Monet's style has changed over the intervening years between these paintings. The brushstrokes are thicker, and he is not afraid to use blocks of color solidly placed on the canvas. Unlike his treatment of Madame Gaudibert's dress, Monet does not paint his son's clothing in detail.

**Portrait de Madame Gaudibert (1868)**
**Portrait of Madame Gaudibert**
*Musée d'Orsay. Courtesy of Image Select. (See p. 45)*

## LE JARDIN DE VÉTHEUIL (1881)
## THE GARDEN AT VÉTHEUIL

*Courtesy of Christie's Images*

HERE, Monet shows an unruly and untamed garden. When compared with the earlier work *Jeanne-Marguerite, le Cadre au Jardin* (1866), this disorder is particularly marked. The regularity and structure provided by the steps and the china-blue plantpots on the terrace are fighting a losing battle with the foliage. The tree on the left of the painting snakes across the canvas and virtually obliterates the house. The shadow on the lawn is irregular in shape and adds to the sense of chaos. In *Jeanne-Marguerite, le Cadre au Jardin,* the shadows of the woman and the flowerbeds are neat blocks of black. In this later painting, the garden is trained and controlled, the beds and trees providing a safe environment to walk in. In *Le Jardin de Vétheuil* there is no one walking in the garden; its unruly appearance suggests that nature has gone wild.

**Jeanne-Marguerite, Le Cadre au Jardin (1866)**
***Jeanne-Marguerite, the Image in the Garden***
*The Hermitage, St Petersburg. Courtesy of Topham.*
*(See p. 30)*

The colors used in *Jeanne-Marguerite, le Cadre au Jardin* are laid on to the canvas as separate blocks so that the woman forms a block of white, the lawn a block of green and so on. This distinction is lost in *Le Jardin de Vétheuil,* where colors merge into each other, making one element difficult to differentiate from the next; the white of the house, for example, becomes the white on the tree leaves.

# *Fleurs à Vétheuil* (1881)
## Flowers at Vétheuil
*Courtesy of Christie's Images*

THE town depicted in *Fleurs à Vétheuil* is small and vulnerable on the canvas, isolated by a gray sky that matches the gray water in front of it. The same is not true in *Vétheuil* (1901), where the town has a strong presence on the canvas and attracts the eye to its jumble of colorful rooftops.

In contrast, the eye is drawn to the riot of color formed by the flowers in the foreground of *Fleurs à Vétheuil*. In fact, the flowers are not restricted to the foreground but threaten to envelop the picture. They are so bright that the town in the background seems washed out in comparison. Although the opening in the bushes provides a vista of Vétheuil, the tall flowers that spike up from the general melee of color that covers the bottom half of the canvas are threatening to close over the gap. Vétheuil is in danger of being swallowed up by nature, but in *Vétheuil*, the little town is serenity itself.

The colors used in *Fleurs à Vétheuil* form connections between themselves. The red flowers that band across the picture are repeated in color on the spiked flowers. These also have the rosy-white color of the flowers in the foreground. This provides them with a unity out of the confusion of colors.

**Vétheuil (1901)**
*Pushkin Museum, Moscow.*
*Courtesy of Topham. (See p. 216)*

## *BARQUES DE PÊCHE DEVANT LA PLAGE ET LES FALAISES DE POURVILLE* (1882)
## FISHING BOATS IN FRONT OF THE BEACH AND THE CLIFFS OF POURVILLE
*Courtesy of Christie's Images*

IN ORDER to paint this picture, Monet made a great effort to reach the exact location that he thought was necessary for the best viewpoint. It is recorded that he was seen clambering over cliffs and rocks dragging six or seven canvases with him. This would be in keeping with his ideals concerning *plein-air* technique, although the reality was that he finished most of the canvases in his studio.

*Barques de Pêche devant la Plage et les Falaises de Pourville* and *La Falaise de Ste.-Adresse* (1873) seem to lack some of the obvious spontaneity evident in other paintings, although the scurrying clouds in the former have some sense of being captured on canvas on location. The painting depicts sailing boats, which had already proved a popular subject when Monet lived at Argenteuil. Here the lonely figure on the shore is isolated by being detached from the fun of the boats at sea. This isolation

is emphasized by the careful blocking Monet adopts with each element. Strong lines separate the shore from the sea and the sea from the sky. There is no blurring of the boundaries in either painting, as has been seen in other work. Instead, each element is clearly differentiated from its neighbor.

**La Falaise de Ste.-Adresse (1873)**
*The Ste.-Adresse Cliffs*
*Courtesy of Christie's Images. (See p. 66)*

## CHEMIN DANS LES BLÉS À POURVILLE (1882)
## PATH THROUGH THE CORN AT POURVILLE
*Courtesy of Christie's Images*

WHAT is most noticeable about this painting are the strong, bright colors. The blue of the sea is reminiscent of some of Monet's paintings from the Mediterranean. What he set out to do was to capture the effects of a brilliant summer's day on the beach landscape.

By using strong colors that contrast with each other rather than blend together, he achieves the effect of each color appearing even stronger. Thus, where the red of the wheat touches the blue of the sea, each benefits from the contrast; the same is true where the sea meets the shore. This time, the effect of the sun is to render the sand a brilliant white. These blocks of colors work together to create an impression on the viewer. There is actually very little detail in the picture itself.

This painting has strong lines that form horizontals and verticals. In the picture the curved path not only draws the eye toward the sea but also provides a vertical curve that meets the sand and continues to the horizon. This balances the horizontal of the sea and cliff.

## *LA PLAGE À POURVILLE, SOLEIL COUCHANT* (1882)
## THE BEACH AT POURVILLE, AT SUNSET

*Musée Marmottan. Courtesy of Giraudon*

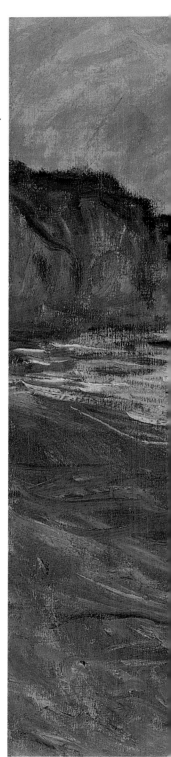

*T*HE effect of the sun setting on the beach is entirely decorative. The sweep of the beach across the bottom of the painting is balanced in equal measure by the sea and the sky. Unlike other paintings from this period, there is no sense of drama between the three elements.

*La Plage à Pourville, Soleil Couchant* is harmonized by the colors used. The orange and yellows of the sun in the sky are reflected on to the water beneath and again in the colors used on the beach. This strengthens the link between the three elements and harmonizes the picture. Similarly, blue paint is used on the shore as well as the sea and sky. The painting has been produced purely for the pleasure of viewing it. Monet has dispensed with the previously held beliefs of the official French art world that paintings need to have a purpose other than beauty. Prior to the appearance of the Impressionist artists, only paintings with moral or religious significance were considered correct subjects for art.

The painting is purely concerned with the harmony of nature. No humans are present in the painting, and no message is intended. "Art for art's sake" was soon to become one of Monet's central beliefs.

## *LES GALETTES* (1882)
## THE CAKES
*Courtesy of Giraudon*

ALTHOUGH Monet did not paint many still lifes, he chose to present one to the Municipal Council of Le Havre. This suggests that he felt strongly that they were of significance within the portfolio of his work. His still life paintings tended to appear in the earlier part of his career, from the late 1860s to the early 1880s.

This later work in the period shows evidence of his changing technique. The treatment of the tablecloth compared with *Nature Morte au Melon* (1876) reveals much more vigorous brushwork and thicker strokes. Similarly the cakes are painted with obvious brushwork and are not attempting to be an exact copy of the subject in the same way as was Monet's treatment of the grapes in *Nature Morte au Melon*. More startling still is his use of perspective. The earlier work shows the subjects on a tablecloth with a wall behind; the plate leaning against the wall helps the viewer understand the perspective. No such aid is provided in *Les Galettes*. The cakes are painted onto a tablecloth which is merely a flat background of color. No sense of depth is given to the picture, so that the cakes are in danger of sliding off what appears to be a sloping plane. This is a huge step forward in terms of Monet's perception of his subjects.

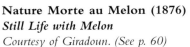

**Nature Morte au Melon (1876)**
***Still Life with Melon***
*Courtesy of Giradoun. (See p. 60)*

## *EGLISE DE VARENGEVILLE, EFFET DU MATIN* (1882)
## VARENGEVILLE CHURCH, MORNING EFFECT

*Courtesy of Christie's Images*

THIS remarkable painting is unusual for its composition. Many of Monet's paintings from this period were created from the top of the cliffs looking down or along, but here he has broken that precedent and chosen to paint the cliffs at their base, and face on.

To reach this position Monet would have had to make strenuous efforts, dragging his canvas with him. His desire to paint this particular subject is expressed in the enthusiastic manner in which the paint is applied to the canvas. Swift strokes of varying colors are laid side by side. The cliff face in particular is a medley of color. No effort to tone in the

paint is made, so each color stands in stark contrast to its neighbor. This gives the painting its sense of drama and an overall brilliancy of color. This lack of washing colors together and, instead, contrasting them with each other has become synonymous with Impressionist work.

Monet creates a sense of the scale of the cliffs by using long vertical brushstrokes on the cliff face, their height is emphasized by the small strip of canvas reserved for the sky, so that the cliffs completely dominate the space. Finally, the perilous nature of the cliffs is expressed by the church that stands at their apex; it is almost threatening to tip over.

## LA CHEMIN CREUX
## DANS LA FALAISE DE VARENGEVILLE (1882)
## THE PATH THROUGH THE HOLLOW
## IN VARENGEVILLE CLIFF

*Walsall Art Gallery. Courtesy of Topham*

WHAT must have appealed to Monet about this scene has to be the strong geometric shapes that are formed by the valley and the sea. This is in contrast to the cliff paintings such as *Sur la Falaise près de Dieppe* (1897), where the view of the coastline does not lend itself to such shapes.

The triangular shape of the hills is complemented by the inverted triangle of the sea. The top of the cliffs and the horizon form horizontal lines that are counterbalanced by the vertical path. This path draws the eye forward toward the sea. It is now that the viewer realizes that the perspective cannot be accurate. The sea appears to be about to fall on to the heads of the women walking along. Monet must have manipulated the scene in order to emphasize the geometric qualities of the landscape. A similar problem occurs with the Dieppe painting where, in order to understand the perspective of the cliff banking on the right in relation to the cliffs on the horizon, the viewer assumes the viewpoint to be taken from a hollow.

The minute figures in the Varengeville painting appear to be overwhelmed by the land swelling around them and by the sea in front of them. They are tiny and derive their importance only as a focal point to draw the observer's eye forward along the path.

**Sur la Falaise près de Dieppe (1897)**
*On the Cliffs near Dieppe*
Courtesy of Image Select. (See p. 210)

## *LA SEINE À PORT-VILLEZ* (1883)
## THE SEINE AT PORT-VILLEZ
*Courtesy of Christie's Images*

**I**N this picture of 1883, Monet chose to paint the view without including either buildings or people in it, unlike his recreation of the same subject in 1908–09. The result is a tranquil picture that focuses on the contours of the land.

The tranquility is matched by the water, which is calm and reflects the scene around it almost perfectly. The shorter brushwork on the surface of the water differentiates it from the land. The whole blends together to form a harmonized view of nature. The same cannot be said for the later piece with an identical title. In this, Monet has included the town as the central focus. The simplicity of the scene in the 1883 painting has been extended to a simplicity of color and style in the 1908–09 work. Here colors are applied as thick bands on the canvas in contrasting tones to each other so that harmony is not the object of the piece.

The artist chose warm gold and yellow tones to complement the green of the land in the earlier work. The water reflects the tones of the land. The result is a very restful painting.

**La Seine à Port-Villez (1908–09)**
*The Seine at Port-Villez*
*Courtesy of Christie's Images. (See p. 218)*

# LE CHÂTEAU DE DOLCEACQUA (1884)
## THE DOLCEACQUA CHÂTEAU

*Musée Marmottan. Courtesy of Giraudon*

PAINTED in 1884, this winter scene of the château has a symmetry to it that makes it aesthetically pleasing. The curve of the bridge, which cuts horizontally across the painting, is counter-balanced by the curve of the river bed, which moves from the front to the back of the painting.

The buildings on the right of the valley are a sign of human life, but the opposite side of the river is free to nature. The green of the left bank has encroached on the right and is creeping up the sides of the château. This suggests that, rather than man dominating nature, nature is claiming back the land. This theme occurs increasingly in the artist's later work. Monet's preoccupation with the power of nature is particularly evident in the paintings that he did of the Creuse Valley. *Vallée de la Creuse, Effet du Soir* (1889) is typical of these, perfectly capturing the barrenness of the wild landscape.

In *Le Château de Dolceacqua* Monet suggests that, in a few years' time, nature will have completely reclaimed the land and the valley will be like the Creuse. The comparison is furthered by the sweep of the river bed in both pictures, forming the central dissection of the canvas.

**Vallée de la Creuse, Effet du Soir (1889)**
*Creuse Valley, Evening Effect*
*Musée Marmottan. Courtesy of Giraudon. (See p. 178)*

## *ETREAT, LA PLAGE ET LA FALAISE D'AVAL* (1884)
## ETREAT, THE BEACH AND THE AVAL CLIFF
*Courtesy of Christie's Images*

*T*HERE is evidence from Monet's sketchbook that, in 1884, he was experimenting with the idea of "framing" within a picture. In this painting the cliff juts into the picture on the left, creating a frame. In the earlier work, *Chemin dans les Blés à Pourville* (1882), there is no attempt to frame the piece; instead, the landscape fills the canvas to the edge.

The cliff frame in *La Plage et la Falaise d'Aval* gives the painting some depth. The composition establishes a relationship between the cliffs and the sea in two ways. First, the horizontal lines of the waves are paralleled in the horizontal shading on the far cliffs and on the shore. Although their purpose on the sea is to denote movement and on the shore unevenness, they do help to establish a relationship between the two. In a black and white reproduction of this painting, it is almost impossible to distinguish where the sea ends and the shore begins.

A second relationship is established by the use of shade and light. Using purple to indicate the effect of light softens the solidity of the rock. This is especially evident around the base of the rock on the shore. The sea in turn has patches of dark color, indicating shadow and the rippling of the waves.

**Chemin dans les Blés à Pourville (1882)**
*Path through the Corn at Pourville*
*Courtesy of Christie's Images.*
*(See p. 127)*

## *BORDIGHERA* (1884)

*Chicago Art Institute. Courtesy of Giraudon*

*T*HIS painting of a view of Bordighera is dominated by the trees in the foreground. Their trunks rhythmically twist across the picture, dissecting the view of the town and preventing the strong blue of the sea from forming a solid band of color across the canvas.

This is in contrast to *Bras de la Seine près de Giverny* (1897), where the trees are used as a frame to the view. The contrast in styles between these paintings is obvious. For the earlier landscape Monet uses a palette of vibrant colors that mark out each element against each other; the green of the trees contrasts with the blue of the sea. With the Seine painting, Monet concentrates on harmonizing the color. The colors are subtler and flow together so that it becomes difficult to identify where one color ends and another begins. Across the whole, a pale blue seems to hang. In *Bordighera* the landscape is sharp in comparison. No one color pervades the whole painting.

The tangle and shape of the trees form a contrast to the solid squares and oblongs of the town. The brushstrokes on the leaves are rounded with flecks of white paint. The surface of the sea is expressed using several horizontal lines of contrasting blue.

**Bras de la Seine près de Giverny (1897)**
***Branch of the Seine near Giverny***
*Musée Ile de France. Courtesy of Giraudon. (See p. 204)*

## LE CAP MARTIN (1884)

*Musée des Beaux Arts, Tournai. Courtesy of Giraudon*

MONET first discovered the beauties of this headland when he came here with Renoir. They intended to paint it together, but in 1884 Monet secretly visited the area on his own. The resulting pictures are full of energy and color.

The roughness of the rocks complements the uneven brushstrokes used on the sea. The strokes are laid on quickly and thickly, the sea has odd, broad, white dashes of color on it to represent the waves and the horizontal lines of the sea contrast with the rocks, with brushstrokes painted in several directions. The trees provide the vertical mass that balances the horizon. The horizontal and vertical are particularly emphasized in this painting by the contrasting techniques used on the sky, sea, and trees. The sky is painted as a smooth surface, making use of pale colors; the sea and trees are painted in stronger colors using shorter brushstrokes, and a definite line is formed where they each meet the sky.

On the sea, a single vertical white line is highlighted against the pink skyline, this represents a sail. When compared with Monet's earlier detailed paintings of boats at Argenteuil, it is obvious how his technique and composition have changed. By 1884, Monet was content to represent the boat as a dash of white paint, an impression on the horizon.

## PORTRAIT DE L'ARTIST DANS SON ATELIER (1884)
## PORTRAIT OF THE ARTIST IN HIS STUDIO

*Musée Marmottan. Courtesy of Giraudon*

*T*HIS painting is unsigned, and the bottom half of the canvas has been worked on only slightly. It can, therefore, be assumed that this is an unfinished work. Monet did other self-portraits, but what makes this interesting is its setting in his studio.

Unlike the 1880 portrait of Michel (*Portrait de Michel en Bonnet à Pompon*), Monet felt the need to include a background to his own portrait. Significantly, he does not refer to this as a self-portrait but titles it in the third person. This is a portrait of him as artist, not as a private individual; his definition comes from his art. Also, unlike the portrait of his son, his eyes are averted from the viewer, not inviting an intimate response as Michel's do. Thus, although the viewer is being given access to the artist's studio, the experience is not an intimate one, and the viewer of the painting is slightly removed from the subject of the picture.

Despite this, the portrait of Michel appears more formal than this painting. Michel is posed, whereas Monet is pictured caught at an idle moment, his look distant and his hands relaxed onto his legs. It is interesting that Monet chose to paint himself as an artist at a moment when he is not actually working.

**Portrait de Michel en Bonnet à Pompon (1880)**
*Portrait of Michel in a Pompom Hat*
*Courtesy of Giraudon. (See p. 116)*

## PORTRAIT DE POLY (1886)
## PORTRAIT OF POLY

*Musée Marmottan. Courtesy of Giraudon*

WHILE Monet was working at Belle-Ile, the fisherman Guillaume Poly frequently visited the inn where he was staying. Monet painted this portrait during that period.

What appears to have attracted Monet to Poly as a subject was his features—he began his career as a caricaturist, earning money to go to Paris from selling caricatures of well-known people in his home town. This makes it surprizing that Monet did not produce very many portraits, as he was clearly interested in the human face. Unlike portraits of his children or of himself, as depicted in *Portrait de l'Artist dans son Atelier* (1884), this portrait of Poly is full of character. The eyes are turned toward the viewer, the nose is rounded and the cheeks are ruddy; the hat and beard add character to the face.

In Monet's own portrait he is also wearing a cap and has a beard, but there is no sense of his personality. He is defined as an artist by the canvases in the background. With the painting of Poly, it is easy to read a story into the portrait; his face invites the viewer to read it, and he requires no background to generate interest.

**Portrait de l'Artist dans son Atelier (1884)**
*Portrait of the Artist in his Studio*
*Musée Marmottan. Courtesy of Giraudon. (See p. 146)*

## *L'Eglise à Bellecoeur* (1885)
## THE CHURCH AT BELLECOEUR
*Courtesy of Image Select*

PAINTED only a few years apart, both *L'Eglise à Bellecoeur* and *L'Escalier* (1878) are intimate, close views of a rural setting. Both are devoid of people and concentrate on the beauty of the buildings. In *L'Eglise à Bellecoeur*, Monet shows a little more of the village, which seems sleepy in the warm sun.

The difference between the two paintings is that *L'Eglise à Bellecoeur* appears to have a greater preoccupation with shapes and patterns than *L'Escalier*. The buildings form a pattern of oblongs, squares, and triangles. They are all, apart from the church, depicted with the slant of their roofs facing the viewer, creating a contrast between the red of the roof and the white of the walls that emphasizes the geometric shapes. The low walls running around the properties echo this. *L'Escalier* does have a similar pattern with its walls and roof, but because the viewer is positioned closer to a single building, this pattern is more difficult to appreciate.

In the later painting, the clouds in the sky provide a contrast to the shapes below. The tree in the foreground helps to disrupt the regular pattern. The amount of space given over to the blue sky helps to prevent the complex of buildings from overwhelming the painting.

**L'Escalier (1878)**
*The Stairs*
Courtesy of Christie's Images. (See p. 102)

## *GLAÏEULS* (1882–85)
### GLADIOLI
*Private Collection, Paris. Courtesy of Image Select*

THE agent Durand-Ruel commissioned Monet to paint a set of decorative panels; it took the artist over two years to complete them. They each depicted either fruit or flowers and were designed to reflect the changing seasons.

The shape of the gladioli is perfect for an upright panel. Painted positioned on what appears to be a tabletop, the background is very simple, unlike in *Chrysanthèmes* (1878), where the wallpaper pattern is clearly in evidence behind the flowers. By placing the gladioli against a blue background the colors of the flowers are revealed to startling effect. In contrast, the chrysanthemums lose impact to the effect created by the flowers on the wallpaper. Whereas the chrysanthemums move across the canvas, the gladioli form vertical lines counterbalanced by the edge of the table.

The strange vase that the flowers are presented in forms a second focal point, drawing the eye away from the gladioli and down the canvas to the white flowers on the vase. With the chrysanthemums it is the wallpaper that draws the eye up. The vertical linear rhythm of the gladioli painting is pleasing to the eye.

**Chrysanthèmes (1878)**
***Chrysanthemums***
*Courtesy of Christie's Images.* (See p. 100)

## *TEMPÊTE, CÔTES DE BELLE-ILE* (1886)
## STORM ON THE COAST OF BELLE-ILE
*Courtesy of Giraudon*

MONET found the changing weather conditions on the Brittany coast very exciting. In particular, when the weather was rough, he was impatient to capture the moment on canvass. The swiftness of the brushstrokes in these Belle-Ile paintings adds to the air of dashing the pictures off in a frenzy of excitement.

In both paintings, a sense of drama is created by moving the horizon very high up the canvas, making the sea appear to be flooding into the sky. *Tempéte, Côtes de Belle-Ile* in particular exaggerates this effect by using similar colors for both the sky and the sea. The swift brushwork on the sea versus the more solid strokes of the sky help the viewer to identify the horizon. In *Les Roches de Belle-Ile* (1886) Monet uses a bank of cloud to identify the dividing line.

In *Tempéte, Côtes de Belle-Ile*, the sea itself is painted with a lot of white, to create the turbulence of the waves hitting the rocks. Because the painting has been cropped on the left, the viewer feels that he has been placed on a level with this turbulence. In *Les Roches de Belle-Ile* the artist's viewpoint is higher, which helps to maintain a distance from the water, leaving the observer removed from the intensity of the action.

**Les Roches de Belle-Ile (1886)**
***The Belle-Ile Rocks***
*Musée d'Orsay. Courtesy of Giraudon.*
(See p. 156)

## *LES ROCHES DE BELLE-ILE* (1886)
## THE BELLE-ILE ROCKS
*Musée d'Orsay. Courtesy of Giraudon*

*T*HE wildness of the sea is captured here by Monet's use of color, the dark blues and greens typical of a stormy sea. In contrast, when the sea is viewed on a calm day, as in *La Plage à Pourville, Soleil Couchant* (1882), the sea has softer tones. The color of the sea in *Les Roches de Belle-Ile* does not indicate a specific time of day, but the end of day is explicit in the second painting.

**La Plage à Pourville, Soleil Couchant (1882)**
**The Beach at Pourville, at Sunset**
*Musée Marmottan. Courtesy of Giraudon. (See p. 128)*

The drama of this painting lies entirely in the stormy waves of the sea. Their power is complemented by the solid dark mass of the rocks. The movement of the waves is presented by using short brushstrokes and by laying different colors next to each other, so that a dark blue stroke may be placed alongside a green one. In *La Plage à Pourville, Soleil Couchant* Monet lengthens the brushstrokes along the surface of the sea to produce a more regular surface and manages to create the impression of tranquility.

The menacing presence of the rocks actually takes up nearly the same amount of canvas space as the sea. By painting them encroaching across to the bottom left of the painting, but losing ground to the sea in the top right-hand corner, Monet depicts the eternal battle between land and sea.

### CHAMP DE TULIPES, HOLLANDE (1886)
### TULIP FIELD, HOLLAND
*Courtesy of Giraudon*

MONET was inspired by the flatness of Holland when he visited the country in 1871. This picture emphasizes that flatness by the equal split between land and sky. The windmill at the center helps break up the never-ending horizon and gives a perspective to the view.

It was not just the flat landscape that inspired Monet; he was animated by the colors he saw as well. This is evident in the quick brushwork that switches from color to color. Such chaos of color is echoed in *Le Bassin aux Nympheas, les Iris d'Eau* (1900–01), where contrasting colors are painted on to the canvas side by side. The result in both works is an explosion of color that floods the viewer's sensations. So inspired by the color was Monet that he did not feel it necessary to give the flowers form. Their color is their essence, so it was sufficient to represent them by a patch of red or purple. This is especially noticeable in *Champ de Tulipes, Hollande*, where the scope of a view does not require a detailed rendition of a flower as if viewed from up close.

**Le Bassin aux Nymphéas, les Iris d'Eau (1900–01)**
*Water Lily Pond, Water Irises*
*Courtesy of Christie's Images. (See p. 214)*

## *ESSAI DE FIGURE EN PLEIN AIR*
## *(VERS LA GAUCHE)* (1886)
## STUDY OF A FIGURE OUTDOORS (FACING LEFT)
*Courtesy of Giraudon*

MONET painted a pair of figure pictures, one depicting a woman turned to the left and one to the right, in 1886. The model for both was Suzanne Hoschedé, the daughter of his friends Ernest and Alice. Following Camille's death, Suzanne had become Monet's favorite model. This painting is reminiscent of one of Camille produced in 1873.

Suzanne's features are blurred, making her an anonymous figure.

Monet deliberately did not want the viewer to be looking for a personality or story in this painting. Because she has no expression, the woman becomes a part of the overall picture and should be viewed as part of the landscape. The wind is seen to affect her in a similar manner as it does the grass. Her skirt is being blown against her legs, and the ribbon from her hat is blowing forward. The majority of the short brushstrokes representing the grass are moving in the same direction. The grass on the brow of the hill is more defined and can be seen clearly to bend in the wind.

The colors used on the grass are very different from those in Monet's earlier work. This time they include pinks and whites, as well as green and yellow. This helps to harmonize the figure with her environment. The flecks of white from the grass make a connection with the white of her dress and with the clouds.

## *LA BARQUE* (1887)
## IN THE ROWING BOAT
*Courtesy of Topham*

FOR some critics, this painting is concerned with the nature of girls passing into womanhood. Their looks and bodies are undergoing constant change. This perpetual development is illustrated in the three girls by the lack of features shown. Even when compared with Blanche Hoschedé's face in *Blanche Hoschedé Peignant* (1892), which is only rendered in the vaguest terms, these girls' faces are sparse of detail.

Their association with nature is strong. Not only is Monet recording them at their most transient and developmental period in their lives, but, unlike Blanche Hoschedé, their clothing identifies them with the natural background they are in. The pink on their dresses is a reflection of the pink in the grassy bank behind the boat. For some critics this is symbolic of nature often being referred to as a female; to them Monet was using the women as a representation of nature.

Whether this was his aim is impossible to assert. What is certain is that this picture is one of harmony and balance. The boat is equally balanced by its reflection in the water, and all the colors work with the subject to create a tranquil painting.

**Blanche Hoschedé Peignant (1892)**
*Blanche Hoschedé Painting*
*Courtesy of Christie's Images. (See p. 182)*

## CHAMP D'IRIS JAUNES A GIVERNY (1887)
## FIELD OF YELLOW IRISES AT GIVERNY

*Musée Marmottan. Courtesy of Giraudon*

DESPITE the fact that this painting is entitled *Champ d'Iris Jaunes à Giverny*, two colors dominate—yellow and purple. The purple in the foreground is repeated in the hedges that span the middle of the painting. This is a very different treatment of the iris compared with the later *Iris Jaunes* (1924–25). In that painting, the yellow of the flower is the main focus; here it has been dampened in effect by being mixed with purple.

A second obvious difference is that the flowers themselves are the primary focus of *Iris Jaunes*. Deprived of a background, it is the essence of the plants that Monet is demonstrating. In the 1887 work,

Monet is putting the flowers in their context. They are painted in their natural habitat with a hedge and sky as background. They have none of the Oriental style that can be found in *Iris Jaunes* when placed back in a natural background.

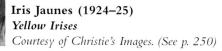

This painting has the horizontal banding found in many other paintings by Monet. The field of flowers forms the first band, the hedge the second and the sky the third. Painted in landscape format, this linear design is very obvious.

**Iris Jaunes (1924–25)**
***Yellow Irises***
*Courtesy of Christie's Images. (See p. 250)*

### *PRAIRIE DE LIMETZ* (1887)
### LIMETZ MEADOW
*Courtesy of Christie's Images*

*T*HE figure in the foreground is believed to be Alice Hoschedé, later to become Alice Monet. The two boys following her are her sons. This is one of the few paintings where Alice acted as model.

A natural scene, it captures the moment when the family is walking from Giverny. This summer outing is a theme that frequently recurs in Monet's work. The warmth of the day is made explicit by the parasol Alice carries; the use of yellow on the field adds to the warmth of the painting. The brushwork reflects the angle of the different planes it is used to depict: thus, horizontal brushstrokes are used on the field because it is a flat plane and diagonal ones are used on the hill in the background to emphasize the angle of the slope. Monet is trying to capture the nature of each element not only in terms of color but also its substance. The grass seems long and wild in the foreground precisely because it is painted with quick strokes that dart in all directions. This is of more importance to Monet than a detailed, accurate picture of the grass.

## *VUE D'ANTIBES* (1888)
## VIEW OF ANTIBES
*Courtesy of Image Select*

THE trees in the painting frame this distant view of the coastal town of Antibes. The blue of the sea and sky are so similar that they provide a backdrop against which to display the tree. It is the shape of the branches of the tree and its leaves that interests Monet.

In contrast, the bushes in the foreground of *Antibes, Vue de Cap, Vent de Mistral* (1888) are used for perspective purposes and to add to the linear quality of the painting. The tree in the *Vue d'Antibes* is the focus, its strong solid trunk and branches contrasting with the soft, almost translucent quality of the leaves. By placing the tree so prominently in the foreground, Monet emphasizes the subtlety of the colors and light that surround the city. The solid structure of the tree makes Antibes dreamlike in contrast. It floats on the water in a wash of gold and pink that creates a haze around it. In the second painting, thicker strokes and vibrant colors are used so that Antibes is not surrounded by the same mystical air.

A great deal of space on the canvas is given to the sky, which allows the tree to be emphasized and results in Antibes appearing small and delicate. This is one of four paintings of this composition, which forms a mini-series.

**Antibes, Vue de Cap, Vent de Mistral (1888)**
*Antibes, View of the Cape in the Mistral Wind*
*Courtesy of Christie's Images.* *(See p. 170)*

## *ANTIBES, VUE DE CAP, VENT DE MISTRAL* (1888)
## ANTIBES, VIEW OF THE CAPE IN THE MISTRAL WIND
*Courtesy of Christie's Images*

*W*HEN Monet arrived in Antibes, he wrote to Alice Hoschedé complaining about the difficulties that he was having capturing the unusual color of the local light. He wrote: "You swim in blue air, it's frightful."

This one is an example of the jewel-like colors he used in many of his Mediterranean paintings. The blue of the sea is almost unreal and is perhaps a symbol of what he was seeing rather than an accurate rendition. When compared with the pale sea in *Antibes, Vue de la Salis* (1888) it is even more startling. It is not allowed to dominate the painting too much by being kept in check by the bushes in the foreground. These form a horizontal line across the bottom of the work made up of yellows, greens, and pinks. The bushes are allowed to push into the band of color that is the sea and to break up its horizontal dominance. The sky, mountains, and city all form striking horizontals across the canvas. This trait is present in *Antibes, Vue de la Salis*, but the subtler colors prevent it from seeming so obvious.

Monet's palette of colors during this trip became enriched with new tones. In his earlier work he would never have used such a strong blue to represent the sea. This painting is testimony to Monet's confidence in his work.

**Antibes, Vue de la Salis (1888)**
*Antibes, View of the Fort*
*Courtesy of Christie's Images. (See p. 172)*

## ANTIBES, VUE DE LA SALIS (1888)
## ANTIBES, VIEW OF THE FORT

*Courtesy of Christie's Images*

MONET'S motifs are said to shift between the rough and the soft. *Antibes, Vue de la Salis* is definitely a soft subject. The colors glow with hints of gold, pink, and turquoise.

The harmonization of colors present in this painting appears again 20 years later in *Le Grand Canal et Santa Maria della Salute* (1908). The composition is also very similar. Both paintings feature a large expanse of water in the foreground, a building that appears to be floating on the water's surface and an expanse of sky above. This similarity arises from Monet's preoccupation with buildings next to water. His treatment of reflection in both works demonstrates how he was fascinated by the effect of light on a solid structure when it is placed by water. The reflection is reduced to the reflection of color rather than shape, so that the fort's reflection is created with lines of gold and that of Santa Maria della Salute becomes shimmers of pink.

The colors used in both are soft and pastel in tone. However, the Venetian work is dominated by blue and pink to the point that water, sky, and building are all represented in these colors. A*ntibes, Vue de la Salis* has more variety using rose, gold, white, blues, and greens. Each part of the picture is painted as distinct from its neighbor rather than fused together.

**Le Grand Canal et Santa Maria della Salute (1908)**
***The Grand Canal and Santa Maria della Salute***
*Courtesy of the Tate Gallery.*
*(See p. 228)*

## *PAYSAGE AVEC FIGURES, GIVERNY* (1888)
## LANDSCAPE WITH FIGURES, GIVERNY
*Courtesy of Image Select*

*I*N the second half of the 1880s, Monet returned to figure painting. He painted 16 pictures of his family between 1885 and 1889; striving to capture figures in a natural background in true *plein-air* style. Monet started trying to achieve this initially in 1865, with *Le Déjeuner sur l'Herbe*. His aim was to approach figure painting in the same spontaneous manner in which he worked on landscapes.

Monet tries to do this in *Le Déjeuner sur l'Herbe* by presenting the figures as if unrelated to each other, using strong blocks of color on the women, with little interest in shading. They are caught in the middle of an action rather than in a posed setting. In *Paysage avec Figures, Giverny* there is the same detachment between the figures. The first and second group are separated by a large space, the three figures in the foreground apparently unconcerned with each other. The viewer is positioned uncomfortably close to the first three people. This unusual angle adds to the air of spontaneity.

The colors used to signify the figures are repeated in the tones of the grass, trees, and hills in the background. Here Monet is using color to incorporate the figures as an integral part of the landscape.

**Le Déjeuner sur l'Herbe (1865)**
*The Picnic under the Trees*
*Pushkin Museum, Moscow. Courtesy of Giradoun.*
(See p. 24)

### CREUSE, SOLEIL COUCHANT (1889)
### THE CREUSE AT SUNSET
*Courtesy of Christie's Images*

WHEN Monet visited the Massif Central region of France, its bleakness and savagery instantly impressed him. He decided to paint the region around the River Creuse and try to capture that barren and dramatic landscape. When he started it was winter. To his horror, while he was still working on the details of a tree, spring arrived, causing the tree to bud. Unable to cope with his subject changing into a green and leafy tree, Monet paid the owner to strip the buds off. This demonstrates that Monet was perhaps not so receptive or reactive to nature as he would have liked his public to believe.

**Vallée de la Creuse, Effet du Soir (1889)**
*Valley of the Creuse, Evening Effect*
*Musée Marmottan. Courtesy of Giradoun. (See p. 178)*

The river and the rocks around it appear in many of the pictures of the region. This one depicts the river in the glory of a late afternoon. The effect of the light is to make the hills form a solid, dark mass against which the sky and water stand out. In contrast, the same view is cooler but allows the features of the hillside to emerge. The bleakness of the area is enhanced by the lack of vegetation, and the only source of warmth comes from the sky. This glow has gone from the hills once the sun has gone down.

### *VALLÉE DE LA CREUSE, EFFET DU SOIR* (1889)
### VALLEY OF THE CREUSE, EVENING EFFECT
*Musée Marmottan. Courtesy of Giraudon*

THE barren landscape of the Creuse Valley intrigued Monet, and he sought to capture its savagery. This is in contrast to other work from the period, such as *Sur la Falaise près de Dieppe* (1897). In that painting, Monet renders a rough landscape soft. Here the Creuse is empty and cold.

The strange blue light of the evening adds to the coldness of the painting. The blue touches the hills and the water. In contrast the hills seem red. They swell up on the canvas to form imposing round forms that seem to be never-ending. The sense of infinity that surrounds them is achieved by having them stretch right across the canvas and by giving them the appearance of forcing the sky back so that only a slim strip is left. In *Sur la Falaise près de Dieppe*, the expanse of sky adds to the sense of tranquility.

**Sur la Falaise près de Dieppe (1897)**
*On the Cliffs near Dieppe*
*Courtesy of Image Select. (See p. 210)*

What is interesting about the Creuse paintings is the range of effects Monet creates from the same subject. His study of different light at different times of day produced a set of pictures that come alive through the variety of colors used. Here blue has a strong presence; in others, orange, red, or purple are the dominant colors. In this way Monet maintains the interest of the viewer.

## *Peupliers au Bord de L'Epte* (1891)
## Poplars on the Bank of the Epte
*Courtesy of the Tate Gallery*

AS with the grainstack series of paintings, Monet often used poplars in his work. Like the subject of his first series, poplars were of great commercial importance to the rural community. The very trees that Monet was painting were due to be harvested for timber before he had completed the series. Monet struck a deal with the timber merchant, and together they bought them on condition that the merchant left them standing until Monet had completed his series of paintings.

Most of the 24 paintings in the series were made on board Monet's boat studio. They are painted at a point where the river bends back on itself to form an "S." Hence the double line of trees. By painting from on board his boat, Monet's vantage point is low, allowing the trees' height to be emphasized. They soar across the painting. The strong vertical trunks are contrasted by the soft curves of the leaves at the top, the billowing clouds echoing the shape of the treetops.

By painting a foreground of water, Monet creates the sensation for viewers that they are floating in the middle of the river. This has been described as a "duck's-eye" perspective. He is attempting to immerse his viewers into the landscape, as opposed to holding them back from it.

### *BLANCHE HOSCHEDÉ PEIGNANT* (1892)
### BLANCHE HOSCHEDÉ PAINTING
*Courtesy of Christie's Images*

I N the painting *Paysage avec Figures, Giverny* (1888) Monet uses short strokes across the canvas. The same technique is used in this picture. However, unlike the earlier painting, *Blanche Hoschedé Peignant* does not form connections between the background and the figures using similar colors. Here Blanche is in contrast with her surroundings rather than blending in.

Although there is a similar air of spontaneously catching the moment, this painting is less concerned with people as an integrated aspect of the landscape. The red of the jackets and hats on the women are strikingly in contrast to their background. However, Monet's brushwork is the same for the figures and their surroundings. Both people and trees are blurred. The face of Blanche Hoschedé is not dealt with in any kind of detail, and her hand is represented only by a dash of paint. The leaves on the trees are treated in the same way.

As in *Paysage avec Figures, Giverny*, in *Blanche Hoschedé Peignant* Monet uses two groups of people to give the painting a sense of depth and perspective. In this painting, the red clothes worn by both women forms a connection that invites the eye forward into the painting.

**Paysage avec Figures, Giverny (1888)**
***Landscape with Figures, Giverny***
*Courtesy of Image Select. (See p. 174)*

## VUE DE ROUEN DEPUIS LA CÔTE DE STE.-CATHERINE (c. 1892) VIEW OF ROUEN NEAR THE COAST OF ST. CATHERINE
*Courtesy of Christie's Images*

*T*HIS work was probably left unfinished. It is not signed and it is possible to identify the outlines of buildings that Monet was obviously intending to include. However, this does not detract from the work, which is fascinating because of its choice of subject.

Monet painted very few industrial scenes in his career, preferring quieter rural landscapes or the modern buildings of cities as subject matter. In both the paintings shown on this page, the subject is modern and industrial. The paintings share a similar color palette, so that the scene has been painted with primarily dark or subdued colors. This gives the whole a somber air. *Vue de Rouen depuis la Côte de Ste. Catherine* lacks the regularity and machine quality that the men evenly spaced on the ramps provide in *Les Déchargeurs de Charbon* (1875). Each man mimics the next in posture, adding to the balance of the painting.

In the main picture, Rouen is shown from a slight distance and its smoking chimneys feature prominently. This again is unusual. Chimneys have appeared in other works by Monet, but usually they are found in the background, romanticized by shrouds of fog and smoke. Here they dominate the skyline forcing the viewer to acknowledge their presence and providing the pivot around which the industrial town is set.

**Les Déchargeurs de Charbon (1875)**
**Unloading Coal**
*Courtesy of Giraudon. (See p. 86)*

## *LA SEINE À BENNICOURT, HIVER* (1893)
## THE SEINE AT BENNICOURT, WINTER
*Courtesy of Christie's Images*

IN January 1893, the ice floes that had been carried downriver stuck at Bennicourt. Monet painted several pictures of this scene over the next few weeks, of which this was the first. At this stage the river is almost frozen over.

This view of the Seine is very different from the one that Monet was to produce four years later. In this painting Monet is still using the formula of horizontal planes of color contrasted with vertical subjects. As can be seen, the trees on the island provide the vertical balance to the horizontal bands of the sky, the hills, and the snow. In *Matinée sur la Seine, Effet de Brume* (1897) the use of horizontals and verticals is still there but in a subtler manner. The water forms one band of color but because the trees frame either side of the river, the water draws the eye forward toward the horizon rather than across along its width.

**Matinée sur la Seine, Effet de Brume (1897)**
*Morning on the Seine, Mist Effect*
*Courtesy of Christie's Images. (See p. 206)*

The use of color contrasts in both works. The later painting centers around different tones of blue and purple. This has the effect of harmonizing the picture. *La Seine a Bennicourt, Hiver* uses a range of colors placed next to each other to form a contrast.

### *LES MEULES, EFFET DU SOIR* (1884)
### HAYSTACKS, EVENING EFFECT
*Pushkin Museum, Moscow. Courtesy of Giraudon*

IN 1890 Monet began a series of paintings that had a central motif of the grainstacks. He chose to depict them at varying times of day and season, creating intimate portraits of a traditional French symbol.

This painting is a forerunner to that series, and is similar to it in many aspects. He has chosen to depict a single haystack in the foreground with a second one further away; likewise the Grainstacks series mainly concentrates on a single stack or two stacks. However, this painting has placed the haystack in a detailed background context. The viewer is not just responding to the changing colors of light on a single motif. Instead, Monet has painted a background of poplars, hills and sky that also demand the viewer's attention. The poplars would have been of equal symbolic importance to French viewers as the haystacks and are painted in as much detail.

The technique used on the grass in the foreground is also similar to that used in the Grainstacks series. Small strokes of paint are laid next to each other, in varying shades of color, in order to create an overall effect. However, although this work can be seen as a forerunner to the important Grainstacks series, it was not painted as part of a group of paintings designed to be viewed together.

### *LES MEULES* (1887)
### THE HAYSHEAVES
*Courtesy of Image Select*

*T*HIS is a contrasting view of haysheaves to many of the others that Monet painted. The angle is similar in both paintings so that the viewer is taken quite close to the haysheaves and is given an intimate view. However, these paintings do have an empty feeling to them. They are devoid of people or any evidence of them. The strange regularity of the sheaves in this work has a disquieting effect.

The primary focus of the work is the haysheaves, unlike in *Les Meules, Effet du Soir* (1884) where it can be argued that the poplars are equally as important. Here, the sheaves' triangular shape is in keeping with the geometry of the overall picture. Broad bands of color representing grass, hedge, and sky are emphasized by the lines of the sheaves. In the earlier work, the rounded shape of the stacks and the rounded heads of the poplars are a counterbalance to the lines of the trees, hills, and grass. The effect of the sun dappling across the field also helps to prevent the strength of the linearity from dominating. One of the most striking aspects of this painting is its simplicity of composition, which Monet also employed in the Grainstacks series of the 1890s.

**Les Meules, Effet du Soir (1884)**
*Haysheaves, Evening Effect*
*Pushkin Museum, Moscow. Courtesy of Giraudon. (See p. 188)*

## *LA SEINE PRÈS DE GIVERNY* (1894)
## THE SEINE NEAR GIVERNY
*Courtesy of Christie's Images*

THE main feature of this work is the water. The viewer is on a level with the river, which flows forward, drawing the eye along its course. It fills the bottom of the canvas; in fact the water dissects the canvas virtually in a straight line. Above that line, its color is echoed in the color of the sky. A comparison of the bottom left and top left corner reveals almost identical brushwork and tone.

The land that divides the water and sky prevents them from becoming one. It is only where the land is reflected onto the water that any indication of movement on the water's surface occurs. The brushstrokes become long, horizontal lines of varying colors to indicate the ripples, in contrast to the water away from the dark reflection, where the color is almost one block of paint.

This treatment of the Seine is different from that in *La Seine à Port-Ville* (1908–09). Here there is no sense of perspective. The arrangement of water, land, and sky present in the main painting is simplified into three broad bands of color. This is broken only by the circular strokes of green for the trees, the yellow for the shore, and black strokes indicating the surface of the water.

**La Seine à Port-Ville (1908–09)**
*The Seine at Port-Ville*
*Courtesy of Christie's Images. (See p. 218)*

## *LA CATHÉDRALE DE ROUEN, EFFET DE SOLEIL* (1893)
## ROUEN CATHEDRAL, SUNLIGHT EFFECT

*Clark Art Institute, Williamstown. Courtesy of Image Select*

ROUEN Cathedral became the subject of another series of paintings by Monet, and the first to concentrate so exclusively on an architectural subject. The rationale behind his choice of Rouen Cathedral was in line with his subjects for previous series of paintings, in that it is distinctly French.

Monet's letters of the time describe the struggle he had with his subject: this series took three years to reach completion. As can be seen by comparing *Le Château de Dolceacqua* (1884), Monet has abandoned the conventions of setting and taken the viewer uncomfortably close to Rouen cathedral. Unlike the château, Monet does not paint in the entire building; only a part of the cathedral is shown. Neither painting dwells on architectural detail but aims to capture the effect of a moment. In *Cathédrale de Rouen* in particular the primary interest is the effect of light on the surface of the building. The cathedral is shown here in full sunlight, which creates a golden glow on the building.

As Monet took a year's break between painting the pictures in this series, he often painted over sections again, so the canvases have a crustation of paint on them. Some critics have found this suggestive of the actual stonework of the building.

**Le Château de Dolceacqua (1884)**
*The Dolceacqua Chateau*
*Musée Marmottan. Courtesy of Giraudon. (See p. 138)*

### Norvège, les Maisons Rouges à Bjornegaard (1895)
### Norway, the Red Houses at Bjornegaard
*Courtesy of Giraudon*

*P*ART of the commercially unsuccessful series of Norwegian paintings, both of these canvases depict snow landscapes. In contrast to *Paysage Norvège, les Maisons Bleues* (1895), this painting has a more complex arrangement. Rather than taking a viewpoint of the buildings as a part of the landscape, Monet has moved in close so that the buildings dominate the picture.

Although not as simplistic in arrangement as *Paysage Norvège, les Maisons Bleue, Norvège, les Maisons Rouges a Bjornegaard* does have a symmetry to it. The blocks of colors used on the buildings and the lack of architectural detail allow the geometric shapes to emerge from the canvas. The result is that the buildings become secondary to the pattern of squares and oblongs that they make. The redness of the walls is striking in contrast with the deep blue of the sky. Painted at a different time of day, there is little evidence of the rosiness that the sun causes in *Paysage Norvège, les Maisons Bleues*. The contrasting colors help to emphasize the geometry of the painting.

The overall effect is one of remoteness, with no human figures disturbing the white landscape. However, there is a pervading sense of calm that is shared with some of Monet's seascapes.

**Paysage Norvège, les Maisons Bleues (1895)**
**Norwegian Landscape, the Blue Houses**
*Courtesy of Giraudon.* (See p. 198)

## PAYSAGE NORVÈGE, LES MAISONS BLEUES (1895)
## NORWEGIAN LANDSCAPE, THE BLUE HOUSES
*Courtesy of Giraudon*

THE simplicity of the content of this painting means that the true subject matter is the effect of the light and the snow. Monet had been looking forward to painting the snow of Norway because he found the effects of light on snow exciting. However, when he arrived in Norway he found the realities of painting snow in the northern light very difficult. The flatness of the painting is perhaps testimony to those difficulties. The snow blankets all features, making it difficult for distinct shapes to emerge.

So determined was he to capture the strange light of Norway that Monet actually painted many of these pictures in defiance of the cold, with icicles forming in his beard as he worked. In this painting, he has concentrated on showing the effect of light upon the colors of the snowscene. Hence the snow is not pure white but blue and pink, and the sky is yellow and pink. In terms of composition, the painting is reminiscent of the haystack painting of 1884.

The composition—a band of ground with houses set in the center against a line of hills and a band of sky above—is identical in both pictures. The haystacks are painted from a viewpoint closer to the subject, which gives the stacks greater prominence than the houses in the Norwegian work, but the similarity in composition cannot be denied.

**Les Meules, Effet du Soir (1884)**
*Haystacks, Evening Effect*
*Pushkin Museum, Moscow. Courtesy of Giraudon. (See p. 188)*

## *Le Mont Kolsaas en Norvège* (1895)
## Mount Kolsaas in Norway
*Courtesy of Giraudon*

*I*N 1895, Monet decided to take a trip to Norway. His purpose was two-fold: he wished to visit his stepson, Jacques Hoschedé, who lived there; and he was looking for inspiring new subject matter.

On arriving, Monet struggled to paint the snowy scenes in the strange Scandinavian light. His problems were solved on discovering Mount Kolsaas. Eventually he painted 13 canvases of this subject, marking the different light effects at various times of day. Unlike previous series paintings, these were all painted from the same viewpoint. Despite this, the paintings are not identical in composition. This can be attributed to Monet's desire to capture the impression of the moment rather than the detail. These two paintings demonstrate how the light at different times of day makes the mountain appear with a rosy hue in the main picture and with more blue in the second image. The main painting uses more vertical brushstrokes, which create a blurred effect, whereas the smaller format image is more sharply defined.

Painted on canvases almost identical in size these Mount Kolsaas pictures are considered most powerful when displayed as a series next to each

other. They then resemble a range of mountains. Although attractive, the paintings lack the complex palette of colors from previous paintings, and their non-French subject matter made them unpopular when exhibited.

**Le Mont Kolsaas en Norvège (1895)**
***Mount Kolsaas in Norway***
*Musée Marmottan. Courtesy of Giraudon.* (See p. 202)

*Claude Monet*

## *LE MONT KOLSAAS EN NORVÈGE* (1895)
## MOUNT KOLSAAS IN NORWAY
*Musée Marmottan. Courtesy of Giraudon*

PAINTED within a year of each other, *Le Mont Kolsaas en Norvège* and *La Cathédrale de Rouen, Effet de Soleil* (1893) are each part of their own series. What is of interest here is the different approaches to the use of a single motif.

The painting of Mount Kolsaas is a more conventional composition in the sense that the viewer is placed at a distance from the subject and can see the entire mountain. To a certain extent the mountain is given a context, with sky above and snow at its base. With *Cathédrale de Rouen*, a less traditional stance is taken. The viewer is thrust close to the subject. The whole of the building cannot be seen, and little context is provided, to the point that only a small amount of sky is shown. The mountain is painted in a simpler style, comprising bands of colors that contrast and merge together at different points.

The colors used in the Norwegian picture are either placed in contrast to each other, as with the green line near the base next to the purple line above it, or whirled together, such as at the tip where violet, blue, and white merge. The whole is harmonized through either brushstrokes or color.

**La Cathédrale de Rouen, Effet de Soleil (1893)**
***Rouen Cathedral, Sunlight***
*Clark Art Institute. Courtesy of Image Select. (See p. 194)*

## *BRAS DE SEINE PRÈS DE GIVERNY* (1897)
## BRANCH OF THE SEINE NEAR GIVERNY

*Musée Ile-de-France. Courtesy of Giraudon*

*T*HE Seine, a symbol of France, features in so many of Monet's work that it became his most used motif. Between 1896 and 1897, Monet decided to use the river in a remarkable series of paintings. In all he produced 21 pictures.

What makes this series like no other is that it records the dawn on the river, moment by moment, within one period of time. Although critics had assumed this was what Monet was attempting in other series paintings, none of the previous series had been concerned with the changing light within such a tight time-frame. As can be seen in both *Bras de Seine près de Giverny* and *Matinée sur la Seine, Effet de Brume* (1897), the dawn on the river causes varying tones to appear and disappear. The former has a soft blue, almost lilac color that hangs across the whole of the painting but centralizes where the river meets the sky. In comparison, *Matinée sur la Seine, Effet de Brume* was painted a little later in the morning, when the sun begins to rise. The blue tones are beginning to disappear and the green of the trees, especially in the foreground, to emerge. On the horizon, the sky is starting to glow. Although these two paintings record changes in light that are easy to identify, the differences between other paintings in the series are less clear.

**Matinée sur la Seine, Effet de Brume (1897)**
*Morning on the Seine, Mist Effect*
*Courtesy of Christie's Images. (See p. 206)*

### *Matinée sur la Seine, Effet de Brume* (1897)
### Morning on the Seine, Mist Effect

*Courtesy of Christie's Images*

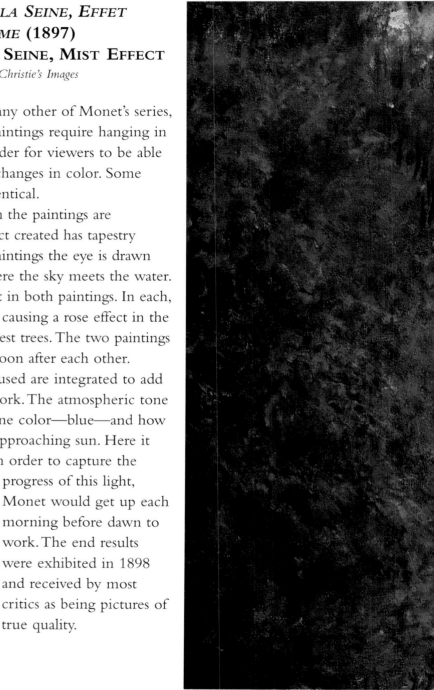

MORE than any other of Monet's series, the Seine paintings require hanging in a specific order for viewers to be able to appreciate the subtle changes in color. Some appear to be virtually identical.

The colors used in the paintings are harmonious, and the effect created has tapestry qualities. In both these paintings the eye is drawn through the work to where the sky meets the water. This is the source of light in both paintings. In each, the sun is starting to rise, causing a rose effect in the sky and a tint to the nearest trees. The two paintings must have been painted soon after each other.

The brushstrokes used are integrated to add to the harmony of the work. The atmospheric tone of each centers around one color—blue—and how it fades slowly with the approaching sun. Here it has almost disappeared. In order to capture the progress of this light, Monet would get up each morning before dawn to work. The end results were exhibited in 1898 and received by most critics as being pictures of true quality.

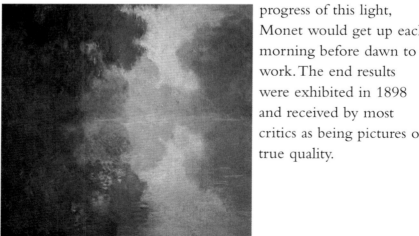

**Matinée sur la Seine, Effet de Brume (1897)**
**Morning on the Seine, Mist Effect**
*Private Collection. Courtesy of Image Select*
(See p. 208)

### *MATINÉE SUR LA SEINE, EFFET DE BRUME* (1897)
### MORNING ON THE SEINE, MIST EFFECT
*Private Collection. Courtesy of Image Select*

*T*HE effect created in the Seine series is purely decorative. The colors are manipulated from reality in order to create different combinations. This can make some of the paintings seem very pale when reproduced on the page.

For Monet, the Seine provided the challenge of capturing the changing qualities of light on water. As these two paintings show, his treatment of reflection changed over the years. In *La Seine près de Giverny* (1894), the reflection of the trees is not rendered in detail, instead it is a dark patch that is comparable to the subject only in outline. Monet uses strokes of white paint in th dark reflection to represent the effect of light on water, sparkling off the surface.

In the Seine paintings the nature of reflection has changed. The water has become a mirror image of the subject both in color and density. There is a solidity around the reflection that is missing in other work. In addition, the trees framing the water give the work an enclosed feeling that is lacking in the open landscape of *La Seine près de Giverny*.

**La Seine près de Giverny (1894)**
*The Seine near Giverny*
*Courtesy of Christie's Images. (See p. 192)*

## *Sur la Falaise près de Dieppe* (1897)
## On the Cliffs Near Dieppe

*Courtesy of Image Select*

THE beauty of Monet's cliff-top paintings lies in their simplicity. The basic elements are sky, sea, and land. No particular time of day can be attributed to them and so they are imbued with a timeless quality.

In this painting, it is not the strength of the sea that is on show; instead, it is a calm image that demonstrates a softer view of nature than that present in the paintings of the Creuse. In those, Monet wanted to capture the savagery of nature; in this painting he wants to depict an equally harsh landscape—but in a gentler manner. The soft curves of the cliff as it swells into the picture and gently falls into the sea are softened even further by the pastel colors that are used.

The viewpoint taken from the top of the cliff is repeated in many other paintings. In some it is used to more dramatic effect than it is here. In this way the cliff pictures are similar to some of Monet's earlier work such as *Boulevard des Capucines* (1873). His obvious interest in perspectives from higher viewpoints is still in evidence with these cliff paintings. However, the earlier work is concerned with capturing the business of a moment. Here the impression of serenity is what is most important.

**Boulevard des Capucines (1873)**
*Capucines Boulevard*
*Courtesy of the Visual Arts
Library, London. (See p. 68)*

## LE BASSIN AUX NYMPHÉAS, HARMONIE VERTE (1899)
## WATER-LILY POND, HARMONY IN GREEN

*Pushkin Museum, Moscow. Courtesy of Giraudon*

MONET began building his water-lily garden at Giverny in the 1890s as an oriental complement to the more traditional western flower garden that he had already designed. A keen gardener, Monet employed a team of workers to maintain the gardens even when he claimed he had very little money.

His gardens at Giverny became virtually his only subject for painting for the remaining 26 years of his life. Monet had long believed that a close relationship with nature on an almost primitive level helped to develop an individual's understanding of himself and the world around him. The Japanese were thought to be a nation that particularly understood this regenerative relationship. His choice of an oriental garden as a theme effectively underlines his beliefs.

Although the subject is distinctly un-French, the color palettes Monet chose for it are, nevertheless, quite traditional. The water draws the eye of the viewer into the distance through a world harmonized in green and blue. The serenity of the scene is derived from the subject matter and the complementary colors. In addition, balance is provided by the water that ends almost exactly at the center of the picture and reflects the foliage in the top half. The bridge spanning the pond forms a symmetrical rounded shape that adds to this balance.

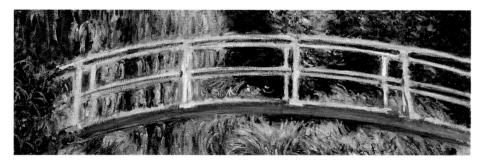

## *LE BASSIN AUX NYMPHÉAS, LES IRIS D'EAU* (1900–01)
## WATER-LILY POND, WATER IRISES
*Courtesy of Christie's Images*

THIS painting is rich in color and tone. Some of this riot of color is present in the earlier picture *Fleurs à Vétheuil* (1881), hinting at the extraordinary use of color employed in Monet's later work. The bottom half of the painting shows a vast mixture of flowers of different colors.

By the time Monet painted *Le Bassin aux Nymphéas, les Iris d'Eau*, the flowers and foliage are dominating nearly the entire canvas. The later painting uses a wider variety of colors that clash to increase the drama. Each flower is painted with less detail but becomes a splash of color. The colors of the irises by the pond are repeated on the footpath and on the water where the lilies are. Even the sky has a tint of pink to it so that the entire area is suffused with color.

**Fleurs à Vétheuil (1881)**
*Flowers at Vétheuil*
*Courtesy of Christie's Images. (See p. 122)*

The earlier painting shows a view of Vétheuil, which is about to be swallowed up by the flowers and bushes. In the *Le Bassin aux Nymphéas*, the garden appears to have won the battle. Although the bridge and the footpath suggest the presence of humans, the lack of people or buildings gives the garden an air of wilderness. Only a tiny square of sky is left, and even that looks destined to be covered over by the willow. Nature in both paintings is seen as a strong force.

# *VÉTHEUIL* (1901)

*Pushkin Museum, Moscow. Courtesy of Topham*

WHEN Monet moved to Vétheuil, he moved his family to a more rural town than they had previously encountered. Unlike their previous home of Argenteuil, there was no industry at Vétheuil and the people who lived there were mainly agricultural workers.

This rural setting meant Monet changed his approach to the subject matter. In *Au Pont d'Argenteuil* (1874), the artist celebrated the harmony of nature and industry. In Vétheuil there is no sign of industry. The town exists against a backdrop of hills. The presence of people has been reduced, in physical size: the boat is tiny and the figures unidentifiable. In many of Monet's paintings from this period people are absent altogether. The town provides the focus, the viewer's eye being led up to it by the flow of the water. The town's reflection in the water helps its presence to dominate the work; similarly, the spire of the church thrusts up into the sky. The town is equal to all elements. In *Au Pont d'Argenteuil*, the bridge forms a dominant line across the canvas and, in the foreground, a woman and child are depicted taking a leisurely walk. The scene in *Vétheuil* is restful, with the water calm and the boat helping to break up its expanse. The colors here are muted and warm, with none of the cold, gray tones found in *Au Pont d'Argenteuil*.

**Au Pont d'Argenteuil (1874)**
*The Bridge at Argenteuil*
Courtesy of Image Select. (See p. 83)

## *LA SEINE À PORT-VILLE* (1908–09)
## THE SEINE AT PORT-VILLE
*Courtesy of Christie's Images*

THIS painting represents Impressionism taken to the borders of Abstract art. The whole view has been simplified around three bands of color; the sea is turquoise, the land purple, and the sky a very pale blue. Against these, details, such as the boat on the shore, are added without any attempt at complexity.

The surface of the water is indicated by irregular brushstrokes and the occasional black line. Similarly, the trees are represented by swirls of green, brown, and yellow. Some similarities in technique can be seen in *Antibes, Vue du Cap, Vent de Mistral* (1888), in which the sea is a broad band of color, with the town, mountains, and sky beyond. The sea in both has been painted with a strong color, but in the earlier picture Monet has detailed the town and mountains more clearly than in Port-Ville. In addition, he gives the viewer some sense of depth to the painting by including the tree in the foreground.

In La *Seine à Port-Ville* there is no clear indication of time of day or season, but the weather is clear and the sky is blue. With the Antibes work, however, Monet took great care to record the sunlight on the hills and the wind in the trees. His representation of nature is strongly conventional in comparison with the Port-Ville painting.

**Antibes, Vue du Cap, Vent de Mistral (1888)**
*Antibes, View of the Cape in the Mistral Wind*
*Courtesy of Christie's Images. (See p. 170)*

## WATERLOO BRIDGE (1902)
*Courtesy of Christie's Images*

THE mirage quality of the bridge in this painting is taken to the point where it virtually disappears from view. The ethereal quality of the painting can be explained partly by the London fog; Monet was attracted to the constantly changing light that it created. The painting is an example of Monet trying to capture what he referred to as the "envelope" of light that seeps from the subject and surrounds it, giving movement to a static object. He struggled to understand the ever-changing effects that the London climate created.

Here, there is a shroud of romance around the familiar landmark. The boatman in the foreground adding to the sense of mystery, and the bridge shimmers in the background as if it is in close danger of disappearing altogether. Reality tempers the romance in the form of the smoking chimneys just visible in the background. The bridge itself is reduced to a silhouette. The eye is automatically drawn to the boat, which is highlighted by a patch of lighter yellow and white flecks on the canvas.

The real subject of the painting is not the bridge but the fog and the way in which it constantly changes the landscape around it, so that at one moment one area is given prominence, at the next another.

### CHARING CROSS BRIDGE, LA TAMISE
### (1903)
### CHARING CROSS BRIDGE, THE THAMES
*Courtesy of Christie's Images*

*P*AINTED during Monet's second trip to London, this picture is in the same style as the others produced around this time. The London fog is used to distort colors and cloud buildings so that only outlines appear. It reflects the color of the sun across the whole of the painting so that the canvas is transfused with a pink glow.

The unreal quality that the fog gives the painting is similar to that created in some of the water lily paintings. As with *Nymphéas* (1903), the water lilies often appear as if they are hovering over the canvas. There is no reflection in the water, and their presence is not put into any context. *Charing Cross Bridge, La Tamise* clearly has a context in that the Houses of Parliament are recognizable landmarks, but their ghostly appearance does not give them a solid presence in the painting. The trains crossing the bridge are equally as insubstantial, represented purely by plumes of smoke.

The difference between the two works is that *Nymphéas* is an intimate painting that forces the viewer close to the subject. *Charing Cross Bridge, La Tamise* lacks that intimacy because it is painted from an obscured distance.

**Nymphéas (1914–17)**
*Water Lilies*
*Courtesy of Christie's Images. (See p. 234)*

## LE PARLEMENT, COUCHANT DE SOLEIL (1904)
## THE HOUSES OF PARLIAMENT AT SUNSET
*Courtesy of Christie's Images*

*T*HIS image was among the most controversial subjects from Monet's London trip, because J.M.W. Turner (1775–1851) had, prior to Monet, successfully painted this among his London scenes. By choosing London as a subject and including in the series landmarks already painted by such an acknowledged master as Turner, Monet was deliberately laying down a challenge. He wanted to prove that his method of painting was the superior.

Monet undoubtedly admired Turner's work and was influenced by him, but he felt that art had moved since his time. His London paintings have also been compared to James Whistler's (1834–1903) *Nocturnes* (subsequently accepted as groundbreaking art although at the time of their creation, they received a mixed reception). Monet had been friendly with Whistler and was, therefore, familiar with his work.

Here Monet is concentrating on the cumulative atmosphere created when architecture is placed near water and suffused with an eerie light. The Gothic spires of the Houses of Parliament have almost succeeded in piercing through the fog, but they are still reduced to a vague image that does not create a strong reflection in the water. The sun and its reflection cast a warm glow upon the scene and provide two focal points; one at the top of the painting and another at the bottom. The whole work adheres to Monet's aesthetic principles of being pleasing to the eye.

## GONDOLE À VENICE (1908–09)
## GONDOLAS IN VENICE

*Musée des Beaux Arts, Nantes. Courtesy of Giraudon*

*T*HIS is an unfinished piece of work and it is possible to trace the shadowing of outlines for the gondola beyond the finished end. In this unfinished state it lacks the harmony of the completed *Le Grand Canal et Santa Maria della Salute* (1908).

The gondola and water are painted, like the finished work, using mainly greens and blues, but the tones are much darker, giving the painting a moody air. The patch of purple that represents another boat helps to lift the atmosphere slightly. The reflection of the gondola in the water is painted simply as a dark patch. As with *Santa Maria della Salute*, Monet is not interested in painting a water surface that reflects like a mirror. The water itself has been treated differently in the two paintings: the finished work uses short, horizontal strokes in a variety of colors, which help to capture the movement of the water and the varying colors. In *Gondole à Venice*, the water is painted horizontally again, but with long swirls of paint that represent the reflections. The rest of the water, where painted, is created from one color laid on the canvas in a variety of directions.

Although it is hard to judge from an unfinished work, it would seem that Monet was trying out a different style in this painting from his earlier Venetian subjects.

**Le Grand Canal et Santa Maria della Salute (1908)**
*The Grand Canal and Santa Maria della Salute*
*Courtesy of the Tate Gallery. (See p. 228)*

## LE GRAND CANAL ET SANTA MARIA DELLA SALUTE (1908)
## THE GRAND CANAL AND SANTA MARIA DELLA SALUTE

*Courtesy of the Tate Gallery*

MONET visited Venice for the first time in 1908. Staying with a friend of the artist John Singer Sargent (1856–1925), Monet was inspired by the magical effects of the light. It is surprizing that he had not visited Venice before, as with its unusual combination of water, architecture, and sky it had all the elements Monet often sought in his work.

Venice has proved fertile ground for artists stretching back across the centuries, but Monet was not interested in recording the city in a conventional style. He was more concerned with the effects of light on the buildings. In this picture the architectural details of the Santa Maria della Salute are reduced to outlines. The strong lines of the edges of the building create a vertical and horizontal grid in the right-hand corner. The vertical lines of the painting are emphasized by the gondola poles rearing out of the water and reaching for the sky.

Painted from the center of the canal, Monet has thrust the viewer on to the water with very little land to act as a boundary. Santa Maria della Salute seems to be floating on the water, an effect furthered by the water reflecting greens and blues on to the side of the building and the white of the stonework reflecting back down on to the water.

### *LE PALAIS DE MULA* (1908)
### VENICE, PALAZZO DA MULA

*National Gallery, Washington, D.C.. Courtesy of Image Select*

AFTER the close intimacy of Monet's garden paintings from Giverny, these dramatic pictures from Venice mark a return to painting on a monumental scale. This extraordinary work confirms that Monet's main interest was the effect of light. Traditionally the *Palazzo da Mula* would have been depicted in all its glory as the primary focus of a painting, with its architectural details accurately recorded. Here, Monet has dispensed with this notion; the building has been cropped short so that the top floors are not shown and, by removing the sky and showing only part of the palazzo, he has disassociated it from its surroundings. The horizontal and vertical lines of the architecture provide him with a grid which he deconstructs. By focusing on the relationship between the colors of the water and the colors of the building, Monet has made the palazzo a part of nature rather than being apart from nature.

Some critics have found elements of abstract design in this painting. The emphasis on the grid work of the building and the fading away to nothing of the actual details of the stonework has led them to connect this with work by more established Abstract artists.

# *NYMPHÉAS* (1907)
# WATER LILIES
*Courtesy of Christie's Images*

*T*HERE is a sense of suspension about many of the water lily paintings, particularly those that depict water without land or sky above it, as both these paintings do. The viewer is suspended in this strange place where surroundings have been dispensed with and all that remains is the world of water.

The 1907 painting is a prime example of this world of water. The reflection of clouds can just be made out, and what appears to be the reflection of willow trees appears on the left and right. However, by filling the canvas entirely with water, the planes of the water and of the canvas have become one. The water lilies are carefully laid on the canvas in horizontal lines in both this picture and the later *Nymphéas* (1914–17).

Both the 1907 and the 1914–17 paintings are intimate to Monet because they not only represent his own private garden but also his peculiar vision of that garden. By having a subject that is so intimate, Monet pulls the viewer into sharing his own experience. The brushstrokes in the later works become progressively broader, which was primarily a result of his failing eyesight.

**Nymphéas (1914–17)**
*Water Lilies*
*Courtesy of Christie's Images. (See p. 234)*

## *NYMPHÉAS* (1914–17)
## WATER LILIES
*Courtesy of Christie's Images*

PRIME Minister Clemenceau had always been a loyal supporter of Monet's work. In 1914 he urged the artist to work on a larger project, which became a formal state commission in 1916. This was for a set of large canvases depicting water lilies that would be displayed together permanently. Between now and his death this was to be the main preoccupation of Monet's work.

The paintings were destined to be hung in two basement rooms of the Orangerie in Paris. The paintings were hung together all the way around the two oval rooms so that the viewer was completely surrounded by Monet's water lilies. This style of painting extends the experience the artist has had with the subject out to the viewer. It was the ultimate resolution of all of Monet's series work.

A comparison between this intimate painting and the earlier *En Promenade près d'Argenteuil* (1875) demonstrates how far Monet's style had changed. The earlier landscape is open, balanced, and keeps the viewer at a distance. The use of horizontals is common to both paintings but *Nymphéas* forces the viewer close to the subject so all that is visible is the flower in a background of water. Nothing else exists.

**En Promenade près d'Argenteuil (1875)**
*Walking near Argenteuil*
*Courtesy of Giraudon. (See p. 92)*

## *NYMPHÉAS* (1914–17)
## WATER LILIES
*Courtesy of Christie's Images*

DURING the course of this painting, Monet's cataracts were getting progressively worse. He could see so badly that he had to read the names on the tubes of paint to find out which colors he was using. Nevertheless, his sense of color and harmony was not affected, and this painting is a stunning testimony to that.

The effects of the cataracts can be seen primarily in the brushstrokes. A comparison between this and the painting of c. 1919 shows that this one has been painted with thicker strokes. There is a mixture of broad, horizontal and vertical brushwork that is especially noticeable in the top of the painting, which suggests a sense of urgency on the part of the artist. There is also a pervading sense of darkness that is missing from the second picture. This is a result of dark colors used in heavy strokes, causing the delicacy of the lilies to be lost. Monet was so concerned that his cataracts would ruin the water lily paintings that he abandoned work on them until he had had an operation on his eye. These two paintings together provide an excellent study of how he could treat the same subject in a completely different way. One is tranquil and calm, the other full of drama and frenzy.

**Nympheas (c.1919)**
***Water Lilies***
*Courtesy of Christie's Images. (See p. 239)*

## NYMPHÉAS (c. 1919)
## WATER LILIES
*Courtesy of Christie's Images*

MONET returned time and again to his garden for inspiration. Between the years 1903 and 1908 he had painted numerous canvases of water lilies—48 were exhibited by Durand-Ruel in 1909. Contemporary critics exclaimed over the beauty of the paintings. He came back to the subject towards the end of his life.

In all of these paintings, Monet focuses on the surface of the water. He dispenses with any representation of the land or sky, only showing their reflection in the water. This painting is typical, with the willows visible only as a reflection. The sky, with its white clouds, is reflected in the water, so the blue of the sky and the blue of the water are one. Only the presence of the water lilies helps the observer to understand that this is a reflection. The painting is done in such a way that it is difficult to judge depth and it becomes a very flat canvas.

As the sky has clouds in it, the surface of the water is hard to identify. The wispiness of the edges of clouds could be the ripples of the water. The overall effect is of a harmonized world where water and sky have truly become one, and land has almost disappeared.

# LES HEMEROCALLES (1914–17)
## HERMEROCALLIS

*Musée Marmottan. Courtesy of Giraudon*

LIKE others in Monet's series of flower paintings, this depicts the plant in isolation. Unlike others, however, this picture has a variety of colors and shadings as background. There is the merest hint that other plants are present, particularly on the left-hand side, where the blue brushstrokes may represent their leaves.

The flowers erupt from the central bush of leaves and are painted without any detail to the flower head. Once again Monet is striving to give an overall impression rather than to represent any specific detail. The brushwork was quickly and roughly applied, and the same technique can be seen in *Nymphéas* also painted in the same time. This technique has the effect of blurring the central image so that the colors merge together. However, in *Les Hemerocalles*, the plant can still be seen in isolation from its surroundings. In *Nymphéas* the flowers were painted on to a background of water which becomes part of the essence of the flowers; the downward strokes on the surface cut across both the water and the flowers.

The colors used in the painting are vibrant, testifying to the problems that Monet was encountering as a result of his cataracts. The strong red and the yellow in the background indicate this in particular.

**Nymphéas (1914–17)**
*Water Lilies*
*Courtesy of Christie's Images.*
*(See p. 236)*

# LE PONT JAPONAIS (1918–24)
## THE JAPANESE BRIDGE

*Musée Marmottan. Courtesy of Giraudon*

THE colors and brushstrokes date this picture to the time that Monet was most affected by cataracts. His strong use of yellows and reds had been growing over the years as his sight declined. The effect of the chosen paints is to create a chaos of bright, contrasting colors on the canvas from which the outline of the bridge emerges as a shadowy presence. This is in stark contrast to *Le Bassin aux Nymphéas, Harmonie Verte* (1899), which shows the same bridge harmonized in green and blue. The earlier painting was made before the introduction of the wisteria bower over the bridge, visible in *Le Pont Japonais* as a higher green line. Even when studying the bridge and the foliage above it, Monet still sees some red and yellow so that brushstrokes in these strong colors are present in the greenest part of the painting.

The artist's treatment of the bridge has changed to the point where the structure is not easy to distinguish. This is typical of the Expressionist response to nature that occurs more and more in Monet's work at this time. The angle he painted from is closer to the bridge than in the earlier work and the overall spatial structure still seen there has collapsed here.

**Le Bassin aux Nymphéas, Harmonie Verte (1899)**
*The Water Lily Pond, Harmony in Green*
*Pushkin Museum, Moscow. Courtesy of Giraudon. (See p. 213)*

## LE PONT JAPONAIS (1918–19)
## THE JAPANESE BRIDGE
*Courtesy of Giraudon*

ERE Monet's treatment of the Japanese bridge changes dramatically from the earlier pictures. Following the very green paintings of the late 1890s and early 1900s, Monet has painted the bridge with a blue cast over it. In terms of color, a comparison between this version of the bridge and the later version (1918–24) is striking. Monet moves from a still-harmonious blue and green palette of colors to a riot of red and yellow.

This painting may not indicate the brighter colors that were to appear in Monet's later work, but it does contain some of the Expressionist elements that emerged in force in the later work. The brushstrokes have become wilder and the bridge is merging with its surroundings, making it harder to define than in earlier works. There is still some sense of spatial awareness created by the plant positioned in the foreground, but this is not as strong as in earlier paintings. The flatness that appears in the later work is present in this picture.

Both paintings were created from a similar viewpoint, which makes it easier to appreciate how much Monet's work changed and developed over the intervening years.

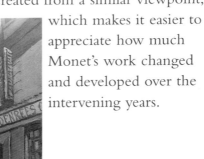

**La Rue de la Bavolle, à Honfleur (c. 1864)**
*Bavolle Street, at Honfleur*
*Mannheim Stadtische Kunsthalle.*
*Courtesy of Giraudon. (See p. 22)*

## LA MAISON D'ARTIST VUE DE JARDIN AUX ROSES (1922–24)
## THE ARTIST'S HOUSE SEEN FROM THE ROSE GARDEN
*Bavaria Bildagentur. Courtesy of Giraudon*

*I*N 1923, Monet was finally persuaded to have one of the cataracts that were affecting his vision removed. The cataracts had distorted his vision since around 1908, and his sense of color had been disrupted. The effect of the cataracts had made the world appear as if he were looking through a yellow lens. As they grew worse, his vision became browner and browner.

This painting is evidence of that effect. The colors that dominate are yellow and red, with very little blue in the picture. It is not easy to identify any subject in the painting, but the chimney and part of the roof of the house are visible in the left corner, painted in pink. The thick brushstrokes and extremes of color are thought by some to be indicative of the anguish Monet was feeling about his inability to see properly. Paintings like this have been called early examples of Abstract Expressionism rather than Impressionism.

Monet's despair over his vision meant that he suspended work on the Orangerie *Nymphéas* paintings until he was confident he would not ruin them with his poor vision. Prime Minister Clemenceau finally persuaded him to put aside his fear of the operation and have the cataract removed from one of his eyes.

## *LA MAISON VUE DU JARDIN AUX ROSES* (1922–24)
## THE HOUSE SEEN FROM THE ROSE GARDEN

*Musée Marmottan. Courtesy of Giraudon*

*T*HE effects of Monet's eye operation are seen instantly in this painting. The color that virtually screams from the canvas is blue. This is dramatic when compared with the pre-operation painting *La Maison d'Artist Vue du Jardin Aux Roses* (1922–24). The riot of pink and yellow in that painting has completely disappeared.

Although it is easier to identify objects in this later painting, the overall effect is a cacophony of color rather than a concentration on subject matter. Monet found great difficulty in coping with the sudden transformation of his perception of color. He resorted to wearing yellow-tinted glasses to help prevent him from being overwhelmed by blue. However, because only one eye had been operated on, he was struggling to focus properly, so he resorted to wearing a patch over his affected eye. This had the effect of taking away his binocular vision, and as a result he lost an appreciation of depth.

The artist chose to destroy many of his paintings from this period, and he fought hard to return to a style that he desired. Paintings from these years are sometimes referred to as Monet's "blue period;" very few of them remain.

**La Maison d'Artist Vue du Jardin aux Roses (1922–24)**
***The Artist's House Seen from the Rose Garden***
*Bavaria Bildagentur. Courtesy of Giraudon.* *(See p. 247)*

## *IRIS JAUNES* (1924–25)
## YELLOW IRISES
*Courtesy of Christie's Images*

THIS painting's strength lies in Monet's use of color. The brilliance of the yellow flower is enhanced by being placed against a strong blue background. It is the flower that attracts the eye; unlike the painting *Iris* (1924–25), where the flower itself is secondary to the pattern formed by the leaves.

The straight stems and leaves in *Iris Jaunes* is reminiscent of the poplars in *Peupliers au Bord de l'Epte* (1891). As with those, the heads of the flowers form parallel horizontal lines to counter the vertical green lines. This is an even simpler pattern than that in *Iris*. What both paintings share is not just a common subject but a common treatment of it. Neither is given a background to put it in context; the plant exists entirely in isolation.

The simplicity of *Iris Jaunes* coupled with the grid formation used gives it an oriental tone. By choosing a flower as a subject set against a single-color background, the effects of Monet's interest in Japanese art can be seen. Several of Monet's paintings of flowers have these traditional Japanese elements within them.

**Iris (1924-25)**
*Musée Marmottan. Courtesy of Giraudon. (See p. 252)*

## *IRIS* (1924–25)

*Musée Marmottan. Courtesy of Giraudon*

*T*HIS painting is among the last that Monet worked on. Even at this late stage in his career he was still developing as an artist and trying new techniques. This is one of the many reasons why he has gained the respect of critics over the years.

With *Iris*, Monet has moved in to give an intimate view of the plant. The background is a swirl of color that is indecipherable as representative of anything in particular, so the plant exists without any distractions to the eye. It is a depiction of an iris in its purist form. Unlike his earlier paintings, it is not the amazing violet and lilac tones of the flowers that have caught Monet's eye. Instead it is the shape of the leaves; their greenness, and even orange on one leaf, that are the focus of the painting.

What interests Monet, as can be seen in work dating back to the beginning of his career, is the grid of horizontal and vertical lines created by the leaves; the sweep of the leaves forming horizontal and vertical lines that cross each other. The informality of the symmetry is further emphasized by the curves of the leaves, ensuring that the whole has a softened and harmonized effect.

### *LES ROSES* (1925–26)
### THE ROSES
*Courtesy of Giraudon*

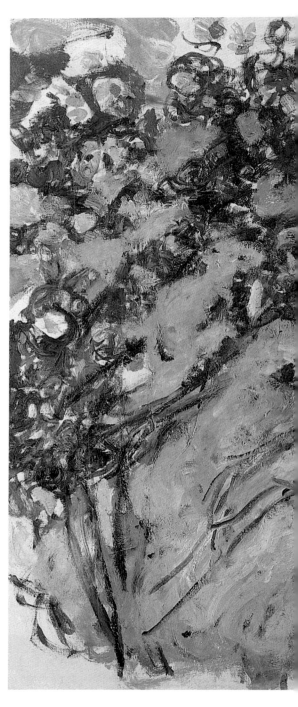

*L*ES *Roses* has an obvious oriental
influence. The tree is painted against a
blue background that could represent
the sky, although it is so anonymous it would
be difficult to state that for certain. The shape
of the tree as it curves across the canvas is
reminiscent of Japanese art. In particular, an
examination of the branches reveals that they
are represented by thin black lines that barely
connect with each other. This willowy effect,
combined with the depiction of flowers by
simple touches of color, is synonymous with
oriental art.

Water lilies are also a traditional oriental
theme. Monet's treatment of them in *Nymphéas*
(1914–17) is similar to that of the roses; the
main difference between the two being the fact
that the tree branches have a defined end,
whereas the water lilies float to the edge of the
canvas and create the illusion that they continue
floating further than the artist
(or the viewer) can see.

The colors used here are
soft pastels and light blues,
creating the effect of color for
the sake of it. Monet chose this
subject because of the beauty of
the combination of colors. The
pattern they create together was
more important to him than an
accurate representation of the tree.

**Nympheas (1914–17)**
*Water Lilies*
*Courtesy of Christie's Images.*
*(See p. 234)*

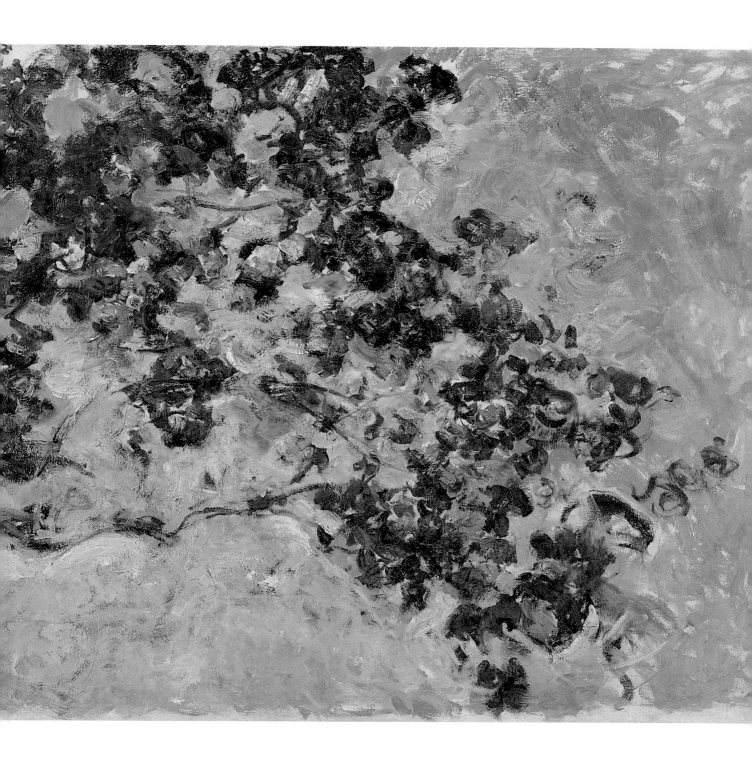

# AUTHOR BIOGRAPHIES AND ACKNOWLEDGMENTS

*To Greg, with love and gratitude.*

**Vanessa Potts** was born in Sunderland in 1971. She completed a B.A. Honours in English and American Literature at Warwick University in 1992. Since then she has completed an M.A. in Literature and the Visual Arts 1840–1940 at Reading University, from where she graduated in 1998. Vanessa currently combines her writing career with her job as a buyer for a major retail company.

*For my father, for sharing his love of landscape.*

**Dr. Claire I. R. O'Mahony** has a B.A. from the University of California at Berkeley and an M.A. and PhD from London's Courtauld Institute of Art. Her specialty is nineteenth-century art, in particular mural decoration in Third Republic France and images of the life model in the artist's studio. She is a visiting lecturer at the Courtauld Institute and Curator for the nineteenth-century exhibitions at the Richard Green Gallery, London.

While every endeavor has been made to ensure the accuracy of the reproduction of the images in this book, we would be grateful to receive any comments or suggestions for inclusion in future reprints.

With thanks to Image Select and Christie's Images for assistance with sourcing the pictures for this series of books. Grateful thanks also to Frances Banfield, Lucinda Hawksley, and Sasha Heseltine.